Best Foot Forward

Best Foot Forward

ADAM HILLS

HODDER &
STOUGHTON

First published in Great Britain in 2018 by Hodder & Stoughton
An Hachette UK company

1

A CIP catalogue record for this title is available from the British Library

Hardback ISBN 9781473681316
Trade Paperback ISBN 9781473681323

Typeset in Sabon MT by Hewer Text UK Ltd, Edinburgh
Printed and bound by CPI Group (UK) Ltd, Croydon, CR0 4YY

Hodder & Stoughton policy is to use papers that are natural, renewable
and recyclable products and made from wood grown in sustainable
forests. The logging and manufacturing processes are expected to
conform to the environmental regulations of the country of origin.

Hodder & Stoughton Ltd
Carmelite House
50 Victoria Embankment
London EC4Y 0DZ

www.hodder.co.uk

For my family

Contents

PART FOUR: STRANGE DAYS INDEED

PART FIVE: HEY DAYS

Best Foot Foreword

Hi there.

Before you start reading my book, I thought I'd let you know what you're in for.

In essence, this is a compilation of stories from a life of comedy. Nearly thirty years of tales from the road, the stage, and the screen.

My original idea was that you could pick up the book at any time, read a wee chapter, and come back to it whenever you felt the need. Ideally, I imagined you leaving this book beside the toilet, and delving in and out as time permitted. Literally, a 'wee' chapter at a time.

However, as I compiled story after story, I came to realise that this isn't just a random collection of adventures. It's a journey, as every life is.

When I started doing comedy, I had no idea where it would lead me, or what it would teach me about myself. I just wanted to make people laugh. I still do. Along the way though, I found laughter had some positive side effects: May cause happiness, may improve your mood, may have health benefits, may change the way you look at yourself and the world around you.

All of those side effects have held true for me.

I've seen authors use a profound quote to start their book, and my first instinct was to drop a bit of Mark Twain on you:

'The two most important days in your life are the day you are born, and the day you find out why.'

However, a quick internet search tells me that Twain may not actually be responsible for that sentiment after all. And I'd hate to start a book about comedy by misappropriating someone's line.

So instead, I'd like to paraphrase from the character Hawkeye in the TV Series MASH:

'I don't want to change the world. Just my little corner of it.'

What does all of this mean?

Well, I guess it means I hope you enjoy this book, and that you get something out of reading it. Because I got a lot out of writing it. More than I expected.

Happy reading

Adam

Part One

Early Days

The Hillsy Kids

When I first told my mum I was going to try stand-up comedy, she simply said, 'But you're not funny.'

It just made me all the more determined to do it.

She hates it when I tell that story, but I can see why she did it. As the words left my mouth, I'm sure she had visions of me chucking in my university degree, foregoing my plans to become a journalist, and winding up celebrating my fortieth birthday rummaging through a mini skip for a candle.

For the record – I did finish the degree, my dreams of journalism were put on hold, and I celebrated my fortieth birthday by watching *Toy Story 3* in 3D with family and friends.

Maybe at nineteen, comedy was my way of rebelling against my parents. Not alcohol, nor drugs, or even girls – but comedy, the most addictive vice of them all.

It is ironic really, since comedy had always been what bound us together as a family. If you were to ask me when I was at my happiest as a child, I'd say it was sitting in the car with my mum, dad and younger brother Brad, listening and laughing along to comedy tapes.

Whenever the school holidays rolled around, we'd pile into our beige (Dad swore the colour was called 'Sahara Tan') Ford Fairmont, with the pinstriping up the side, and begin the four-hour drive down the coast from the southern suburbs of

Sydney to my grandparents' house in the seaside town of Tuross Head, in New South Wales.

Home to around two thousand residents, Tuross Head gave the world Eva Mylott, an internationally acclaimed opera singer of the early 1900s, whose grandson went on to become an internationally acclaimed actor. You may have heard of Mel Gibson.

There is also a rumour that the parents of Flea from the band Red Hot Chili Peppers now reside in Tuross Head, and that occasionally he can be spotted at the bar of the local golf club. You can recognise him because he's naked, with a 3-wood cover over his willy.

To Australians, our holidays were nothing out of the ordinary, but to British people they were the most Australian thing anyone ever did, ever!

When my dad's parents retired, they left Sydney for Tuross, and a four-bedroom, two-storey brick house, built specifically to be invaded sporadically by their children and grandchildren. If you walked out the front door, crossed the road, and followed the street for ten minutes, you had a choice of beaches at which to spend your day.

There was One Tree Beach (so named because it was overlooked by a headland with one tree on it), Rock Beach (it had lots of rocks around it) and Whale Beach (a whale once died there).

The whole family would often spend the entire morning bodysurfing, boogie boarding, and sunbathing, before heading back to Nana and Pa's for lunch. Then we'd go back to the beach and do it all again in the afternoon.

Alternatively, Brad and I would walk out the back door in the morning, down to the bottom of the yard, then into the long grass behind the house in search of kangaroos. Sometimes we'd have spotted them already from the top balcony, but by the time we had galumphed our way through the waist-high grass, the roos would scarper.

In which case we'd come home and play backyard cricket. If my cousins had come across from Canberra, we'd have a fine old game that could take an entire afternoon. Occasionally we'd get a visit (and a few tips) from Nana's brother-in-law, a former NSW cricketer by the name of Bill Donaldson, who was legendary in our family for having played alongside the great Don Bradman.

Every now and then the neighbours would join in, and although I don't remember it, my grandfather still delights in telling the story of the time little George Gregan, from a few doors up, came to play. He went on to represent Australia in more Rugby Union games than any other player.

At the time, though, he was just another kid, and would probably have joined us in searching for any balls that were hit over the boundary, into the long grass, for six. Sometimes we'd extend the boundary to the line of trees and place a fielder in the waist-high grass. Of course, the length of the grass made it impossible to run, so the fielder was only effective if the ball was hit directly to them.

Plus they had to be ware of snakes.

If not cricket or bodysurfing, or the odd game of tennis, the other main activity was sailing. Coila Lake was visible from my grandparents' back balcony, and my dad and uncle had gone halves in a twelve-foot catamaran. If the wind was right, we'd hitch it up on a trailer, take it to the lake, and sail to our hearts' content.

When Nana saw the boat make the final run of the day, she'd put the scones in the oven, and they'd be on the table by the time we made it home.

It was idyllic, and throughout it all we laughed, a lot. When we weren't watching *The Two Ronnies* or *The Dick Emery Show*, we were quoting from them. I lost count of the amount of times I saw my grandfather impersonate a Benny Hill character with the phrase, 'Evlybody crapping'.

Like I said though, the laughter started on the way there. As we wound our way through the lush, green, dairy country of the NSW South Coast, with cows on either side of the car and the occasional dead wombat by the edge of the road, Mum, Dad, Brad and I would pop a cassette in the car stereo, and giggle along to the comedy stylings of Bill Cosby.

He was the family-friendly comedian, the one everyone could enjoy, and even when he was a bit risqué, it was funny to hear the squeaky-clean family man be slightly rude.

Oh, how we'd all chuckle at his story of zoning in on the ugly girl at parties, 'cos the ugly ones are always the night ones.' Or the routine about spanish fly, which is apparently an aphrodisiac one puts into a lady's drink to make them more attracted to you.

How were we to know he would later be accused of being a sexual predator, who drugged women's drinks in order to have sex with them?

I mean, it's not like he actually talked about it in his act!

Retrospective inappropriateness aside, those car trips and the family holidays that ensued represent some of the purest moments of a pretty happy childhood. I sometimes think my entire comedy career might be simply an ongoing attempt to recreate those moments of joy.

A *Funny* Foot

I grew up in the leafy southern suburbs of Sydney, in a place called the Sutherland Shire. 'The Shire', as it's now known across Sydney, boasted of being 'The Birthplace of a Nation', since it was here that Captain Cook first came ashore in 1770, on the southern edge of Botany Bay.

Eight years later, when the First Fleet arrived to set up a penal colony, Captain Arthur Phillip surveyed the area and immediately realised it had no fresh water, and was too marshy to sustain a bustling civilisation, so he took his ships around the corner to what is now known as Sydney Harbour.

The Shire has had an inferiority complex ever since.

It also has a reputation for being somewhat 'sheltered', and in the Seventies it reportedly had the highest concentration of white Anglo-Australians of any place in Australia. Author Kathy Lette also grew up in the Shire, and still refers to it as 'the insular peninsula'.

My day-to-day life at home pretty much resembled the holiday life I experienced at my grandparents – except that the city was closer, the beach was further away, and instead of long grass behind the house, we had dense bushland.

Bob and Judy Hills owned a house on a steep, rocky block of land. To park the car in the carport, you had to back it down from the road onto a curving concrete driveway, which dropped away on the right to a native garden of bottlebrush trees, the occasional blue tongue lizard, and a massive gum tree overlooking it all. There was also a native bush whose flowers turn red just before Christmas. It's called a Christmas Bush. We call it like we see it.

Alighting the car, one would walk down three steps and a path, then onto a sloping ramp my mum's father had built out of discarded railway sleepers. The ramp would carry visitors over the rock and shrubs to the front door, a good five or so metres below street level. By the time you exited the back door, you had to take a flight of stairs down to the yard.

The back of the house was raised on brick 'stilts' and underneath was mainly dirt and rubble. Over time that area was enclosed and renovated to become what Aussies of a certain era call a 'rumpus room' – an all-purpose, open-plan entertaining area, that in our case included a pool table, a pot-bellied stove, and Dad's bar.

It goes without saying that a swimming pool was also added to the backyard.

The sounds of summer for me are splashing, running, laughing and more splashing. Of course, while we were making those noises ourselves, our neighbours up and down the street were making the same noises in their pools. Sometimes the water from their splashes would make it over the shared fence and into our yard.

Behind the back fence, though, was the world's best play area – the bush.

Gum trees, wattles, more gum trees, Gymea Lilies, and a whole lot more gum trees; all scrabbling their way down to a creek at the bottom of the valley, then scrabbling their way back up the other side.

Forts were built, games were played, names were carved in rocks, and magazines were stashed in caves; and when our mums wanted us home, all they had to do was call and their voices would echo through the valley.

And the wildlife? Cockatoos would regularly screech overhead, along with kookaburras, magpies, brightly coloured rosellas, and flocks of galahs.

Australian readers may like to look away for a moment while I explain to Brits that (1) galahs do exist, (2) they are a pink and grey bird, (3) they make an almighty high-pitched, raucous screech that is unpleasant to the ear, (4) which is why the term 'galah' is applied to anyone who is a bit of a loud-mouthed fool, (5) which is why Alf in *Home and Away* often called someone a 'flamin' galah'.

It wasn't uncommon to come home from school and see a dozen sulphur-crested cockatoos perching on the railing of the back balcony. One friendly kookaburra took to sitting inside the kitchen window sill while Mum cooked dinner, hoping for a sneaky offcut.

Oh sure, there were snakes as well, and we once caught a deadly funnel-web spider in the swimming pool, but we just accepted it as part of the lifestyle. We all learnt to shake our shoes out before putting them on, in case a spider had crawled in. I mean, it's just common sense.

It didn't occur to me that I only needed to check my left shoe, since my right foot was prosthetic. Any spider sinking its fangs into that rock-hard rubber sole would need an immediate dental appointment. Even though I was born without a right foot, I was raised to do what everyone else did, so I bashed *both* Dunlop Volleys against the front step.

My parents had received the invaluable advice to 'treat him like any other normal kid', so they enrolled me in a gymnastics class at a young age. It taught me coordination, strength and athleticism, and even now I can still do a handy cartwheel.

It wasn't the only advice they received.

Just after I was born, Mum visited a specialist, who told her I would never walk or have a normal life. Distraught, she returned to her GP and told him the news. He suggested she get another opinion, and thankfully the second specialist said that the first specialist was talking bollocks.

The specialist to whom I owe the most, though, was the one who saw me immediately after I was born – Professor Richard Jones.

Whisked away from my mother before she could even hold her baby, I was presented to a group of surgeons who suggested my foot should be amputated directly below the knee. Who knew what the wobbly little thing was at the end of my stump? Best to cut it off.

Professor Jones said he thought the wobbly thing was an ankle of sorts, and keeping it intact would mean I'd have a more natural gait later in life. That one decision enabled me to run, walk, skip and do just about everything that the other kids could do. Sometimes better.

Many years later, when I did my first ever solo stand-up comedy show at the Sydney Opera House, I made sure Professor Jones was there.

And that's the last you'll read of my foot for a while, because in truth, it didn't really enter into my life that much.

Yearly trips to the prosthetist were merely par for the course. I'd have a few days off school, Mum and I would take the train into the city, we'd do puzzles or read while my foot was being made, and we'd have a milkshake afterwards. Sweet!

The other kids didn't treat me any differently, because I didn't do anything different. Half the year you couldn't even see the prosthetic anyway, because I was wearing trousers.

One summer, a kid on my street reacted in shock when I wore shorts for the first time that year.

'What happened to your leg?' he exclaimed, before clocking my expression, then adding, 'Oh yeah, sorry. I forgot you've got one foot.'

It never occurred to me that having a prosthetic foot was anything out of the ordinary. One of my dad's mates came to the house once with his leg in a cast. It was hidden below his jeans, so he knocked on his shin, which then made a loud clunking noise.

'I bet you can't do that!' he dared.

I then reached down and knocked on my jeans, and the exact same sound came from underneath. He looked startled, my parents burst into laughter, and I sat there bemused, wondering what was so funny.

By and large, I considered myself lucky that I could do everything. Except wear thongs. It was Australia in the Seventies. And everyone wore thongs. (For British readers, our thongs are what you call 'flip flops'. At no stage did my lack of a foot preclude me from wearing a G-string.)

My prosthetist once asked if there was anything I really wanted to do, so I said I wanted to wear thongs (stop sniggering, British readers). Nothing fancy, just your standard, blue, rubber thong (seriously, cut it out now).

He made me a foot with toes, but without the ability to grip with those toes, the thong kept flying off whenever I walked. So my mum glued velcro to the bottom of the foot and the top of the thong, to try and keep it on. It didn't work, but it was a valiant effort. Thankfully, a few years later sandals came back into fashion, and I was saved.

OK, *that* is the last you'll read of my foot for a while.

The rest of my childhood was mainly spent playing sport. In the winter it was rugby league, in the summer it was cricket, and all year round it was tennis. Eventually golf entered the picture as well.

Occasionally my prosthetic would break, usually while playing rugby league, and I'd have to hobble home from the local oval with it slung over my shoulder. I once reassured an open-mouthed dog walker with the words, 'Don't worry, mate, it's just a broken leg!'

The irony, of course, is that I was born without a right foot, and yet somehow I am right footed. I don't know why, but it felt like the correct foot to kick with. Until the day I tried to kick a goal from the twenty-metre line, and the prosthetic snapped below the ankle mid-kick.

The ball went five metres, my foot flew ten, and the next day I taught myself to kick left-footed. It still feels unnatural, though.

Alright, alright, THAT is the last you'll read of my foot for a while.

My point is – despite being born with one foot, and growing up surrounded by lethal snakes and spiders, I had a fun, carefree, and relatively sporty childhood.

A Star Is Norm

My dad was responsible for my comedy education, directly and indirectly.

An unfailingly polite man, with sparkling eyes, sandy blond hair, and an inbuilt desire to make sure everyone else was happy, Bob Hills was perfectly suited to his job as a member of the Qantas cabin crew.

Although my father's career meant he spent a lot of time away from us, when he was home he was home all day. So once our homework was done, Dad would sit with us and watch whatever was on TV – usually old episodes of *MASH*, or our favourite, *The Bugs Bunny Show*.

He also had a love of comedy, and together we'd listen to albums by Peter Sellers and Allan Sherman. If I close my eyes, I can hear my dad impersonating an in-character Sellers describing how toothbrushes are made, 'The little holes in the top are put in manually, or in other words, once a year.'

Anyone familiar with my recent work on *The Last Leg* won't be surprised to know that Allan Sherman was famous for putting new words to old tunes to create some of the first comedy song parodies. 'Hello Muddah, hello Faddah, here I am at Camp Grenada,' was one of his hits.

As we grew older, so did our comedic references, and Mel Brooks became a household favourite. There is a scene in

Brooks's *History of the World, Part 1*, where a gathering ends with the call, 'Let's end the meeting on a high note,' at which all involved sing an operatic high note.

Our family ended every get together like that from the moment we saw the movie to the moment my dad died. It was literally the last thing he said to me.

Dad's job also meant we could fly around the world for free on staff travel, but on one condition: we flew standby. That meant rocking up at the airport, bags packed, house locked up, fridge empty – and then hoping there would be four seats available on whatever flight we had chosen. Which is why my first ever international journey was spent sitting three rows in front of my parents.

I was nine, Brad was six, and we were all flying to Los Angeles. As the plane levelled off and the headsets were distributed, I discovered the inflight comedy channel, which featured a Danish comedian and pianist by the name of Victor Borge.

It was the funniest, most amazing thing I'd ever heard – this strange man making people laugh about phonetic punctuation and classical piano. Apparently, I stood up on my seat and yelled three rows back to my parents, 'Mum, Dad, there's a man being funny on the radio!'

Of course, I had heard comedy before at home, and in the car, but this was the first time I became aware that other people listened to it as well. I spent the rest of the flight letting the programme replay over and over, knowing which jokes were about to appear, and marvelling as the audience discovered them for the first time.

Later that year, my first ever comedy appearance took place. It was a school performance day – Sutherland Primary

School to be precise – and I had written a comedy play called *SuperNorm*.

SuperNorm was based on 'Norm', a particularly Australian cartoon character invented for a national get-fit campaign, called 'Life. Be in it.' It is still one of the best ideas for a public campaign I've ever seen.

Norm was a beer-gutted couch potato, constantly exhorted by his sister Libby to do some sort of physical activity. With a jingle every Australian knew by heart, and can still repeat to this day, we as a nation got off our collective asses to: 'Be in it, today. Live more of your life.'

Aaanyway, this gave me the idea for SuperNorm – a super-hero whose only discernible power was that he could deflect anything with his enormous gut. Bullets, beer cans, the slings and arrows of outrageous fortune, were all repelled by his wobbly belly.

From memory, I wrote, directed, cast, starred in, and even designed my own costume – Bonds T-shirt, Stubbies shorts, terry towelling hat, and a pillow for my stomach. I honestly can't remember if it was funny, but I do remember having an absolute ball doing it.

Around the same time, Paul Hogan debuted a TV character called Super Dag, a pillow-gutted superhero in a terry towelling hat and Stubbies shorts who deflected things with his beer gut.

Coincidence? Or did he steal the idea from me? You be the judge.

Stand Up in Front of the Class

Most people think of comedians as being the joker in class, the person who interrupts every lesson with a line that makes all the other kids laugh, and both enrages and tickles the teacher at the same time.

That was not me.

I was the quiet kid, who did all his work, and only spoke when spoken to. But when it was my turn to speak, I made sure it was funny. One presentation to the class took the form of a Morecambe and Wise routine, while another short story was so full of in-jokes about my classmates, it made no sense whatsoever to our teacher.

A report card came home with a comment from my history teacher praising my sense of humour, and I was prouder of that than any of the marks or grades on the entire page.

The closest I came to the entertainment industry was when one of our substitute teachers, Mr Doyle, appeared in a TV ad for Pizza Hut. His one big moment came as he bit into a Super Supreme Pizza, and uttered the line: 'Mmmmm, super.'

As you can imagine, we trailed him around the school for weeks, mocking him with those words, and he left soon after.

Had I known that Mr John Doyle would later team up with a guy called Greig Pickhaver to form a comedy duo called Roy and HG, I would probably have been much nicer to him. Had he known that I would one day be universally mocked for appearing in my own embarrassing advert for KFC, he might have had a decent comeback.

Years later I interviewed John on TV, and he told me off-air that Jannali Boys High was the roughest school at which he ever taught, and was the reason he quit teaching. When he quoted some of the acts he witnessed at the school – like the time one classmate had his teeth knocked out for throwing an orange at another classmate – I was shocked.

Not by the violence, but because it turns out that didn't happen at every school. I thought they were *all* full of thugs and yobbos, with the few nerdy swots sitting in the corner. Turns out it was just mine.

Ask any comedian who it was that bullied them at school and they will instantly reply. I could tell you who my bullies were, but I could also tell you who I picked on. I wasn't at the top of the list of kids to bully, but I certainly wasn't one of the cool kids either.

I was also painfully shy around girls.

Maybe that shyness was what led me to comedy. Deep down, I wanted to be the guy who spoke effortlessly, commanded a room and brought people to laughter whenever I wanted to.

While the other kids were listening to Iron Maiden or AC/DC, I was listening to Kenny Everett and Billy Connolly. While the other kids were smoking behind the bike sheds, I was drawing my own comic strip.

And while other kids might sneak away from a family holiday to meet girls and drink cheap booze, I snuck off with my brother from a family holiday in Las Vegas to see a young Jim Carrey perform at the Comedy Store.

Brad was my comedy compadre. He was, and still is, three years younger than me, and whatever I watched, he watched. I could rattle off the shows we bonded over, or I could tell you that to this day we address each other in all correspondence as two characters played by Hugh Laurie and Stephen Fry in the Ben Elton-penned sitcom, *Filthy Rich & Catflap*.

My daughters think it's hilarious that their Dad and their Uncle send messages to each other that start with 'Dear Poofarty' and end with 'love ya, Nobend'.

I recently told Stephen Fry that story, and he guffawed with laughter, and told me how proud Ben Elton was when he came up with those names. I immediately texted Brad to let him know.

My brother's part in my life can be explained in a story that began when I was seven and he was four.

We had taken a family holiday to Darwin, to visit my mum's brother Kevin, who taught Aboriginal student teachers. One of his students was a friendly and hospitable man named Tom, who took it upon himself to show us around.

At the end of the week, as a gift, he bestowed indigenous names upon Brad and me, after consulting with the elders of his tribe. I was (and still am) called Stingray, and my brother was named Salt Water.

Over time, Tom became a close family friend, and would visit us in Sydney, at first alone, then later with his wife and daughter. It's fair to say he stood out in the white-out that was the Sutherland Shire. The irony is, a quick scan of the local suburbs reveals Kirrawee, Gymea, Woolooware, Caringbah, and Cronulla – all indigenous words.

My dad took Tom clothes shopping one day, and the sales staff had no idea how to deal with him. It didn't help that Tom tried on a pair of dark brown shorts, then joked, 'The good thing is if I need to dress formal, I can just tell people I'm wearing trousers and no one will know the difference.'

Tom became the first Aboriginal person from Arnhem Land to earn a university degree, and became a principal at Yirrkala Community School, where he was committed to combining Western and traditional ways of teaching, and authored books on the subject.

He left teaching to pursue a musical career, and formed the now famous band, Yothu Yindi, whose single 'Treaty' became a huge hit in Australia. Tom, under a new name, went on to be awarded Australian of the Year in 1992, and a few years later, I interviewed him over the phone for a radio station.

I waited until the interview was done, then re-introduced myself as 'Bob and Judy's son'. There was a pause, as I wondered if he still remembered me. After all, it had been at least fifteen years since he had stayed with my family, and even longer since he had given me my new name.

'Heyyyyyyyy,' he exclaimed with joy. 'Stingray!! How are ya?'

How does all this relate to my brother?

Well, for years I always felt like I got the better name. Stingray is a cool-looking and sounding animal. I've since learned that the stingray is considered to be very family oriented, and a devoted and protective parent, but maybe he only named me that because I have a long barb at the end of one of my legs.

Salt Water, though, always seemed to me to be, well, the daggier of the two names. It's hard to draw a cool picture of salt water, or to identify with it, and I always felt sorry for my brother.

Recently, however, while discussing our names with the actor Shari Sebbens, who happens to be of Bardi Jabirr Jabirr heritage, she corrected me.

'Nah, man,' she opined, 'salt water is way better.'

When I asked why, she put my relationship with my brother into clear perspective.

'Cos stingray can't survive without salt water.'

Love ya Poofarty.

Back at high school, while other kids were looking to careers in medicine, or sport, my main goal was to deliver the farewell to the teachers when we left.

It was a tradition at Jannali Boys High that the vice-captain of the school would deliver a farewell speech/comedy roast to the teachers at their final assembly. From the moment I saw it happen, at age twelve, I knew that was what I wanted to do.

There was only one problem. When I reached my final year, I wasn't vice-captain.

What to do? I really wanted to deliver that speech/comedy routine, but I didn't want to take the mic away from someone else.

As the day approached, I gently raised the topic of the teachers' speech with the vice-captain, who was one of the sportiest guys at the school, but hardly an orator. I, on the other hand, was on the school debating team, and had taken part in a couple of public-speaking competitions.

I loved the act of debating, and tried very hard to perfect the art of getting a laugh while making a point. On at least one occasion we lost a debate because I was more focused on the jokes than the arguments. In fact, it was my enjoyment of public speaking that convinced me to give up my dreams of becoming a veterinarian, and aim instead for a future in journalism.

'So . . . are you gonna do the farewell to the teachers speech this year?' I enquired of our vice-captain, while looking like I didn't care about the answer and was simply making casual conversation.

His face turned to ash.

'I really don't want to,' came the reply. 'Do you wanna do it instead?'

'If you want me to,' I offered, trying to hide my excitement.

His face lit up.

'That would be amazing,' he beamed. 'I've been dreading this speech ever since I became vice-captain.'

It really looked like I had lifted a weight from his shoulders.

A few weeks later I delivered what I now consider to be my first stand-up comedy routine.

The only joke I remember was one that referred to the head librarian, who operated a particularly strict regime, often ejecting students for the most minor of indiscretions.

On the final day of school, some of the senior students had erected barbed wire around the entrance, and put up 'Danger, No Entry' signs, to which I said, 'It backfired, though, cos nobody was able to tell the difference!'

I know. Comedy gold, right?

The point is, the speech went well, got big laughs, and I would confidently describe it as my best moment at high school.

Mum later told me that as she left the stage, her sister turned to her and said, 'He should be a comedian.'

Yep, that was the plan.

Pop Goes the Cherry

And so it was, after a couple more years of listening to and watching Grahame Bond, Rodney Rude and Robin Williams, I arrived at the Sydney Comedy Store on Wednesday 13 July 1989 for my first 'open mic' spot.

I had actually been introduced to 'The Store' by one of my best mates, Dave Smiedt, who used to sing at the club upstairs, and I was immediately smitten (with the club, I mean). It was everything I now know a comedy club should be, and had that lethal combination of being downstairs, and having a low ceiling.

It was once put to me that going 'underground' to a club gives the audience a sense they are going somewhere illicit, where the rules will be well and truly broken. A low ceiling creates a sense of bonding, while also trapping the laughs in the room, allowing them to bounce around the crowd, rather than be lost into the ether above the audience's heads.

It soon became my favourite club in Sydney, and I watched enthralled every time I went. Names like George Smilovici, Vince Sorrenti and Austen Tayshus would headline the shows, but the person that struck me most was Bruno Lucia, under the stage name of Dino Valentino. Assuming an Italian accent and a demeanour that later saw him become a star on a sitcom called *All Together Now* (with the fondly remembered catch-phrase, 'Hey chickybabe'), Bruno was as slick as they come. Put simply, I wanted to do what he did.

But how? How could a sheltered, virginal, eighteen-year-old university student from the Shire take the step to becoming a comedian?

I didn't even know what an open mic night was. I had no idea that anyone could just rock up, put their name on a list, and go on stage that night. Only when I attended my second open mic night, did I realise you didn't have to come up with a new act every time you went on stage.

I spent my long bus rides to Macquarie University dreaming up routines, and would then blurt them out to my classmates, who looked at me as if to say, 'Dude, you're at uni.

You're meant to be smoking joints, drinking beer, and chasing girls. Not working up a stand-up set.'

I waited until the university holidays came around – what was it about comedy and holidays? – and decided on a date to make my stage debut.

At first, I didn't tell my parents that I was going to try stand-up comedy. I told them a group of us were going to the Comedy Store to celebrate my nineteenth birthday, which for all intents and purposes, was true. However, as more and more friends started calling, saying they wanted to see me 'celebrate', it became obvious something was going on.

I think it is fair to say my first gig was stunningly unremarkable. If I had been the MC that night, I wonder what I would have thought of the nineteen-year-old me. A cocky young uni student who thinks he's funny, bringing along a table of mates to laugh at his compilation of smutty old jokes.

Come to think of it, that's pretty much what the compere said after my act. I believe his exact words were, 'Isn't it funny how the guys that talk about sex the most, do it the least.' He received a round of applause for that.

It's even fairer to say I was totally clueless. I think I had a decent amount of stage presence, coming from my few years of high school debating, but there's a big difference between winning over a room of drunk audience members, and convincing a classroom of students that 'Compromise Makes a Good Umbrella'.

When I look back on the 'material' I delivered that night, I actively wince. Even now I couldn't tell you how it went. (Actually, I could, but I'm not going to.) There were a few old jokes, a few more old jokes, and a crappy attempt at a song parody. I'm embarrassed to even remember it, so there's no way in hell I'm going to repeat the act here.

My mates laughed heartily, bless them, then watched the rest of the acts without me as I sat at the comics' table at the back of the room. I figured it would be inappropriate to perform a set, then spend the show sitting at the front table. Unfortunately, it looked like I was snubbing them, but despite my act, I was trying to be vaguely professional.

I remember Ross Daniels was the headliner, but the night was pretty much a blur. As I left the room with my mates in tow, I'm sure nobody thought I'd be back. Again, what would I have said about the nineteen-year-old me as I left the building?

Probably the same thing the MC said as I passed by: 'Yeah, it's all well and good when your mates are here, but next time try it in front of strangers.'

So that's what I did.

Die Another Day

On 29 November 1989, six months after my first stage set (my parents laid down the rule that I could only perform during uni holidays), I turned up to the new Comedy Store premises in Cleveland Street, Surry Hills. This time around I had only three friends with me, who complied with my request to sit demurely at the back of the room. I wanted to go head to head with a roomful of complete strangers and learn once and for all, whether or not I really was funny.

I learnt a new phrase that night – 'to die on your arse'.

It started well enough, in fact my first joke received a decent response. It was a fairly obvious line about a local rugby coach, who had allegedly been caught in a compromising position in a Gents' toilet block. I offered the thought that he originally wanted to become an Aussie Rules football coach, but was turned down because he only knew how to score behinds.

(For British readers, a 'behind' is one point in Aussie rules, as opposed to a 'goal' which is six.)

Hardly comedy gold, but it got a big laugh, which is always handy on your first gag. Even now I tell comics that are just starting out (look at me, the grand old dame of comedy) – open with your second strongest joke, and finish with your strongest.

I was about to launch into joke number two, when I received my first ever heckle: 'That joke's about fourteen years old!'

Silence in the room.

To this day, I swear I wrote the joke myself. Whether or not I was the first person to have *ever* written that joke is a different story; I'm sure it has been told in some form ever since the word 'behind' became a sporting term. Either way, I'd never heard it before. Besides, it was my second ever gig. Whaddya want from me up here?

Even now I'm proud of my response. 'What a coincidence, so is your girlfriend.'

And I received my first ever round of applause. For a brief moment, I felt like the King of the World. I had been challenged to a gunfight in the street, and returned fire with deadly accuracy. In my mind, I blew the smoke from the tip of my pistol and did that swirly thing that cowboys do before placing it back in the holster.

There's a line in the Mel Brooks movie *Blazing Saddles* that describes what happened next. 'If you shoot him, you'll just make him mad.' That guy rode my ass for the rest of the set, and I folded like an origami swan. Not only had I made him look like an idiot, but I had attacked his girlfriend. He criticised my jokes, my shirt, and my existence, and I panicked. I tried to banter with him, failed dismally, and after five minutes of pain, loped off to a smattering of applause.

I am often asked what it's like when people don't laugh. I'll tell you this – they call it dying for a reason. I've died plenty of times since then, and I will probably die plenty more. I am sure you're aware that most people's top fear in life is of speaking in front of an audience. I think the real fear is looking like an idiot in front of other people, but as anyone who has done it will tell you – it's not the end of the world.

At the time, you feel like the world's biggest asshole, and that everyone on the planet knows what a loser you truly are, but the next day you wake up and realise that you're still alive. Gradually, as you go about your business, it dawns on you that the gig wasn't beamed to the entire country, not even to your entire street, and that life does indeed go on. And as a comic, you come to understand that every death carries an inherent lesson.

I was sitting backstage with my head between my knees, trying to work out what had just happened, when the MC came back and gave me his words of advice for dealing with hecklers. 'You went at him too early. It was a great line, but next time, wait until the audience hate him too. Then go for the kill.' Good advice, which was complemented by that of the headliner: 'And always have a few more heckle put-downs ready. Cos they'll keep coming back at you.'

It wasn't until I consoled myself with my mates that they inadvertently showed me what the real lesson was: Don't

Panic. They pointed out to me that the guy gave me the perfect opportunity for a put-down and I missed it. When I asked what he did for a living, he replied, 'I work as an artist.' My friends were convinced I was about to respond, 'You work as an artist. Surely that's a contradiction in terms,' but it never came.

Always remember – you have the microphone and the ability. Trust yourself and you'll find what's funny. And above all, don't panic.

Hug Life

Sometimes I think it's a good thing for a comedian to die early in his or her career. It makes you question whether you truly want to do this job, or whether you're only in it for the good times. That early death shook my confidence like you wouldn't believe, but for some insane reason, I wanted to give it another shot. Somewhere I knew I could do it, and now I wanted to prove it to myself. I wanted to do it properly.

So when a friend suggested I hop up and do five minutes at one of his gigs, I didn't even need the thinking music.

Peter Fox had been performing for a year or so when I started, and was at the support act stage. He was appearing at the Palms Hotel, Chullora, alongside Bazza Banana and the headliner, Austen Tayshus, and I had gone along to watch.

Bazza Banana was a legend of Sydney comedy. Real name Barry Sandford, he was in his seventies, possibly even eighties, and had performed on the early Sydney vaudeville circuit with Roy Rene. He had lived through the advent of radio, film and television, and was still making a living as a live comedian amongst the purveyors of so-called 'alternative comedy'.

With a rubber face that he would contort into an impression of a Pekingese pup, and jokes that could only be described as classics, everyone vaguely associated with the circuit loved him.

'I bought myself a greyhound,' he would wheeze. 'Painted a bus on the side.' Sensational. Occasionally age would take its toll and the joke would come out wrong – 'I bought myself a bus, painted a greyhound on the side' – but his delivery was so good, it would still get a laugh.

Bazz opened the show and introduced Peter, who did a crackin' fifteen minutes. Meanwhile the owner was starting to panic – Austen hadn't arrived. Although three years after his number one hit, 'Australiana', Austen was still the man, and there was a roomful of people who had paid good money to see him.

Bazz got back up and did another fifteen minutes of impressions and jokes, after which Peter suggested I do a five-minute spot. Like I said, no thinking music required. Bazz introduced me, and I delivered my opening gag, the one about the disgraced football coach. Remember? 'He wanted to coach Australian rules, but he only knew how to score behinds.' And a funny thing happened. I got a round of applause. For a joke. A joke that I had written.

A roomful of people liked my joke so much that they laughed and clapped their hands. From that moment on, I was hooked. The rest of the set went well, and when the club owner stood up and told the crowd it was only my third ever gig, there was more applause.

Austen arrived and did his set, but to be honest I didn't pay too much attention. I did it! I had stood before a room of strangers and made them laugh, and it felt amazing. I spent the rest of the night floating. I was more excited than I had ever been, and accepted the congratulations of passing audience members like a proud bridegroom.

I turned to Bazz and asked the only question I really wanted the answer to, and I figured after at least sixty years in the business, he was the person to ask. 'Do you still feel like this when you've had a good gig?'

'All the time,' he replied, without even thinking about it. 'All the time. It's the best job in the world.' And with that, he gave me a hug.

Later, as Peter and I wandered back to the car, he paused as he opened the door. 'You're going to go a long way in comedy. A long way.'

'What makes you say that,' I asked.

'Because Barry Sandford gave you a hug.'

And so a career, and an addiction, was born.

Acting Up

It is fair to say my parents weren't entirely enamoured by my new career path, and yet they also made me the comedian I am today.

After three or four attempts at stand-up, I brought home a video tape of one of my performances. In an attempt at encouragement, Mum persuaded Dad to sit down and watch my five minutes of poorly delivered sex jokes. I couldn't bring myself to watch it with them, so I hid away in my bedroom.

After three minutes, I heard my Dad storm out, saying, 'It's not even funny, it's just filth.'

Mum handed me back the tape with a look of pity on her face.

'Maybe I should play a character,' I said forlornly.

'No,' she said, 'just be yourself. You *are* funny.'

I took both of their opinions on board and came up with new material – about them.

The first proper routine I delivered was about how embarrassing it was when your parents used to drop you at school in front of the other kids, and would insist on a kiss goodbye.

The bit ended with: 'One day I thought, right, I've had enough. So I stuck the tongue in. Hey, it was the last time Dad ever dropped me to school.'

Finally, a bit of comedy that was clean.

The first time I delivered it, one of the Comedy Store regulars, a gentleman called Jim Burnett, who famously produced the Australian TV show *Hey, Hey It's Saturday*, took me aside and said, 'That's better. Keep talking about what you know.'

I talked about my grandparents, my childhood, and even started to chat to the crowd a little bit. By the time a journalist from the *Sydney Morning Herald* came along to review an open mic night, I was singled out as 'the highlight of the night' with 'a fine ability to ad-lib under pressure and a penchant for talking about his family.'

The original agreement was that I could only perform stand-up in my uni holidays, but after the summer break of 1989/90, I managed to convince my parents that comedy was the one career choice I was going to stick with. Not like that short-lived astronomy phase.

They relented and said I could perform each Wednesday at the Comedy Store's open mic night.

Every week I'd turn up an hour before the show, put my name into a hat, and await the outcome of the order. There were ten spots on offer every night, five minutes each, and if more than ten open mikers arrived, the first out of the hat were on. The rest were guaranteed a spot the following week.

I know now that we were lucky. I've heard that the Los Angeles Comedy Store often has up to a hundred open spots arrive at three in the afternoon to vie for a position. In New York apparently there is a three-month wait to do an open spot, and the same goes for the Comedy Store in London. In Sydney, though, in those pre-Fox Studios days where it was highly unlikely a film producer would drop in to scout for talent, there were about a dozen of us.

The open mikers became a fairly close-knit bunch, and our ranks included John Philpott (the Bush Psychiatrist from Dunnedoo), Peter Berner, James O'Loghlin, Haskel Daniel and his amazing sound effects, Peter Saleh (later to be known as Akmal), Gary Eck, Anthony Mir and Dan McCartan (the last four later formed a show called 'All Aussie Are Boofta'). There was Belinda Franks, Ian Triffitt, Sylvia Karlov, Steady Eddy, and a softly spoken but exceedingly funny Irishman called Jimeoin.

On the weekends, some of us would drop in to watch the professionals in action. We'd beg and plead for a five-minute spot, and if the manager, a brilliant, gorgeous, nurturing young woman called Ingrid, was feeling generous, she would let us on stage.

The Comedy Store was the only full-time comedy club in Sydney, and I missed it when I wasn't there. If I was out and about with friends on a Saturday night, I'd drop in to the Store on my way home to check out the late show. Once the audience had left, the comics on the bill and any others who had also dropped in, would sit around, raid the bar, and swap gig stories.

In many ways, this book is merely a collection of those stories. Every comedian has them, I was just sober enough to remember them, and nerdy enough to write them all down.

Like the time a couple of local actors appeared, wanting to try their hands at stand-up. Ooh, the tension. It was as if a group of rabbis had asked to join a pilgrimage to Mecca.

These young upstarts reckoned they could do comedy, not because they had a love of the art form, but because they weren't getting acting work and considered it a last resort. (That's how we saw it anyway.) To make matters worse, they had even brought along a group of friends to laugh at them. None of us would ever sink that low . . . Ahem.

To be fair, they weren't bad. The guy did a fairly amusing comedy lecture about his girlfriend, and the girl performed a skit as some sort of schoolgirl character. Their friends laughed, as did the audience, but we knew they wouldn't be back.

Hah! Not as easy as it looks is it? Maybe you should go back to your little acting classes and see if that makes you famous, we thought, but were too afraid to say.

The schoolgirl character was a woman named Gia Carides, who went on to appear alongside Mike Myers in *Austin Powers: The Spy Who Shagged Me*.

Lecture-boy, aka John Polson, co-starred with Russell Crowe in one of my all-time favourite movies *The Sum of Us*, as well as *Mission: Impossible 2* with Tom Cruise. He's also the man behind Sydney's Tropfest Short Film Festival.

As for those in the audience, Naomi Watts is one of the movie world's hottest stars, appearing in David Lynch's *Mulholland Drive* and *Twin Peaks*, and giving an Oscar-nominated performance in *21 Grams*.

I've since come to learn that actors and stand-up comics are different animals. Each with different talents and skills, and each unable to understand fully what the other does. A friend told me recently of a wedding he attended, in which the bride was an actor and the groom a comedian.

One of the bride's thespian friends read a poem, and delivered it with passion, pathos, poignancy and pride. As he returned to his seat, every actor in the room jumped to their feet, in tears, applauding and nudging each other to say, 'Wasn't he brilliant?'

Every comedian in the room looked at each other and said, 'What a wanker.'

The Hardest Job in the World

'Oh my God, is that what I think it is?' asked the young male waiter, who was staring over our shoulders, eyes locked on the stage. We followed his gaze and immediately gasped. From where we were sitting, side on to the performer, it appeared that he had a full, well . . . nah, it couldn't be. Maybe his pants were sticking out at an odd angle.

'Nope,' countered the waiter, 'that's definitely a hard-on.' (Another gasp.)

A swarm of questions buzzed around the table. Was he aroused by someone in the audience? Was it a prop? Did it develop while on stage or did he bring it on with him? And finally, 'Do you think it happens every time?'

Now this thought was too bizarre to even contemplate. I mean, I've felt a certain degree of excitement while performing, and to be brutally honest, have occasionally been slightly turned on by certain faces in the crowd, but I've never raised the Union Jack, so to speak. Surely he wouldn't be able to think straight?

Besides, we'd been performing with him for at least eighteen months now. You'd think we'd have noticed if he was always, you know, pitching a tent. He finished his five-minute set, and exited the stage, to a bemused and strangely silent green room.

The following week, the open mikers' table was packed. At least a dozen comedy meerkats had assembled, to check out act number three's, um, material, and I have to say, it was one of the most remarkable things I've ever seen. The performer in question (whose name in all good conscience I could never divulge) stood before the microphone, side on to us, and began his act.

Sure enough, a bulge began to form in his pants. The bulge became a lump, the lump became a rod, and within forty-five seconds (although to be fair, I wasn't actually looking at my watch) he was sporting a fully fitted, hundred per cent, bona fide, put the glasses down, the horse has bolted, erection.

It was a moment of pure majesty that should have been accompanied by the theme from *2001: A Space Odyssey*.

Not only did he manage to, ahem, raise the Titanic, but he kept it out of the water for the entire five-minute set. A remarkable achievement, but one that also raised a few more questions. How on earth can one perform while sexually aroused? Was he even aware of his own erection? Did the audience ever notice? Was that why his on-stage manner was so laid back?

I'm afraid to say not one of these questions was ever answered, because none of us knew quite how to broach the subject. I mean, what do you say? 'Hey, great gig, mate. Like your stuff. What's with the horn?' To compound matters, he had just been booked for his first fifteen-minute spot. Would he be able to keep it up for that long? Sadly, the answer to that one was – no.

To be perfectly blunt, the little engine that could began to lose steam at around the eight-minute mark. By ten minutes he was flagging, and by fifteen it was everyone off at Pancake City.

The bizarre thing (as if the rest of this was entirely by the by) was that the laughs died off at exactly the same rate as his arousal. Could it be that he was actually turned on by the laughs? Or was his falling stock affecting his delivery, and therefore losing the audience?

Sadly, we'll never find out. He is no longer involved in comedy, having never managed to keep the laughs up for a solid fifteen minutes. How he'd have handled a full ninety-minute show, with interval, I will never know. Perhaps he'd have cranked out a killer ten minutes, then had a break for half an hour to recharge. Maybe some sort of tantric arrangement was needed. Either way, he was the only performer I ever saw who truly embodied the phrase 'stand-up comedy'.

Mr X and Mr Y

There is a performer's maxim: 'What happens on tour stays on tour.' Basically, it means exactly that. In the heady, wound-up world of performing, things happen, people get carried away, and the madness of the whole situation can take hold of you – with horrible consequences. The saying can also be extended to: 'What happens backstage, stays backstage.' Either way, I probably shouldn't tell you this next story.

It was early 1990, and I was still doing open mic nights, although after five months of solid performances was on the verge of snaring my first professional booking. The show was about to kick off when a particularly well-known and respected headline act, let's call him Mr X, wandered through the front door accompanied by a relatively talented Australian actor, Mr Y. Now, when I say 'wandered' through the front door, I really mean 'careered like disoriented rhinos', for they were inebriated, soused, hammered, and all things in-between.

The show started, and the demolished duo took their seats at the back of the room. Although rowdy, rambunctious, even a little rude (and unnecessarily alliterative), they were well-enough behaved. Until 'she' took to the stage.

'She' was a first-timer, fairly cute, but obviously inexperienced. Backstage she was shy, petite, and painfully hopeful. On stage she had just delivered her first tentative joke when from the back of the room came the bellowing direction, 'Why don't you fuck off home?'

Any heckle is confronting, sometimes more so for the audience than for the performer, but it is an unwritten rule that you don't heckle a first-timer. It is also an unwritten rule that you don't heckle another performer. I find the defendant, an Australian actor by the name of Mr Y, guilty on both counts, m'lud.

As 'she' tried to regain some composure and dignity, and any vague memory she may still have had of which joke came next, he followed up, 'I said, why don't you fuck off home where you belong?'

Even now the memory of it makes me nervous and edgy. It was an all-out, unprovoked attack on a totally defenceless woman. Imagine a Rottweiler savaging a goldfish, or the US Military dropping cluster bombs on a stone hut.

It continued, 'What makes you think you're funny? You should be at home cooking dinner for the kids. Get off stage and don't ever come back.' All the while, Mr X looked on in glee.

'Listen,' she countered, but was stopped.

'No, you listen, love. You're not funny, you're shit. You shouldn't be doing comedy. You should be at home in the kitchen.'

It was truly horrible, and there was nothing anyone could do. She folded, left the stage to the pity of the audience, and the unmitigated hatred of an obscure actor. As the next act launched into his set, to an audience still in shock, I wandered – and by 'wandered', I mean tiptoed – backstage to prepare for my set, and perhaps offer some sort of condolence. But someone had beaten me to it.

Somehow, Mr X had ensconced himself next to her and was offering words of support. That's right, the man who had just watched as his mate decimated this poor woman. Her head on his shoulder, his arm around her shoulder, she was nestled into him like a frightened bird. And I realised what was happening.

He had set Mr Y up to heckle her, so that he could provide a shoulder to cry on. He had ridden in as the knight in shining armour, not letting on he was actually in cahoots with the dragon. And now he was hitting on her, in her time of need. I was incensed, outraged, affronted, and I did what any self-respecting nineteen-year-old would do. I sat quietly in the corner.

Until Mr X caught my gaze and turned on me. 'You. Fuck off. Now.' (Pause) 'You heard me. Fuck off.'

'But I'm on next.'

'I don't care. Fuck off now.'

To his eternal credit, the compere protested, 'But Adam's on next. He's supposed to be backstage.'

'I said I don't care. Leave the room. Now.' Once again, I did what any self-respecting nineteen-year-old would do when faced with a drunk bear in the midst of a mating ritual. I left the room.

I was still shaking when I walked on stage. Horrified by what I had seen, cursing myself for not doing anything about it, and desperately trying to hold it together in front of a hundred strangers, I struggled through my set, and returned to the comics' table, where I sat until the interval. At which time, Mr X approached me.

'What's wrong?' he asked.

I decided it was time to make a stand. 'I'm not used to being told to fuck off right before a gig.' And I did it. I made a stand. Not much of a stand, but a stand nevertheless. Screw you Mister-I'm-a-big-name-headliner-and-I-can-treat-people-like-shit, I saw what you did, and I'm calling you on it. I'm mad as hell, and I'm not going to . . .

'Well, GET used to it, asshole!' was not the response I was hoping for. 'Cos until you crawl your way out of the slime of talentless pricks that inhabit this place, you're gonna get treated like shit.'

I'm sure there were at least three more sentences, but to be honest I can't remember what they were. I only remember the viciousness of what was said. The anger, the invective, as he stood above me like an angered god, striking shards of lightning upon me. OK, maybe I'm getting carried away with my analogies, but you get the gist.

I waited for him to finish, and make his way to the toilets, before I left the table and headed into the office with tears in my eyes. I was angry at him for what he had said, I was angry at his mate for what he did, but mainly I was angry at myself for letting it all get to me. For being a shaking, intimidated, weak nineteen-year-old, and for letting it affect my performance.

For years after that night, I thought the moral of the story was: it doesn't matter what happens in the dressing room, don't bring it on stage with you. Leave it at the curtains, you can pick it up when you return. What happens backstage, stays backstage.

Recently, though, in a world of sexually abusive behaviour being called out for what it is, I've realised there is more I should have done.

I wish now I had stood up backstage and told the woman who had just been heckled that the man consoling her was mates with the man who heckled her. That she shouldn't be dissuaded from doing comedy because two drunk performers decided to take her down publicly, and then take advantage of her afterwards.

I could have told the performer in question how out of line he was being.

But I was nineteen. And he was drunk. And a hell of a lot bigger than me.

The woman went home alone, and the man in question later took to the stage to give a drunken, barely coherent performance, before being legitimately heckled off by genuine audience members.

Karma's great. But I could have done better.

Day of the Triffitt

My first ever paid gig was a piece of shit. There's no other way to put it. It was in a nightclub in North Sydney, and being a uni night, I had to beg and plead with my parents to let me do it.

I was still studying, and my courses included Linguistics, Telecommunications, Journalism, and Australian Cinema.

Often, I'd be analysing an Aussie actor in a film during a tutorial by day, then performing with them the following night.

My parents relented, and I delivered my first professional set to about forty financial sector suits (mainly blokes) boozed up after work, in a club with disco lighting, a temporary stage, a nearby bar area making the world's noisiest cocktails, and thumping music from the room next door.

To be fair, only the headline act, Austen Tayshus, had a decent gig, but I received absolutely no laughs, had beer coasters thrown at me (and when they come spinning out of the glare of the spotlight and ricochet off the microphone, it can be quite a shock) and left the stage after about ten minutes.

A week later, I had my first paid spot at the Comedy Store, and it was a lot better and a lot worse. A Saturday night, a full house, and a stag party seated on the upper level.

To this day, I, and every comedian on the planet, shudder when told there's a stag night in – or a buck's night, as we call them in Australia. A bunch of pumped-up lads, full to the brim of testosterone and alcohol, and with no women in the group to try to impress. Add to this a roomful of strangers in front of which to show off, and a lone performer in a spotlight – a lamb and a slaughter anyone?

Years later, I ran into an old schoolmate who was at the Store on a buck's night, and asked him why they had chosen a comedy night. His answer: 'Well, we couldn't decide whether to go out and get hammered, or come to the Comedy Store and fuck up a comedian's act. So we decided to do both.' Ah, the glamour, the respect, the adulation.

The first act was summarily booed off. Even after thirteen years of comedy, I reckon I've seen only about a dozen acts booed so loudly they had to leave the stage. This particular act was Iain Triffitt, an incredible writer, who as far as I know actually invented the joke that I've seen repeated endlessly around the world – 'My grandfather is so old, his phone number is seven.'

Sadly for Ian, he was also quite shy, well-mannered, and intelligent. They hated him. They actively hated him and cheered when he left the stage. The next act was more experienced, and managed to deal with it, and although constantly heckled, he made it through his twenty minutes.

During the interval I sat backstage, head in my hands, going over my act. I wasn't scared. I think 'determined' was the word.

To this day, I'm never really afraid of a rough audience. Fired up, maybe, but not afraid. What's the worst that can happen? Sure, they might yell and boo, but hey, they're doing that to everyone anyway. I don't mind dying in front of a rough crowd; it's dying in front of an easy crowd that hurts.

Anyway, as I sat there gritting my teeth and preparing for a battle, but also kinda enjoying it, Ingrid the manager spoke up. 'Look at Adam, having kittens in the corner,' and then she laughed. I looked at her, and around the room, and realised – they don't think I can handle it.

Here was I, a fairly sheltered nineteen-year-old mass communications student, facing one of the toughest audiences the Store had seen, and in their eyes, about to go down in flames.

If ever there was a sentence that was going to fire me up, 'look at Adam having kittens' was it. Not only did I decide I was gonna kick that audience's ass, but I was determined to show Ingrid and the rest of the comics that I could do this shit.

The compere opened the second half, and was just launching into my introduction, when Iain Triffitt approached me.

'I just realised what I should have said,' he began. 'The bucks are sitting right outside the men's toilets. I should have said, "Hey, isn't it slightly suspicious that a table of blokes are sitting right outside the men's toilets?"'

Then, in an act of pure generosity for which I'll forever be in his debt, Ian added, 'If you need to use it, it's all yours.'

Before I even got to the microphone, they started on me. From memory, they yelled my name in a childish/sarcastic way, criticised my shirt, and offered other generic insults, some of which entailed my mum.

I waited for a pause, and with more attitude than I had any right to possess, I said, 'Hey, isn't it a little suspicious that a table of blokes is sitting right outside the men's toilets?'

Even the bucks broke into applause. And they didn't say a word for the rest of my set. See, that's the weird thing about buck's parties – once you put them in their place, they generally shut up. They have issued the challenge, stood raking the ground with their hooves, brandished their horns, charged, and been knocked backwards onto their butts. Nine times out of ten, they will simply acknowledge the victor, show due respect, and behave themselves until another stag steps forward.

Hen nights on the other hand, are a riddle wrapped in a Doberman. An attack on one is an attack on all, and believe me, once you issue a put-down you will never hear the end of it. Sadly, it took me years of comedy to learn that one.

So, there it was. Potentially the roughest gig of my career, but I had a killer, thanks to a combination of a backstage slur (that Ingrid swears was a disguised pep talk), a determination to stand tall in the face of danger, and a little false bravado. Oh yeah, and an act of generosity from a man who stopped performing less than a year later, and whom I haven't seen since. The next month Ingrid booked me for four gigs, and I've been a paid professional ever since.

Mr Iain Triffitt, wherever you are, I owe you one.

Big Yin and I (Part One)

The first time I met Billy Connolly, he was standing outside the Sydney Opera House. He was due to perform there that night, and I had bought tickets to see him, but I didn't expect him to be standing in front of the venue (and I say venue in the same way someone might naively call the Taj Mahal 'a building').

I was excited enough about seeing him perform, but to bump into him before the show, casually window shopping . . . well, I had to have a chat. Like a star-struck waif, I introduced myself, told him I was coming to the show, and asked if he still got nervous before performing.

It was the only question I wanted to ask, and is one of the most common questions I am asked now. My general answer is – God, yes. If I'm nervous, it means I care about doing a good show. I actually start to worry when I'm not nervous.

Billy's answer was pretty much the same.

'I don't actually get nervous, so much as anxious,' he said in that unmistakeable accent. 'I just want to get out there and do it, y'know.'

What struck me was that he spoke to me as he would a friend – chatty, open, and obviously quite used to strangers starting up conversations with him on the street.

44

I was about to tell him that I had just started stand-up myself, when I heard my name called from across the courtyard. It was a professional comic, Lawrie Coy. He acts and directs now, but in those days he went by the stage name of Pat McGroin – 'I've got a brother who does bikini lines, Nick McGroin, and a sister who is a prostitute, Cher McGroin.'

Lawrie was doing a show in the Opera House studio venue along with some other bigger name Sydney comics, and assumed I was there to see them. I awkwardly informed him I had come to see, um, Mr Connolly, whom he had failed to recognise. Lawrie apologised, introduced himself, and invited Billy along to see their show one night.

'I'd love to, but I don't go to comedy shows, cos I find I accidentally steal the material.' (The worst crime a comic can commit.) 'I'll find myself on stage six months later, chatting away about something and suddenly think – hang on, that's someone else's joke. So thanks for the invite, but you'll understand if I'm not there.'

'Don't worry about it,' joked Lawrie. 'We'll probably nick all *your* jokes.'

At which point Billy placed a hand on my shoulder, and in all sincerity, said, 'Oh, by all means dooo. If you see something you like, just take it. It's all yours.'

Not only was he conscious of not taking anyone's material, but he was offering us his. That's unheard of. Of course, we could never get away with doing his jokes, because everyone would know whose they were. Either way, it was a fairly generous offer.

At that point a theatre manager came to collect him, and he patted both of us on the shoulder and bade us farewell.

Was it a sign from above that comedy really was the right career path?

A few months earlier I had been sitting in the front row of a show by the Irish comedian Dave Allen. As he ended the first half, he called to me in the audience, 'Are you a drinking man, sir?'

I nodded, and he offered me a glass of champagne, which I duly took. At no point until then had he interacted with me, but for some reason he offered me a drink. Was that a sign, too?

Probably not, but I was young and obsessed with comedy. First Dave Allen gave me his champagne, now Billy Connolly gives me a pat on the shoulder.

Connolly's show was wonderful – two and a half hours with no interval – and as I sat there entranced, I probably had visions of meeting Billy again someday and telling him how great his show was.

The nineteen-year-old me would have loved the thought of Billy Connolly popping up occasionally throughout my career, like a Hairy Godmother, pointing me in the right direction, or offering words of advice.

Maybe he would even see me perform one day.

Not for a second would I have considered that it might actually happen. Then again, I never assumed that it wouldn't.

Badoom–Tish

As well as the regular gigs at the Comedy Store (yes, I was chuffed to consider myself a 'regular'), a few outside bookings started coming in. Self-labelled 'promoters' would turn up to open mic nights, looking for comics that were willing to work for petrol money and a bag of crisps, but were also decent enough to keep an audience seated for ten minutes.

We strutted our stuff like preening peacocks, and every now and again would be rewarded with a spot at (for instance) the Campbelltown Catholic Club Talent Show. Oh yes, my friend, the big time. Ten acts, one compere, and an on-stage band.

Basically, they were getting ten singers turn up every week, and wanted to break up the competitors with some comedy. I'd still have to compete like everyone else, but I would also receive a twenty-dollar appearance fee.

I asked one of the professional comics, Graham Pugh, if I should take the gig, and was told I should for two reasons.

First, every gig is a learning experience, especially when you're starting out, and second, to prove his theory that every talent show compere was legally required to sing a standard tune called 'Water'. I needed experience, and I'd never heard the song 'Water', so either way I figured I'd be a winner.

I schlepped my way out to the venue, using at least half of my gig money in petrol, negotiated the valley of gambling machines, and wandered backstage. Oh my God. The dressing room was a psychologist's wet dream. Over-protective mothers fluffed their oh-so-pretentious daughters, trying desperately to attain some sense of achievement in their lives by encouraging their offspring, whether they wanted it or not.

Nerdy wannabes (like me) mingled with those who had gorgeous singing voices but the stage presence of a black hole, or alternatively, the charisma of Robert De Niro combined with the singing voice of a galah. The band tuned up, the organiser slipped me a twenty, and the MC took to the stage.

To be fair, some of the acts weren't too bad and the audience was extremely supportive. I strode to the mic and told my first gag (which at this point was still the one about the disgraced Rugby coach). The response was not quite what I had expected. The crowd laughed, thank the Lord, but in amongst it there was another noise I had heard before, but never after one of my own jokes.

It couldn't be, could it? I told another, this time keeping an ear out, and sure enough it was there again. I turned to face the band, and saw the drummer gleaming with joy. He was giving me what can only be described as a 'badoom–tish' after each joke. You know what I mean. Technically called a rimshot, it's the noise associated with any and every corny, vaudeville, mother-in-law gag ever written. And I was getting them.

What can you do in a situation like that? One can hardly turn mid-gig to an on-stage performer and ask, 'Can you not do that, please?' So, at the age of nineteen, I did an entire five-minute set accompanied by my own 'badoom–tish' drummer. To make matters worse, he sometimes came in too early and drummed before I had said the funny bit. By the end of the set, I was telling stories to the crowd, but pausing to say, 'Wait for it, wait for ittt . . .' to the drummer.

I stayed to the end of the gig, partly out of respect for the other performers (a habit I try to maintain to this day), but also because we all had to reassemble on stage for the awards ceremony. First place went to a ten-year-old girl, who sang 'I Think We're Alone Now' by Tiffany. I came in third and won another thirty dollars to go with my twenty-buck appearance fee.

As I left the stage and the venue, the band kicked in, and the compere began a song I had never heard before, and have never heard since. I waited for the chorus, and sure enough it was 'Water'.

Mission accomplished.

Three Part Harmony

In the late 1980s, Sydney comedy was experiencing a slight upswing, and Steve Harmony (not his real name) decided his 'Promotions' company deserved a piece of the action. You see, when comedy is out of fashion, only those truly devoted to the craft attempt to run gigs. But when comedy hits a boom, every promoter in town thinks he can bung a milk crate and a microphone in the corner of a pub and *voilà* – The Guildford Arms Comedy Night.

The best way to describe Steve is to tell you of a phone conversation he once had, while in a meeting with some Sydney stand-ups. Steve had called them in to discuss establishing a comedy night in one of his clients' pubs, and mid-chat, his phone rang.

'Hello, SH Promotions.'

(*Pause*)

'Well, yes, we do have some strippers.'

(*Pause*)

'Oh no, they're very classy. None of your smut.'

(*Pause*)

'Nah, nah, nah, they stay in lingerie the entire time,
they make no physical contact with the customers,
and there are no props of any sort.'

(*Pause*)

'What?'

(*Pause*)

'Oh, they can do all that stuff if you want! Oh, shit
yeah, mate, we do full frontal, spreados, cream on the
tits, dry rooting – you want it, mate, they'll do it.'

(*Pause*)

'Top stuff, listen, I'm in a meeting at the moment. You
work out what you want and give me a call back, OK?
Good on ya, mate, bye.'

(*Hangs up receiver and turns to the comics.*)

'Right, now about this comedy.'

* * *

I didn't know of this previous encounter until after I agreed to play the Guildford Hotel and, to be honest, I would probably still have taken the booking. When you're a nineteen-year-old comic with eleven months' experience, any gig will do, and besides, who can turn down eighty bucks?

You know it's going to be a rough gig when the only advice given to you by another comic is: 'Make sure you can see your car from the stage.' Sadly, this was made possible by the fact that the backdrop for the stage was the window that faced onto the street. This also meant that the front door was directly to the right of the stage – anyone entering the pub mid-show would look like they were the next act on.

The room itself was, well, shit. The stage was a board balanced on milk crates, there was a microphone, and a spotlight. That was it. Oh, and a pool table: the natural born enemy of the stand-up comic. You'd be surprised how easily a punchline can be drowned out by the sound of a fifteen-ball break.

When it was gently suggested to the four blokes playing pool that the noise of the game would interfere with the show, they responded with, 'Well, looks like there won't be a fuckin' show then.'

They were enticed away from the table by the promise of a few free beers, and they joined the rest of the audience. When I say audience, I mean the twenty-three people scattered randomly throughout the room. At a guess, I'd say there were at least fifteen mullets in that place, along with five goatees, two handlebar moustaches, three shaved heads and seventy-eight tattoos. Of the twenty-three audience members, nine were women. I refer you to the previous mullet count.

Steve Harmony had appointed himself the MC, and introduced me thus: 'Righto, your first act, well, he's pretty new, here he is – Adam Hills.' Not the most auspicious of introductions, and to be fair, I did OK. I had told myself beforehand not to expect any laughs, and to do my material as if it were a monologue. If by chance someone did laugh, I'd pause, but otherwise I'd plough on through.

It seemed to work, in fact they kinda enjoyed it, and before they knew what hit them, I'd compressed a fifteen-minute set into eleven, said thank you and goodnight. The next act was comedian and juggler Nick Penn. After receiving the same lukewarm reaction as me, he pulled out the big guns – colour and movement.

'OK, ladies and gentlemen, it's time for some juggling,' he began, as he reached into a prop bag and pulled out three bowling pins. 'I'm going to start with these clubs.'

Before a single projectile had left his hand, a short wiry man of about fifty staggered to the stage, dressed resplendently in Stubbies shorts and a T-shirt, with a face that had been soaked in beer for the best part of a decade, and yelled, 'Why don't you juggle some balls?'

Without missing a beat, Nick responded, 'I dunno, why don't you juggle yours?'

Now normally this retort would be seen by an audience member to be the end of the exchange, a quick and witty comeback that lets the comedian get on with his job. At the Guildford Arms, this particular scenario was seen as a request.

Old leather face reached down towards the bottom of his Stubbies, which to be fair wasn't that far from his navel, and pulled aside a shorts-leg to reveal that he was in fact sans-underwear. Quelle surprise.

With a cheeky wink and a toothless grin, he then used his free hand to, literally, 'juggle his balls'. Sure, it was a fairly basic one-handed juggle, no tricks or behind-the-back flamboyance, but hey, he was using his own testicles. After a minute or so, he retired to the bar, accompanied by the cheers of the crowd. Strangely, the rest of Nick's set was a relative anti-climax.

An interval was called, during which a befuddled elderly gentleman joined us at the comedians' table. Unshaven, and with a confused manner, he didn't seem to understand that the table was reserved for comedians. In fact, he didn't seem to understand he would be watching comedians. A plastic wristband with a phone number on it drew our attention, and it was decided that the manager would call the number just in case.

Meanwhile the second half swung into action, with Gary Latham, another newer comic with a distinctly surreal style of comedy. It is fair to say that surrealism probably hadn't made it to Guildford at that point. I'd hazard a guess the majority of the audience thought Dali was an Indian side dish.

Gary battled on regardless, until an obviously disgruntled audience member strode from the back of the room, past the stage and out the door, pausing only to say, 'You're shit, mate.'

Stung, Gary's gaze followed the mulletted (is that a word?) critic onto the street, past the window, and on past my car until he was out of sight. At which point Gary said, very quietly, 'Yeah well, you're a prick, mate. You're a fuckin' prick. What would you know, you dickhead.' Fully aware of the futility of his volume, Gary turned to the audience and countered, 'Well, that showed him.'

At which point the door swung open, and the whirlwind of flannelette returned, spitting, 'What did you call me, what did you fuckin' say? I'll fuckin' do ya, mate.'

Gary retreated even further, and could only respond with, 'It was just a joke, mate. Just a joke. I didn't say anything. Really.' Perhaps realising the inherent irony (although probably not) of punching a comedian, our Wildean punter backed away, warily threatening, 'Just watch yourself, OK.'

The final act of the night was Rob McHugh, a true ruffian with a heart of gold. Dressed in black T-shirt and jeans, he looked to be the saviour of the night. After some warmly received material on sex, he moved on to the coup de grass – the drug jokes. Rob had ten minutes of cracking drug material that was hitting home with the assembled mob.

Suddenly the stage-side door swung open, and two uniformed police officers entered – to be met by the booming words, 'So I was lighting up this massive joint . . .'

A local rest home had alerted the officers that one of their patients had escaped and was sitting at the comics' table at the Guildford Hotel. The next ten minutes were spent watching the simultaneous events of (1) Two policemen trying to convince a seventy-year-old man in pyjamas to leave a pub and (2) A stand-up comic telling every clean joke he could think of, most of which began with, 'Two guys walk into a bar . . .'

When Rob finally left the stage, there was a cheer of massive proportions, but I think that may have been because the old fella was threatening to fight both policemen at once. Eventually the three left, and it was left to Steve to mop up proceedings. 'This is only the first night, ladies and gents. Tell your friends, there'll be comedy here every week.'

* * *

The following week, Steve introduced a young female comic by saying, 'This next chick on, well, she's not real funny, but I fucked her and she was good at that . . .'

He never ran a comedy night again.

Best Foot Forward

If you're getting the impression that the Sydney comedy scene in the early Nineties was like the Wild West, you're kinda right.

From what I've heard, though, it was nowhere near as bad as it used to be. Legend has it that the early days of the Comedy Store were compered by Rodney Rude, who would sit side of stage with a water pistol. If an act wasn't going well, he'd fire at their genitals, making it look to the audience like they were wetting themselves.

The Store had since moved premises, and matured, but only slightly.

The attitude was summed up by some graffiti written on the backstage walls. As I sat there one night, shitting a thousand bricks before a gig, I noticed the following gem.

A comic is only as good as the audience.

A lovely thought, but I felt it meant one could blame an audience if a gig went badly. So I added (and quite cleverly, I reckoned) one of my own.

An audience is only as bad as the comic.

A witty riposte, thought I, and went on my way contentedly. The next time I appeared there, underneath it all was scrawled something that summed this entire business up.

Who gives two country fucks. Just be funny and they will laugh.

I took every gig I could, from an afternoon show in a strip club, to an Italian christening that I remember like this:

Eight o'clock at night. Guests leaving. Dance floor, children as young as three running around at my feet. Old Italian men that don't speak English. Helium balloons, and an in-house PA that interrupted me to say, 'Number forty-two, your steak's ready.' Eighty dollars, no laughs, and a girlfriend watching on, thinking, is this the way he's gonna provide for me for the rest of my life?

Early on in my career, my ability to ad-lib held me in good stead. I only did it because Robin Williams did, and I wanted to be like him, but it was a handy talent to have, especially as an MC.

The MC, or compere, is the person who starts the show off, and introduces each act to the audience. It sounds like a simple job, but there are some sneaky facets to it that make it more difficult than it appears.

For starters, you're walking out to a cold audience. They haven't laughed yet, they haven't really looked at the stage, and some of them don't know what's about to happen.

Your job is to tell them how the show is gonna work, get them laughing, help them make the transition from a disparate roomful of people having a rowdy chat to a friendly and united mob all focusing on the stage, and convince them that they're in the hands of a professional.

That way, even if an act goes badly, the audience know you'll be there to pick up the pieces.

The hardest part of all this is – you can't be the star of the show. The worst MC in the world is the one who absolutely storms it, kills the audience, leaves them breathless, exhausted and wanting no more laughter – then brings on an act.

You have to get the audience to just the right place, then hand them over to an act to get the job done.

If that acts kills it, you have to let the audience cool down a little before bringing on the next act. I've seen some MCs purposely be a bit average, solely to make it easier for the next act. On the other hand, if an act dies, your job is to go back out there and get the audience back on side.

It's a weird job, and no matter how well it goes, someone will approach you at the end of the night and say, 'You were great. You should be a comedian like the other acts.'

The other thing the MC must do is chat to the crowd. Find out who's celebrating a birthday or a stag night. Or more accurately, find out how many stag nights are in. One night I counted four stag parties and a hen do in a three-hundred-seat venue.

Gradually my ad-libbing skills, combined with my ability to turn up on time, run the show well, and generally be a safe pair of hands, meant that I got a lot of MC work.

Other comics with the same experience were getting three or four gigs a month, while I was doing two to three shows a week. Some of them were much better than me, but didn't have the ability to chat to a crowd.

Often, I would MC the early and the late show, with different acts on each. It was on one of these occasions that I received a major comedy lesson, which I carried with me for thirteen years.

The first show had gone well, to a decent-sized audience of around two hundred and fifty people, including one particularly large group of twenty, who were celebrating a birthday.

The late show, however, was about to start, and it comprised around twenty-eight people – including the same particularly large group of twenty, who had decided to stay on to watch the second show.

The main problem here was that I only had about twenty minutes of material, and I had used it all in the first show.

Now, here's the question: do I go out on stage and do the same material, to an audience of eight newbies and twenty people who had just seen it; or do I try to ad-lib my way through the show?

I attempted a bit of both.

The ad-libbing was OK, but eventually I needed to tell some jokes. So I started to repeat some of the act from the first show.

The twenty were fine with it, but only just fine. It is hard to laugh genuinely at a run of jokes you sat through only a couple of hours beforehand.

I quickly recalculated and decided to try out some new material. A few bits and pieces I had written down, but hadn't really turned into jokes yet.

One of them was an observation about having a prosthetic foot.

'So, I've got an artificial foot,' I began, 'which is weird, because people always ask strange questions about it. One time I was at a party and a woman asked, "Can you still have sex?" '

It got a laugh. Not a major laugh, but a good laugh.

I tried a few other bits and bobs, but that was the only joke about my foot in the set.

Afterwards I was approached by one of the elder comics on the scene, a bear of a man by the name of Richard Carter.

'You shouldn't talk about your leg,' he said gruffly.

'Why not?' I meekly replied.

'Cos you're not good enough yet,' was not the answer I was expecting.

'What do you mean?'

'You're still plying your trade. Working out how to be properly funny. You're not good enough yet to talk about your leg, and make it count.'

He was off and running now.

'One day, you'll work out the best way to talk about your leg, how to make it really funny and, more importantly, how to use it to actually say something. But right now, you're just making a joke about it because you can. Wait till you get really good at this shit. Wait till you find a reason to talk about it. Then put it together, and something really good will happen.'

Bloody. Great. Advice.

I mean it.

It was bloody great advice.

I ran all that past an agent of mine at the time, who added, 'If you talk about your leg now, you'll forever be known as the one-legged comedian, and that's all you'll be able to talk about. Wait until you've proven yourself, until you know you can talk about anything and make it funny. Become known as the really funny guy first, then talk about your leg.'

Those two pieces of advice shaped my career more than I could ever have imagined.

I knew bugger all about the industry when I got into it, but I knew that I knew bugger all. So I listened to smart people around me.

I didn't talk about my prosthetic foot on stage for another thirteen years. I plied my trade, and worked hard at being the funniest comedian I could be, without having to use my foot as a crutch, pun intended.

On stage, I concentrated on the jokes, wondering if one day I'd be good enough to use my foot in my act, and make it really work. Maybe there'd come a time. Maybe I'd eventually feel accomplished enough to broach the topic again, and maybe I'd find something to say with it, rather than simply use it as a punchline.

For now, though, I decided to put my best foot forward.

Radio Ga Ga

'Why don't we try writing for radio?' Belinda offered. It was a very tempting thought.

Belinda Franks had started doing comedy a few months before me, and together we had made our way through the open mic nights. She had a softly spoken, gentle manner on stage, and was a joy to be around off-stage as well.

We were supporting Peter Powers, billed as 'Britain's Naughtiest Hypnotist', in a two-week run at the Hilton Hotel in Sydney.

I say 'supporting'. Actor's Equity required any international act to have a local support act, so in reality, we were keeping up the local quota. As well as doing a ten-minute set, it was also my job to perform the hypnosis equivalent of a 'fluffer' on a porn film.

Every night, about two-thirds of the way through the show, Peter would select two audience members, who would be sent backstage (still under hypnosis) and told to obey every order they were given, no matter what. It was my job to tell them, without flinching, to put on a pair of tights each, and then give a wig and a tutu to whoever looked the most masculine. I would then inform them that as soon as they entered the stage, they would become the best ballet dancers in the world.

They could leap, pirouette, twirl, and even jump into each other's arms, so long as they didn't do anything dangerous, or go too close to the edge of the stage. It was the most bizarre power trip I had ever been on.

At first, I didn't think they'd go with it, but night after night two burly, brawly men would wander backstage, and listen intently while I told them what to do. Within three minutes they'd be wigged-up, stockinged-away, and tutus ahoy.

The show was indeed quite 'naughty', as women faked orgasms, and grown men simulated sex with inflatable dolls, then apologised to their wives in mock Chinese. Unfortunately for us all, the promoter was a weasel in a suit, and the season folded early.

Seriously, he was a scuzz bucket. In an attempt to spice up the show, he hired two strippers who pretended to be hypnotised, then took to the stage and began removing their clothes. Peter, who knew nothing of the plan, and certainly hadn't suggested they should begin to disrobe, was furious.

The following night, Peter couldn't hypnotise anyone. For some reason (I think it was a subconscious protest on Peter's behalf), none of the people he selected to take part in the show would go under.

After thirty minutes of fruitless toil, Peter explained to the audience, 'Sometimes hypnosis doesn't work, but never mind, Adam and Belinda are here to entertain you some more.' He brought me back on to do more jokes. The audience hated me, and an hour later, Belinda and I were contemplating our careers over cappuccinos at a late-night Italian restaurant.

Comedy had given us a bit of a beating, at the ripe old ages of twenty-one and twenty-three respectively. We had become 'disillusioned with the scene', and after closing the show early, with little or no prospects of ever being paid, it was time to get pro-active. To seize the day, carpe the diem, take the bull by the horns, and try to get into radio. We'd been talking about it for months, but now we had the inspiration.

At that time, as it is now, Sydney breakfast radio was a highly paid and publicised form of comedy entertainment.

I had been listening to Doug Mulray on Triple M for years, and he was lauded as the King of the FM breakfast shows. For that reason, we decided to submit some sketches to his main rival, the 2DayFM Morning Crew. We figured that the number one announcer in Sydney probably had all the writers he needed, and that the opposition might be more receptive to an outside hand.

Hyped-up and full of coffee, we waited until the first editions of the next day's papers were available (about 1 a.m.), then headed back to Belinda's place to take our first tentative steps towards a broadcasting career. We sat until 4 a.m., sourced the news, scribbled topical sketches and one-liners onto a notepad, then faxed them off to the station. Oh, the technology.

The next day I received a phone call at my parents' place. (That's right, I was watching women fake orgasms on stage by night, and sleeping in at Ma and Pa's by day.)

'So, you guys saw the ad in the paper then?'

'What ad?'

'The ad for comedy writers in yesterday's paper.'

You're kidding me. The one day we get our asses into gear and submit some sketches to a radio show, just happened to be the exact day the same show had advertised for comedy writers. They thought we had seen the ad, stayed up until four, and rather than calling up for an interview, had submitted our own jokes as an application.

'Oh yeah,' I replied groggily, 'the ad.' Technically it wasn't a lie.

'Listen, we didn't use any of your stuff this morning, but we'd like to record the song parody you wrote.' A song about the danger of skin cancer to the tune of 'Moondance' by Van

Morrison, it began with, 'Well, it's a marvellous day for a sunbake . . .'

'We'd also like you to keep sending us stuff. We can't put you on a wage, but we pay $100 per sketch, and $200 for a song parody.'

And so, the combination of a sleazy promoter, a naughty hypnotist, two strippers, a completely random stroke of timing, and an unintentional white lie, led me to embark upon a career in radio, and a whole new chapter of stories.

By the way, it's twenty-seven years later and I never did get paid for the season at the Hilton. That weasel still owes me a thousand bucks.

Part Two
Radio Daze

Radio Goo Goo

In 1991, two and a half years after starting stand-up comedy, I began working as a freelance comedy writer for 2DayFM Sydney, with Belinda Franks. We would meet up around midnight, often after a gig, collect the early editions of the next day's papers, and start writing jokes, or sketches, or song parodies.

We'd fax them in to the radio station, go back to our respective homes, and hope one or two of them might be used while we were asleep. Meanwhile I was also working as a tennis coach six days a week – every afternoon after school, and every Saturday morning.

I really enjoyed coaching, having played competitive tennis since the age of five. I loved watching the kids progress and got along well with all of them, even when I accidentally knocked someone's teeth out with my racket.

It was a fluke of bad timing – he came up behind me as I looked the other way – but I was dreading the reaction of his parents. Thankfully they knew me well enough to know it was an accident, and even more thankfully, they weren't his adult teeth.

Also, they were Aussies.

'No worries,' said his dad with a pat on the back. 'You're not a kid until you get your teeth knocked out.'

Much as I loved it all, my mother had become concerned that I wasn't putting my university degree to good use, so I applied for, and was given, my first job in television, as a stage hand at Channel Nine.

My job was to help build the sets for various TV shows, run around behind a cameraman making sure he didn't trip over the cable, then when the show was done, help take the sets down again.

Not one bit of it was covered in my university studies, but I guess they saw my degree in communications as evidence that I was interested in the industry, and a sign that once I got my head around the basics, I might come in handy in a more intellectual way.

That hunch paid off, as after only a few weeks I was offered a position on *Australia's Funniest Home Videos*. My job was to decide what pattern the videos would make on the screen behind the presenter. OK, not so much intellectual as I might have hoped, but a start, right?

At the time, I didn't feel like I was doing particularly important work, but now that I've hosted TV shows myself, I am eternally grateful to every single member of the floor crew, and crew generally, for what they bring to each production.

Weird, isn't it? When I did the job, I didn't think much of it.

But now, I realise that every person on set plays a huge part in making me look like I know what I'm doing, and I don't take any of them for granted.

My other jobs at Channel Nine included a rugby league sevens tournament at the Sydney Football Stadium. Once again, my remit was to run behind the cameraman, carrying the cable to the camera, to make sure he didn't trip over it.

This time, however, it was outdoors, in the teeming rain, in front of thirty thousand people, and for some reason whenever I ran past a particular group of blokes, they threw plastic beer cups at me and yelled, 'Run, cord boy!'

More galling was when I was rostered on to clean up after the staff Christmas party, which was held in one of the studios.

As I mopped up a puddle of urine from the corner of the studio (that's right, someone had actually pissed in the corner of the party), I started to wonder what those three years at university had brought me.

It came as a welcome relief when the new year began with a phone call, offering Belinda and me full-time jobs at the radio station. Brilliant, we thought, the on-air crew we'd been writing for must have loved our stuff so much, they want us as permanent writers.

Nope.

Turns out the on-air comedians had been replaced, and we would now be writing for the host Paul Holmes, and his new sidekick, a children's TV character by the name of Agro.

Originally a presenter on morning television, Agro had recently appeared on a late-night chat show, and displayed a very funny 'adult' side. Radio bosses had taken note, and he was immediately offered a job on air.

It should be pointed out that Agro was a puppet.

Belinda and I were chuffed to be offered the job, intrigued to see how we would write for a puppet, and confused by the notion of a puppet on radio.

We took the job.

With one hitch.

We had a one-month trial period, at the end of which they could sack us if we weren't up to scratch. So I decided to keep my job at the TV station, in case things went pear-shaped at the radio station.

The only way to do that, was to do a few late shifts at Channel Nine, which meant for the first week, my diary looked something like this.

> 5.00 p.m. – Start work at Channel Nine. Build the sets for the nightly *A Current Affair* show. Cable run throughout the show, then take the sets down afterwards. Then build the sets for the late-night show. Cable run throughout, then take the sets down again. Build sets for the morning show.
>
> 3.00 a.m. – Finish work at Channel Nine. Drive straight to the radio station.
>
> 4.00 a.m. – Start writing for the Breakfast Show.
>
> 5.30 a.m. – Breakfast Show goes to air.
>
> 9.00 a.m. – Breakfast Show finishes.
>
> 10.30 a.m. – Post-show meetings.
>
> 12.00 p.m. – Drive home.
>
> 1.00 p.m. – Sleep.
>
> 4.00 p.m. – Wake up and drive to TV station.
>
> Repeat.

Some mornings I turned up to the radio station in a paint-splattered shirt and tracksuit pants, because I didn't have time to get changed after the TV shift.

It nearly killed me. Literally.

I remember driving home one afternoon wondering why it was raining inside the car. I had just driven over Tom Ugly's Bridge (honestly, that's what it's called) and had started my ascent up the bit of road that cambers perfectly to the right, when I noticed little drops falling in front of my eyes.

I put the windscreen wipers on, but to no avail. The drops kept falling. That's when I realised my vision was getting foggy, and I was starting to fall asleep. I pulled the car over, took in some fresh air, and a few days later took a punt and quit the TV job.

I later found out that my joke-writing performance that week was so poor, the radio station had contacted the old on-air crew to see if they would come back as writers. Thankfully, they told the station they would only do it if they were paid the same as when they were on-air.

The following week, with decent sleep and a clear head, I returned to 2DayFM, and bit by bit I somehow worked out what I was doing.

Belinda and I were kept on at the end of the one-month trial, thanks to the mentorship of the head writer, Tim Pye. We started to work out how to write for both Agro, and the man behind him – Jamie Dunn, who remains one of the most naturally funny people I've ever met.

'The secret to showbiz,' he used to pronounce, 'is to find a way to make money while you sleep. Every afternoon, while I'm having a nap, someone is buying Agro's breakfast cereal.'

'Never forget the golden rule – where there's a till there's a way!'

Gradually I found my feet and we all found a routine of some sort. We'd come together around 4.30 a.m. in the writers' room, bounce around some ideas for sketches, and try to record one or two of them during the show.

Every writers' room can be the most fun place in the world, and the most depressing – often within a few minutes. There will be a table littered with newspapers, copious amounts of coffee, and in those days, a lot of note pads. Nowadays it's laptops.

The goal is for someone to throw up an idea that someone else runs with and adds to, then someone else does the same, and before you know it, the spark of a joke becomes a full-blown blaze, as each offer leads to a bigger laugh. When it happens, it's a joy. You've created something out of nothing – a little comedy miracle.

Most of the time, however, is spent offering suggestions that go absolutely nowhere. Sometimes you know as you say it that it's not the right idea, but it might lead to something. Other times you realise halfway through your own sentence, it's not gonna fly.

The worst are the ideas that you think are brilliant, but no one else can see. Other ideas start off as a gem, but as each person puts in their two cents, the joke gets over-analysed, and eventually no one knows why it was even funny in the first place.

That process is often referred to as Death by Committee.

I managed to come up with a few regular characters – an outdated rock DJ called Dick Starr (using the old on-air name of one of the station's consultants), and a cub reporter called Jimmy Parker. I combined Jimmy Olsen from *Superman* with Peter Parker from *Spiderman*.

We also had regular segments to write jokes for – News of the Future, The Top 5 – as well as the occasional song parody. I tried to sing one of the parodies once, and it was decided soon after that we needed to hire professional singers instead.

Our places at the station were cemented when Belinda and I wrote a parody about the Duchess of York, Sarah Ferguson, taking up with an American cattleman, to the tune of 'Walking in Memphis':

Now she's bonking a Texan, she reckons Andy never
    made her smile,
Now she's bonking a Texan, apparently a Longhorn's
    more her style.

And after an Australian comedian by the name of Andrew
Denton had enticed Rolf Harris to record a version of 'Stairway
to Heaven', we wrote an ad for Led Zeppelin's album of *Rolf
Classics*, including reworked lyrics to 'Rock and Roll':

Got a spare leg, got a spare leg,
Jake's got an extra, extra, extra, extra, extra leg.

There was no doubt that when I started I was absolutely out
of my depth, but somehow an attitude of positivity, enthusiasm, and a genuine willingness to learn got me through.

In fact, two quotes sum up how I survived in that first year.
One comes from an interview I read with the American singer
Chris Isaak, who relayed the best advice his father ever gave
him.

'Turn up on time and be nice to everyone.'

The other came from a radio boss a few years later.

'When you're skating on thin ice, you may as well tap
dance.'

Tunnel of Love

Have you ever walked past a couple on the street, imagined
them both naked, and instantly shivered? I don't do it often,
in fact very rarely, but one morning as I walked from my car
to the station it happened.

Now I should point out that one of the true joys of starting work at 4.30 a.m. is the short walk either from your house to the car (if you don't have off-street parking), or from your car to the station (if you're not big enough to use the station car park). At that time of the morning the streets are generally deserted, but on the odd occasion you do bump into someone, there's every chance they're a little . . . strange.

Even the drive to work can be daunting. It was always a bizarre feeling to cruise through the city streets at 4 a.m. as people wander past on their way home from a night on the town. I remember once seeing a female friend of mine stagger across in front of my car, alone and very much the worse for wear. She later tried to convince me she was conducting a study into how people reacted to a seemingly drunk woman walking the streets alone. I said I believed her.

Sydney is especially strange at 4 a.m., particularly the morning after the Gay and Lesbian Mardi Gras. There's nothing so comically tragic and yet tragically comic as the sight of a tired and emotional drag queen staggering across a median strip, high heels in hand, fake lashes hanging by a thread, and make-up all but smudged away.

So this one morning, as I approached the station, I did a double-take when a slightly out-of-place couple exited the building. Not attractive, but not horribly unattractive, they were . . . well, actually they were fairly unattractive. Imagine if instead of 'The Fly', Jeff Goldblum had become 'The Ferret'. That describes him. She, on the other hand, was just dour.

Clothed, they were less than a sight, but for some reason the image of them making sweet, sweet love flashed inexplicably through my head, and I felt instantly ill. Unfortunately, less than five minutes later, I was watching them do just that.

I had forgotten, on my morning drive, that the newly built Sydney Harbour Tunnel had officially opened three hours earlier, and that as a station we had offered five hundred dollars to the first couple to prove they had 'christened' it. You know, bonked under the harbour. The competition was called 'The Tunnel of Love'. Ah yes, how terribly, terribly witty.

It turned out that the couple I saw in the car park had, well, won, and they had delivered filmed footage to prove it. We turned the video on, and within seconds it had turned us off.

What we saw were Weaselboy and ol' Miss Sourpuss going at it in the back seat of a station wagon, while cars, trucks, and motorbikes whistled past the windows, honking their encouragement. Literally, giving them the horn.

At one point she moaned, and not in a good way, 'Can we stop now, you've filmed enough.'

His response drew the most vocal protest of shock I have ever voiced, and also explained her downcast expression as I walked past her later.

'Hang on, hang on, hang on,' he cried, then 'Agggghhhhh, yep, now we can stop.'

Speak Directly into the Microphone

As far as I know, there is no such thing as International Nude Day. Even if there is, we had no idea what date it was. Nevertheless, on a chilly winter's day in July, it was declared by the 2DayFM Morning Crew that the next morning was indeed International Nude Day, and as such, everyone in the studio would be totally, one hundred per cent, butt-nekked.

The windows that separated the studio from the station hallway were covered over, as were the windows between the studios. Only the windows that overlooked Sydney from the station's eleventh floor would remain clear, which meant we could keep an eye on the weather, but also made the whole scene all the more surreal. Bathrobes were provided for anyone needing to leave the studio, on the strict condition that they disrobed upon re-entering the on-air confines.

I had of late been voicing an on-air character known as Doctor Right, a bumbling medico who made two live studio calls each morning. As such, the good doctor would also be forced to disrobe entirely. So it was, that at six forty-five, and again at eight-fifteen, I went live to air nude, accompanied by two just-as-nude men. To be honest, it was quite liberating.

Since Paul and Jamie were separated from each other by a hulking desk and radio panel, they were spared the sight of the other's genitalia. I had to sit alongside Jamie, however, giving each of us a, well, bird's-eye view of our, well, bird's eyes:

Dr Right: Gee, Jamie, you must be getting a cold draught at the moment.
Jamie: Look who's talking, Captain Carrot.
Paul: So, Doc, what have you got for us this morning?
Dr Right: Well, Paul, I'm afraid one of my patients has passed on.
Paul: Passed on what?

It was an ad-lib, and really, not an especially hilarious line, but for some reason the three of us started laughing. And laughing, and laughing, and suddenly we couldn't stop.

You know when you see one of those *World's Worst Bloopers* TV shows, and for some reason two actors get an attack of the giggles, and every time they think they've composed themselves, they look at each other and collapse again. Imagine that, but naked.

It was the only time I ever really 'corpsed' on air, and the more we tried to regain some semblance of sanity, the worse we made it:

Paul: Doc, try to hold on to it.

Dr Right: Believe me, Paul, I am.

Jamie: I'm sorry, everyone. We just can't seem to pull ourselves together.

After three minutes of what was meant to be a ninety-second segment, we gave up trying and played a song, now hyperventilating through laughter. Later we tried to work out exactly what it was we were laughing at, but nobody really knew.

My theory is that the three of us simultaneously had the same thought. We were three grown men, professionals in our own field, live on air to at least one hundred thousand people, sitting above the rooftops of Sydney, giggling like schoolgirls, completely nude. And we were getting paid for it.

Sydney Harbour Abridged

The rest of the year is a blur of snippets, like a montage from a movie. I was still doing stand-up at night, then starting at the radio station at 4.30 every morning.

That may explain why the year is a blur.

A couple of comedians tried to tell me I'd 'changed' since getting the radio job, but they wouldn't accept that I wasn't blanking them at gigs, I was so desperately tired I could barely make conversation.

My memories include:

(1) Dressing Agro the puppet for an interview with
    Julian Lennon.

Whenever a special guest came in, the station photographer would take press shots, and Agro had to look his best. I even got into an argument with him while dressing him. Apparently I put the arm in the wrong sleeve, and Agro let me know.

Even though he was clearly on the end of Jamie's arm, I somehow found myself yelling at Agro, looking right into his ping-pong-ball eyes.

'You know you're shouting at a puppet, right?' he shot back, and immediately all tension was gone.

(2) Going to the Gold Coast to broadcast live from the
    Indy Car race.

The highlight, or lowlight, of that trip was when my prosthetic foot broke on the golf course one afternoon, and I had to hobble around without it for the rest of the round.

The comedian Peter Moon, who had come with us, left a putt just short of the hole and asked how far away we thought it was. I got my prosthetic out of the golf bag, laid it between the ball and the hole and proclaimed, 'Oh, it's about a foot.'

Once again, Mum came to the rescue, and couriered one of my old prosthetics to me. The look on the hotel porter's face the next day when he delivered a leg to my room, wrapped in sellotape and bubble wrap, was priceless.

(3) Being called into the boss's office on the last day of the year to be told I'd be getting a raise next year, but that Belinda wouldn't be asked back.

It was like being tickled and punched at the same time. I knew Belinda had become unhappy in the job, for a number of reasons that aren't mine to go into, and probably wanted to leave anyway.

But we had joined up together. Should I stay without her, or stick by her side? As I left the room, she was called in and we passed in the hallway. I couldn't look at her.

I honestly can't remember what happened afterwards.

In my best version of my story, I hope we went for a coffee and a chat, and she convinced me to stay at the station without her, that she wanted to go anyway, that I was bound for bigger things.

Truth is, I really don't know.

I know we caught up years later, and Belinda told me I did the right thing by staying. It was my first experience of the cut-throat nature of the radio industry, and it wasn't to be my last.

Looking back, I now realise how difficult it must have been for Belinda, and any woman, in the industry at the time. I know she often felt ignored in writers' meetings because of her gender, and although I didn't notice it, it doesn't mean it didn't happen.

When I think of the incidents involving women I've already mentioned – being heckled off-stage so that someone else can hit on you, being introduced on stage according to some fictional sexual encounter – and combine that with the adrenalin and testosterone-fuelled environment of commercial radio, I can now see I had a vastly different experience to my friend Belinda.

Even though the Sydney Comedy Store at the time was managed by a woman, and Thursday nights had an all-female line up, it didn't stop seventy per cent of female performers having to deal with at least one audience member per show, shouting, 'Show us ya tits!'

Ironically, had Belinda made it to the New Year, she would have found that a comedian by the name of Wendy Harmer had been added to the team. In fact, Wendy was now the star of the team.

Wendy cut her teeth on stage when comedy was even more combative than in my early days, and had recently hosted the ABC comedy and sketch show *The Big Gig* – a show that also gave a platform to the Doug Anthony Allstars.

To put that into perspective: we currently live in a time in which the pay gap between men and women is only now being properly addressed, as is the vast under-representation of women on television, especially in comedy.

Thirty years ago, Wendy Harmer hosted Australia's biggest and best comedy show, and in so doing paved the way for generations of female comedians to follow in her path.

She was experienced, uncompromising and a hard task-master. On one of my first mornings working with her, I walked into the studio and submitted a page of jokes.

'Come on, Adam, you can do better than this,' she admonished, returning the paper. 'Take it away and write something funnier.'

I sulked back to the writer's room like a grumpy teenager, and scribbled out another page of jokes, all the while thinking,

'How dare you tell me I can be funnier than this? I'll show you.'

Half an hour later, I handed her a new page of jokes.

'That's better,' she said.

The worst thing was, she was right. The second lot of jokes was a lot funnier than the first. Turns out I just needed a kick up the arse.

Wendy also taught me one of the golden rules of writing – be specific.

Her example was: 'Don't say, "He went mad and shot a bunch of people," but instead, "He climbed a clocktower and took out fifteen people with an AK-47." '

Both options are dark, but the second one is somehow funnier as a punchline.

I liked writing for Wendy, and it meant the world to me when I made her laugh once while recording a sketch.

By this point, the head writer had left, so my responsibilities now included overseeing the production of the pre-recorded skits, which meant I also had to deliver them to the studio on a cassette cartridge.

One morning we were running particularly late with one of the sketches, which I think was a reworking of Elton John's greatest hits, now that he was sober.

As I ran from the production studio to the on-air studio, I could hear Paul introducing the sketch. But, but, but . . . the sketch was in my hand. On a cassette cartridge.

The run became a sprint, and as I made it to the studio, I swung open the door and threw it to Paul as he was in mid-sentence. The cartridge hurtled across the studio, landing in Paul's hand, who put it in the player, said the words, 'and this is what it sounds like,' then hit play.

The whole time he had a look on his face that said, this better be good.

It was.

But I'm pretty sure if it hadn't been, I would have lost my job.

Adelaide Hills

A few months into my second year of radio, I was told by the boss that an on-air role had come up in Adelaide, and that I should apply for it.

I cobbled together a selection of sketches and songs I had written, and sent them off. A week later, the programme director and a producer from SAFM Adelaide met with me in Sydney and offered me the role of co-host of the breakfast show.

The current host was one of the original 2DayFM breakfast hosts, for whom Belinda and I had written as freelancers. Technically, we had replaced him at the station, but I got along with him well, and was looking forward to being on air with him.

Until I arrived in Adelaide, and found out I was actually replacing him. Again.

Man, radio was a tough business.

Someone once told me that because listeners don't see your face, they don't form as much of an attachment to you, so it's easier to replace you.

In the time I was at SAFM, I was part of:

* The Morning Zoo (with Scott McBain)
* The Morning Crew (with Sean Murphy)

* The Morning Crew (with Toni Tenaglia)
* The Morning Crew (with Toni Tenaglia and John Vincent)
* The Morning Crew (with Toni Tenaglia, John Vincent and Steve Bedwell)
* I then went on holidays for two weeks and came back to find my role on the breakfast show was being reduced. A month later, it was reduced so much that I was no longer required on the breakfast show, so I co-hosted the nine-till-midday slot with Bernie Brittain.
* I then co-hosted that slot with Jason Staveley.
* Then I learnt how to work the radio panel and hosted the Adam Hills Morning Show.

All of this happened in the space of five years.

Once again, I was still doing stand-up on the weekends, so it's fair to say I was absolutely wrecked.

And once again, I was probably out of my depth. A couple of times the station had to apologise for badly judged jokes I had made on air, and I quickly learned the very slight differences in lingo between Adelaide and Sydney.

'Cozzies' became 'bathers', the sandwich meat known as 'Devon' became 'Fritz', 'Chance' and 'Dance' no longer rhymed with 'pants', but had to be pronounced 'Charnce'.

I must have done a convincing job, though, because most South Australians now refer to me as 'Adelaide's Own' – the highest honour they can bestow upon you.

Coincidentally, while I was appearing on Adelaide radio every morning, my brother Brad had auditioned for a role as a presenter on a kids' TV show. The same show that Agro still appeared on. The same Agro for whom I'd been writing jokes in Sydney.

Brad got the job, and when Jamie found out he was my brother, he got a hug as well. Occasionally I'd pop the TV on in the studio while we were on air, and the pride I felt was indescribable as I looked up and saw my 'little' bro on screen.

It was a formative time for me, as I rented my first apartment, made new friends, and established myself in a whole new city – not to mention co-hosting a breakfast radio show at the age of twenty-two.

Over the following five years, I interviewed Sting, the Blues Brothers Band, Chris Isaak and Joan Armatrading.

I became friends with some of the Adelaide Crows footballers, and we ran an on-air competition for our listeners to write a new club song. Our favourite submission was produced up, sung by Jim Keays of Masters Apprentices, and submitted to the club. They still use that song now, and I feel a pang of pride whenever I hear it.

I formed a lifelong bond with one of my favourite cities in the world.

And the whole time I had the words of Sydney comedian Graham Pugh ringing in my head.

When I told him of the Adelaide offer, he said simply, 'Take the job, but make sure you build up your "fuck you" money. Because one day the radio bosses will get sick of you, or you'll get sick of them – and when that happens, you can say, "Fuck you, this is how much money I made out of you." Then go back to stand-up.'

Great advice.

I Gotcha

It started as a dumb idea.

There was a mouse plague in South Australia, and one of the writers suggested we should cull them and use them for meat.

The thought of trying to slice up tiny pieces of mouse steak made us giggle, and it was decided that we would ring a local butcher to see if they were interested in buying some mouse steaks. It was deemed funny enough to become a regular segment, so we began to play harmless prank calls on local businesses.

Eventually the ideas ran thin, so we asked our listeners if there was anyone they wanted pranked. Now this is hardly the most original of ideas, but for some reason it took off, and we were deluged by dozens of faxes a day.

The brilliant thing was, the listeners did the work for us. They'd give us details about a friend who had bought a suit and shirt at a store, but had only been charged for the shirt. They would then suggest we should ring the friend and pretend we were from the police, and were charging them with shoplifting.

They all but wrote the bits for us.

Having said that, it took a lot of effort to get one right. We would pre-record them after we'd finished the live show, but in the days before mobile phones, not everyone would answer.

When they did answer, not everyone would believe us. When they did, not everyone would react with enough energy for the call to go to air. And if they did all of that, the whole thing still had to be edited down to two and half minutes.

The calls themselves bordered on cruel, but we did have a few ground rules, by way of exonerating ourselves:

1. No call went to air without the permission of the person on the other end.
2. We always made sure that revealing it was a prank call was a relief, rather than a letdown. Telling someone they've won the lottery, then revealing it's a prank is not funny. Telling someone they're being charged with shoplifting, then revealing that it's a radio station calling is a relief.
3. We always told the victim who it was that had dobbed them in. That usually got the best reaction of the call, as they suddenly realised Dave from accounts was behind all this (thus letting us off the hook).
4. Wherever possible, I also tried to make the calls more silly than cruel.

My favourite went roughly like this:

Woman: Hello?
Adam: Hello, is that Sharon?
W: Yeah.
A: Sharon, it's Michael Madsen here from the RSPCA. I'm just returning your call from last week about a, um, turtle?
W: Yes?
A: So what seems to be the problem?
W: Well, I put some new weed in the tank a few weeks ago, and ever since then, me turtle's been looking really sick.

A: What kind of weed was it?

W: A kind of bluey-greeny-browny turtle weed.

A: Oh, that's the worst kind.

W: Oh no. Really?

A: Sharon, I'm sorry to say your turtle may be having an allergic reaction to the weed.

W: Oh my Goddd. What should I do?

A: Well, as soon as you get home, you'd better take the weed out straight away. Then you're gonna have to disinfect the turtle.

W: Oh my Goddd. How do I do that?

A: Well, you're gonna have to take him out of his shell and give him a good scrub.

W: Take him out of his shell?

A: Yes.

W: How do I do that?

A: Well, the best thing to do is to gently grab his head with a pair of pliers, right?

W: Right.

A: Then with your other hand, keep a tight grip on the shell . . .

W: Right.

A: Then, just, YANK HIM RIGHT OUTTA THAT SHELL!

W: Oh no, I couldn't do that. It'd hurt him.

A: Well, you're gonna have to disinfect him somehow.

W: Isn't there another way to get him out of the shell?

A: You could try to scare him out.

W: How?

A: You could sneak up behind him and make a loud noise.

W: With what?

A: Blow up a paper bag, then sneak up quietly behind him when he's least expecting it. Pop the bag, he'll jump out of his shell, all you have to do is catch him and bung him in a bath of disinfectant.

W: What if he runs under the couch?

A: *Stifles a laugh.*

W: Couldn't you come around and do it for me?

A: Well, yes, I suppose I could.

W: That'd be great. What was your name again?

A: It's actually Adam Hills from the SAFM Morning Crew.

W: OHH MY GODDDDD!

A Nose by Any Other Name

Picture this – a worshipped Seventies superstar steps off a plane at Adelaide airport, worn out from a long flight, not entirely sure what time of day it is, and is met by the local press. For Barry Manilow it was probably a normal day at the office, until a certain TV reporter thrust a camera in his face and asked a question that probably still makes her shiver.

'What's the best Barry Manilow joke you've ever heard?'

From the moment it was announced Mr Manilow was coming to town, we wanted him on the show. How could we not? The man behind such musical gems as 'Copacabana', and . . . um . . . actually, that alone is enough to make him a legend in my book (and coincidentally, this is my book).

There are few opening lyrics in musical history that evoke the same reaction as, 'Her name was Lola, she was a show-girl . . .' To this day whenever I hear the line, 'he called her over,' I instinctively whistle – an embarrassing habit when sitting in a doctor's waiting room.

The question was: what to do with him. Possibly the daggiest man of our generation, the butt of more nasally centred jokes than Barbra Streisand, but without the gay-icon status, he was ripe for the roasting. That's why John Vincent ('Vinnie' to his friends and listeners) suggested we should take the opposite tack, and actually elevate him to hero status.

'When everyone else is being negative,' he offered, 'the funny thing to do is be positive. Why don't we put together a Barry Manilow fan club, assemble them on a truck outside his hotel, and have them sing "Copacabana" for two hours?'

You know, it was just crazy enough to work.

We had already placed a few calls to his publicist requesting an interview, but when you're as big as Barry, you hardly need the extra publicity of a local radio show – or so we thought. Back at the airport, one simple question was about to make our day.

Now I've heard a few Barry gags in my life ('How do you make Barry Manilow's nose three feet long? Fold it in half') and I'm sure Bazza has, too, but this particular day he'd obviously had enough. That question again, 'What's the best Barry Manilow joke you've ever heard?'

He stopped, gave a look that would make Medusa shiver, and replied (and I know this is true, because they showed it on the news), 'Fuck you. Is that the best question you can find? Fuck. You. I get off a plane in Adelaide and that's the first question I get? Fuck you, lady, fuck you.'

Oh my God. Barry Manilow snapped. The Adelaide general populace couldn't have been more shocked if Cliff Richard had held a virgin sacrifice on the tarmac. Barry stormed off to his awaiting limo, leaving his publicist to pick up the pieces. If only she could find someone to do a positive interview with His Nosiness, guaranteed to leave him and the punters with a happy glow.

Their names were Toni, Adam and Vinnie, they were three DJs.

We were told at 11 a.m., two hours after coming off air, that there was a chance we might have a phone interview with Barry Manilow. The three of us had already been awake since 4 a.m., but there was no way we were going to miss this. The next four hours were spent assuring the publicist that we would be respectful, that we wouldn't mention the airport incident, and that the fans on the truck would sing on key. She in turn did her best to put Barry in the right frame of mind for an interview, promising him there'd be no proboscis-related tomfoolery.

His name was Barry, he called them over (Phwisshht).

At 3 p.m. the call came – Mr Manilow will speak to you. We called his hotel and said the words that still give me butter-flies. 'We'd like to speak to Barry Manilow, please. He's expecting our call.' He answered. HE answered, and one of the strangest and best interviews of my career was underway.

Talking to Barry Manilow was like befriending an abused puppy. He was understandably wary, and often responded to a question with the phrase, 'Is that a joke?' Don't get me wrong, he was a perfect gentleman – personable, funny, inter-esting and even charming, but he was sure we were about to turn on him at any moment.

When he happened to remark that he loved sweet biscuits, Toni responded with, 'We'll have to send you a packet of Iced

Vo Vos then.' There was a pause, and Barry asked warily, 'What are they? Is that a joke?'

We carefully explained that Iced Vo Vos were two strips of pink marshmallow, surrounding a strip of jam, covered in coconut on a biscuit base, and were as Australian as . . . well, lots of other things he wouldn't have heard of. He said he'd like to try some, and the interview was back on track.

To be honest, I can't remember anything else about what was said, only that it was so delicate it made the Middle East peace talks look like a bout of WWE Wrestling. After fifteen minutes of chat, we bade farewell to the Bard of Manilow, and set about the task of editing down the interview.

The following morning was the audio equivalent of a bedroom shrine. Twenty mad 'Fanilows' spent two hours on the back of a flat-bed truck singing 'Copacabana' outside the Adelaide Hilton, while we took listeners' calls to find the best all-time Manilow song, interspersed with the previous day's interview. Not one negative word was said about the great man, and when we came off air at 9 a.m., we were pretty damn happy with ourselves.

At 9.05 a.m. our producer came into the studio with a triumphant smile and announced, 'Barry Manilow's publicist just rang. Barry asked her to say that yesterday's interview was one of his favourites, and that he loved the fans on the truck. He even considered joining them, but he spotted the journalist from the airport and decided to keep his distance. He listened to the show today and really enjoyed it, and just wanted to say thank you.'

Vinnie was right, and I took that lesson with me for the rest of my career – when everyone else is being cynical, a positive slant becomes funny. At 9.25 a.m. we sent Barry Manilow a packet of Iced Vo Vos, and set about planning the next day's programme.

But that was twenty years ago, when there used to be a show.

Good Times and Great Rock 'n' Roll

One of the joys of hosting a breakfast radio show is that you get all the big guests, sometimes in person, sometimes over the phone. We interviewed the Corrs and Savage Garden, sang 'Happy Birthday' to the drummer from Bon Jovi, and played some of Russell Crowe's favourite songs.

Julian Clary said one of the funniest things I have ever heard in an interview. We were pre-recording the whole thing to play on the following morning's show, and although Steve had gone home for the day, he still wanted to be a part of it. So he recorded his own question to be played during the interview.

Julian sashayed into the studio, took his seat, and listened patiently as we explained that halfway through our Q&A session, we would be playing a question from Steve from the tape deck, and could he please act like Steve was still in the studio.

After five minutes of chat – mainly skincare tips – we eventually reached the point of Steve's question. Toni pressed Play, and Steve's recorded voice inquired, 'Now Julian, will you be bringing the lovely Russell on tour with you?'

Our esteemed guest considered the query for a moment, then replied softly, 'I'm sorry, could you rephrase the question please?'

*   *   *

Alice Cooper was brilliant. He was charming, funny, chatty, and referred to his character as 'Alice', as opposed to his real name, Vinnie. Leather jacket, black jeans, long dark hair, he was everything you would hope he's gonna be.

We fired a list of questions at him, including, 'If you could cover one song, what would it be?'

He replied, 'The Beach Boys. "I Get Around."'

'What?' I shot back. 'Alice Cooper, the man who supposedly bit the head off a chicken on stage wants to do a Beach Boys' song?'

'Yeah, man, of course. It's the ultimate rock and roll song. Think about it.' He started to growl the lyrics, and in his voice, they took on a truly grungy tone.

'"None of the guys are goin' steady, cos it wouldn't be right, to leave your best girl home on a Saturday night."' He paused. 'Now that's rock and roll, man.'

* * *

Speaking of rock and roll, one of my on-air partners committed the ultimate sin when he asked Meatloaf, 'A lot of people took you seriously, but you were actually taking the piss out of rock and roll, weren't you?'

'What?' he bellowed down the phone line. 'Taking the piss? ARE YOU KIDDING ME? I took my rock and roll seriously. The only people taking the piss are those candy-ass rock stars who pretend they're tryin' to save the world, or them stinkin' boy bands that have their songs written for them. Rock and roll is about excess, man. It's about big long songs about girls and sex. And anybody who says any different – they're the ones taking the piss, man.'

Right on brother.

* * *

Alexei Sayle was one of my favourite interviewees ever. I was doing the late-night shift at the time, and therefore had less restrictions. After a genuinely lovely and funny chat about his upcoming shows, his career, and comedy in general, I made an admission.

'I'm sorry, Alexei, but there's an ulterior motive to this interview. I think you're really funny, but I really wanted to chat to your warm-up man, Bobby Chariot.'

Bobby Chariot was the world's worst warm-up man. Divorced, on medication, lonely and not particularly funny, he wore an old-style tux, obviously false teeth, and was played by Alexei himself. He saw immediately what I was doing, said his goodbyes as Alexei, and returned to the microphone as blustering northern comic, Bobby.

'So, Bobby, what would be your advice to young, up-and-coming comics listening to the show?'

'Wear shiny shoes,' he bellowed. 'That's the only thing you need to know. It doesn't matter if your jokes are shit, as long as your shoes are shiny.'

I've tried to take that advice with me ever since.

When Whoosh Comes to Shove

I was on my way to the station when I heard that Ayrton Senna had died. The top Formula One driver in the world was much loved in Adelaide, mainly because he professed his love *for* Adelaide, and I felt a real pang when the mid-dawn announcer informed me, and the rest of the 4 a.m. listeners, of his passing.

I also wondered how we should cover it on air. A tragedy like this can be a tricky thing to deal with on radio. On the one hand, it has to be mentioned because it is in the public consciousness, on the other, we were an entertainment-based radio show, and had to keep it bright and breezy.

Do we ask callers their favourite memory of Senna? Do we leave it to the news desk to deal with? Should we give our own personal opinions? It sounds simple now, but Vinnie had the best idea of all: 'Just ask the listeners how they're feeling about it.'

And that's exactly what we did. We asked people to ring in and tell us how they felt. We managed to combine the regular comedy sketches, with calls from genuinely distressed, saddened, and mourning listeners. In amongst all the general radio hype and wank, simply asking people how they felt was the most effective way to deal with a tragedy.

At one point it was suggested that as a mark of respect, anyone in a car should turn their headlights on. I was later told by a mate that he was on a main highway at the time, and it was both eerie and touching to look ahead and see a row of oncoming headlights suddenly come to life.

The combination of national tragedy and FM radio doesn't always go smoothly, however. In 1995, a multiple shooting at Port Arthur in Tasmania rocked Australia. As news filtered in of the senseless deaths of innocent holidaymakers, station bosses pondered how to acknowledge the situation in an appropriate manner.

It was decided that at 11 a.m. the following day, a tribute would be played to the victims. The Annie Lennox song 'Why' was played, and the lyrics were intercut with audio drops from the previous day's events. It is actually a standard radio ploy – as the song's instrumental kicks in, we hear a reporter saying, 'It's hard to believe that only a few hours ago, this was a peaceful town.' In this case, it was a beautiful way to cover a touching and tragic sentiment in an FM radio format. But it so nearly wasn't.

Standard radio procedure after a song is to back announce, i.e., 'That was Annie Lennox and "Why". Now here's the Spin Doctors and "Little Miss Can't Be Wrong" on SAFM.' I think you'll agree that would have been slightly inappropriate.

The alternative is to play a quick station ID, then into the next track. Now, a station ID is a quick, sharp, pre-recorded promo, which may say something like, 'The best music while you work, 107.1 SAFM (Whoosh)' or 'More music, more often. 107.1 SAFM (Whoosh)'. There's always a whoosh. It was decided that a station ID would be played.

Unfortunately, nobody gave much thought as to which particular station ID should follow the tribute. Thankfully, the on-air announcer, Sean Murphy, checked what was cued up and changed it at the last minute. Adelaide listeners very nearly heard a moving tribute to the dozens of victims indiscriminately shot dead by a lone gunman, followed by a booming voice pronouncing: 'Hit, after Hit, after Hit, after Hit. More hits, more often, on 107.1 SAFM (Whoosh).'

This whole scenario was only topped for accidental inappropriateness by an outside broadcast I participated in while in Sydney. We had moved the entire show to the Camperdown Children's Hospital, and went to air live from one of the wards.

The show was spent surrounded by some of the cutest, and sickest, children in Sydney, and more than once various on-air members had to retreat to a quiet corner to succumb to tears. The first break of the morning was an emotional one for all concerned, as Paul and Jamie relayed to the listeners the heartbreaking and at the same time joyous sight of so many spirited and yet desperately ill children.

Paul finished the conversation by dutifully relaying the time, temperature and the name of the station, and someone back in the studio hit the first tune.

'Oh God,' Paul muttered to his sidekick, 'I can't possibly back announce this.'

'Why not?'

'We're in a children's hospital.'

'So?' replied Jamie.

'So . . . what's the name of the song?' shot Paul.

It was Billy Joel. 'Only the Good Die Young.'

Hey, Macarena

Ah, the Macarena. The dance craze that swept a generation, a nation, a planet. What is it about certain songs that inspire teenagers around the world to express their individuality and sense of self by copying the steps of a million other teenagers around the world?

Not only did an obscure Latin American folk song step out of its bedroom as the belle of the ball, but it had somehow acquired two dates for the same prom. You see, as two old blokes who called themselves Los Del Rio went into a recording studio and laid down English vocals to a dance beat, across town a group of younger blokes who called themselves Los Del Mar went into a separate recording studio and laid down Spanish vocals to the same tune.

Both songs took off, and each became a hit in its own right, although the English version became the more popular of the two. Which is probably why Pedro, the singer of the Spanish version, embarked upon a publicity tour of Australia, taking in all the major cities. A press release was sent, accompanied by a biography (both of which I dutifully read) and a live on-air interview scheduled for 8.15 a.m.

As 8.12 ticked past, we found ourselves staring at an empty guest chair. His publicist called, assured us they were in the building, and would be in the studio in two minutes. As prom-ised, they arrived at exactly 8.14 and were ushered in, to be met by the sound of our sphincters returning to normal tension. The publicist – part-cockatiel, part-cocker spaniel – spoke nineteen to the dozen, offering every excuse for their late arrival, while Pedro sat quietly in his seat.

8.15, mic's on, away we go. 'It's the Morning Crew on SAFM (always say the station name). Eight-fifteen right now (always say the time), seventeen degrees in the Parklands (always give the temp) heading for a top of twenty-five today (always give the forecast).

'SAFM's (always claim ownership) Battle of the Sexes coming up in a few minutes (always tease what's coming up), but right now we're joined by Pedro, lead singer of Los Del Mar, the band behind one of the versions of the Macarena on the charts at the moment. Pedro, welcome to Australia.'

Nothing.

'So, you must be happy with the song's success?'

Nothing again.

'Pedro?'

He looked at Toni, then at me, then back at Toni, then at the publicist – all the while with a face like a puppy watching a television. Finally he spoke, to the publicist – in Spanish – who then spoke to us, in English.

'Oh, didn't I tell you? Pedro doesn't speak English.'

What!?! Pedro doesn't speak English? What the hell is he doing on a national publicity tour then? How exactly does he intend to promote the single? With sign language? He can't understand us, and we can't understand him. Do you see? In the words of the Wedding Singer: 'Information that would have come in handy YESTERDAY!'

Of course, no one said that. We smiled politely, gave each other a look that pretty much encapsulated the previous paragraph, and panicked. After all, this was a live interview.

After at least ten seconds of, 'Right', 'OK then', and 'Eight-sixteen right now' (when in doubt, say the time again), I started to smile. 'Well, in that case, we can say what we want and he won't understand.' (Still with a smile) 'Hey buddy, your song sucks.'

He laughed, so I continued. 'As long as I smile, he'll think I'm being nice. Won't you, you no-talent tool?' More laughs from him, and Toni, a horrified look from the publicist.

I was about to launch into an all-out assault of epic proportions when deep, deep in the short-term memory vaults of my mind, a little penny dropped. 'Hang on,' I said, suddenly serious, 'Your biog says you studied linguistics. And that you're fluent in three languages, including English.'

There was a pause so heavily pregnant its waters had broken, then both Pedro and the publicist burst into laughter. 'I don't believe it,' he yelled, 'you're the first person that's ever read the biog!'

Now it was our turn for the confused puppy look.

The publicist piped up, 'Every interview we do, we turn up last minute and pretend for a few minutes that he can't speak

English. You're the only ones that have ever caught us out.' Oh how we laughed, and ended up having a crackin' interview.

We learned a lot that day. Lesson one – always read the biog. Lesson two – never trust a publicist. Lesson three – it's amazing how quickly a no-talent tool with a song that sucks can become a funny guy with a classy top ten hit. A sentence, I believe, that was also the motto for Stock, Aitken and Waterman.

Planes, No Trains, Some Automobiles

The sounds of the jungle echoed in our ears as the large Papuan man with scarlet teeth glared at us across the hut. Slowly he rose from his haunches and dragged his feet towards us across the sandy floor. We were alone – two white men (comedians at that) on a remote island off the east coast of Papua New Guinea, surrounded by locals, and starting to wonder if we would ever see our loved ones again.

Closer the strange man came as we shuffled nervously in our boots, trying to avoid his gaze. Still he advanced, until he was less than a foot from our faces, his eyes narrowed into what I guess was the definition of the word 'glowering'.

Let me explain. I had been asked to support Shane Bourne on a mini-tour of Papua New Guinea. Shane was one of the most recognisable faces on Australian television, thanks to his weekly spots on *Hey Hey It's Saturday*, as co-host of 'The Great Aussie Joke'.

Every Saturday night he would take his place alongside Maurie Fields – the man for whom the word 'entertainer' was invented – and read out jokes sent in by viewers. He was also a crackerjack comedian, and just the person to entertain miners and ex-pats alike on PNG.

We had spent the previous day flying from Sydney to Brisbane to Cairns to Port Moresby. The majority of the trip consisted of me happily listening to Shane's tales of working with Steve Martin on a play called *Picasso at the Lapin Agile*.

We arrived in Port Moresby to a true rock-star reception. A throng of TV cameras, journalists, and beaming locals had gathered, at least three hundred people in all, to catch a glimpse of . . . the Australian rugby league team, who just happened to be on the same flight.

The only person not interested in the team was our contact, who quickly ferried us to an adjoining terminal for our 3.30 p.m. flight to Misima. Now when I say 'terminal', I mean shed, when I say 'ferried', I mean walked, and when I say 3.30 p.m., I mean whenever the pilot's ready.

I'm not kidding – at approximately 4.05 p.m. the pilot (or at least a man who claimed to be a pilot) entered the lounge (and when I say 'lounge' . . .) and informed us we'd be boarding in about half an hour or so.

At around 4.38-ish we boarded the plane, a Twin Otter that seated about fifteen or so. I don't know much about Twin Otters, but we guessed it was probably better than a Single Otter.

It was a small plane. How small? We had to pass out our own inflight meals and serve each other coffee.

How small? The pilot was also the steward. How small?

We were the inflight entertainment. After about an hour, the plane suddenly lurched, dropped, and landed on a dirt airfield.

We were later informed that the sudden nature of the landing was due to the method of navigation.

'We just point the plane in the right direction and fly for an hour. After an hour we look for a gap in the clouds then drop through it, that way we can see if we're about to hit a mountain. Once we're under the clouds, we look around to see how close we are to the airfield, and head towards it.'

Apparently this time, the gap in the clouds had been directly above the runway.

The gig was in the canteen of a mining camp that was cordoned off from the rest of the island by barbed-wire fences. Fifty or so male miners, who generally worked sixteen-hour days, were accompanied by five women in the mess hall to watch Shane Bourne and 'some guy' tell a few comedy jokes, after which we were invited back to Barry's Hut for some 'home brew'. I didn't have a brilliant gig, Shane had a killer, but I don't think they even cared. I believe the whole show was actually a ruse to get some new folks to drink with.

The following day we were shown around the island by one of the miners, who cut such gems of wisdom as: 'If you see a native guy about to throw a rock at you, just wave at him. He'll drop the rock and wave back,' and, 'If you're in your car, and a pig and a child run in front of you, it's better to hit the child. Pigs are worth a lot here, but they can always have another kid.'

My personal favourite was: 'The native women are beautiful. Hard heads, too. Good for carrying stuff on 'em.'

This led Shane and I to refer privately to the majority of white people we encountered as 'The Hard Noggin Brigade'. Anyone we met with a semblance of disrespect for the locals (and believe me there were many), was later mocked in a faux-British Empire accent. 'Yes, yes. Hard noggins the locals. Good for carrying stuff. Another cigar, Jenkins?'

After our island tour we were dropped back at the airport, a building that made the previous day's shed look like the Playboy Mansion, to wait for the 1.30 p.m. flight . . . or 2.15 p.m.

or 3.47 p.m., or whenever the pilot managed to spot a break in the clouds.

It was as we stood in the corner of this thatched hut that Shane turned to me and pondered in his unique Aussie drawl, 'Maaayte. Does anyone know we're here?'

'How do you mean?'

'Well, if the plane arrived, and we weren't here for some reason, would anyone know what had happened to us?'

The gravity of this comment took hold as we scanned our surroundings. The 'ticket desk' was unattended, as was 'check-in' and 'baggage services', although in truth they were all the same table. Outside in the driveway a dozen locals squatted beneath a tree, chewing copious amounts of betel nut. When ingested, this bright red nut gave a calming high, a bit like marijuana and alcohol combined. Locals would sit all day chewing, then spitting the remains onto the ground, creating ominous red splashes.

So, there we were, two white comedians in a dodgy hut, surrounded by half-naked locals, whose red teeth and glazed eyes combined with the puddles of red in the dirt to present a potentially frightening scene.

Now where was I? Oh yeah – the sounds of the jungle echoed in our ears as the large Papuan man with scarlet teeth glared at us across the hut. Slowly he rose from his haunches and dragged his feet towards us across the sandy floor. He didn't say a word. Just fixed his gaze on us as he walked. A gaze that was unavoidable. Eventually he stood with his face a foot from Shane's, and since we were all but huddling together, mine. After an unhealthily long pause, he spoke.

'Hey!'

We shuddered.

'You're that bloke off *Hey Hey It's Saturday*!'

Shane smiled weakly and nodded.

'I've gotta joke for you.'

And there, on a remote island off the eastern coast of Papua New Guinea, in a thatched hut beside a dirt airfield, surrounded by natives glaring at us and chewing betel nut, a large Papuan man told us a joke. To this day I've no idea what he said, and in fact he even followed the punchline by declaring the joke was only funny if you spoke Pidgin English, but I can tell you we laughed like relieved hyenas.

Two nights later, we were invited to share cocktails at the Australian High Commission with the Australian rugby league team. The night after that, I split my forehead open on a microphone on stage. Ah, comedy, will it ever end?

Car Boot Fail

Unlike stand-up comedy, the radio industry seems to encourage the wholesale theft of ideas. I'd say seventy-five per cent of our on-air ideas were stolen directly from another radio station outside the market. I stopped counting the number of times a programme director would play us a tape of WKKZ Missouri and say, 'I want you to do that.'

Of course, WKKZ Missouri had probably stolen it from WRTF Oklahoma, who had in turn appropriated it from Radio Moosejaw Ontario, and so on. We liked to imagine that every radio promotion in the world actually originated from a tiny radio station in Jamaica – the only original radio station in the world.

With the advancement of the internet, it became even easier

to swap ideas with other stations around the globe, and that's how we found the idea that almost got me arrested.

Some DJ at some station somewhere in America had hidden in the boot of a car and pretended to have been kidnapped. While an accomplice drove around town, stopping at garages, drive-thrus and the like, DJ Rick was banging on the boot, screaming that he'd been kidnapped. It was apparently hilarious, and only ended when they were pulled over by the police. A classic radio stunt (and I say that with as much sarcasm-in-hindsight that I can muster).

So it was that three days later, Steve and I drove into the BP service station in Hindmarsh Square – one of the few garages in Australia that still had driveway service. Steve was at the wheel, I was in the boot, and we were both on mobile phones linked back to the studio, where the whole thing was being recorded.

As soon as I heard the petrol cap open, I started with the screaming. 'Help. Help. I've been kidnapped. This guy's locked me in the boot. Let me out,' I yelled, belting the inside of the boot with my fist. The attendant asked Steve what was going on, to which Steve replied, 'Nothing. Don't worry about it. Just ignore it.'

He returned to filling the car, and again I screamed, 'Don't let him drive away. He's locked me in the boot. I don't know what he's gonna do to me.' And again the attendant walked to Steve's side. 'Mate, what's going on?'

This time Steve struggled to keep a straight face. 'Look, don't worry about it. It's just a joke.'

I should tell you that Steve was, and still is, a short, stocky man with a shaved head and a tuft of beard on his chin. Sometimes he looks like your best mate, but with a possible kidnap victim in the boot, the shaved head and beard – plus the fact that he was laughing – made him look, well, homicidal.

The attendant fetched the manager, who approached the car to hear my continued cries for help. He asked Steve what was going on, Steve gave the usual answer, and the manager then informed him that the police would be called as soon as the car left the service station. Steve said he understood, paid his money, and drove off.

Can I point out at this stage that, in retrospect, this is one of the stupidest and most negative things I have ever done in my life? The anguish that must have been felt by both the attendant and the manager were not in any way justified by the fact that it was all for a radio stunt, and I'm sure we could have raised equally as much publicity by engaging in a posi-tive activity.

At the time, however, swept up in the never-ending search for ratings, advertising and listeners, it seemed like a fabulous idea. As we left the service station, and happened to pass a stationary police car outside a café, Steve had a thought.

What if we just went around the block and kept cruising past the police car, to see how long it would take them to catch on to us? The only difference between us and a pair of teenagers pulling a stupid prank was that we were sober and getting paid for it.

First things first, we pulled up around the corner, so I could exit the boot. I suffer from car sickness at the best of times (as a family we never travelled anywhere without an old ice-cream container in the back seat of the car, affectionately known as 'The Chunder Bucket') so an airless, windowless luggage compartment would have quickly led to the evacuation of my lunch.

My phone was switched off, but the hands-free in the car stayed on, and connected to the studio, as we headed slowly back to the 'scene of the crime'. We had barely moved twenty yards when the aforementioned police car swung into view, facing us at the top of the street. As it came closer, we saw the officer in the passenger seat point us out to the driver, who in true movie style instantly accelerated then swung the car around in front of us, blocking our path.

It was as both officers ran from their car, doors open, unclipping holsters, and yelling at us to exit our vehicle that Steve and I realised exactly how inappropriate our behaviour had been.

'Right, you two, up against the wall! Arms outstretched, palms on the wall, feet apart, and don't move.' Oh shit. 'Give me the keys. Now!'

As one officer watched over us, the other unlocked the boot to find . . . a lone tyre. 'One of you blokes wanna tell me what's going on here?'

I turned and offered the only explanation I could, 'It's a radio stunt that's gone horribly wrong.'

Of course, the accurate answer would have been, 'It's a radio stunt that has achieved exactly what we set out to,' but the unclipped holsters made me think better of it. As did the four other police vehicles that had now arrived on the scene.

In total we were surrounded by three squad cars and two paddy wagons – ten of Adelaide's finest, and at this moment in time grumpiest, police officers – and all because we wanted some extra ratings. It wasn't quite the final scene of *The Blues Brothers*, but it's the closest I've ever been to it.

The car's registration was checked and found to belong to

the radio station. Our bosses were called, and managed to confirm that we were indeed station employees. We were summarily informed of the stupidity of our actions, the distress we had caused, and the valuable wastage of police time and money we had instigated. To be fair, a few of the officers were quite friendly, but the majority looked on with well-justified looks of indignation.

We returned to the station and set about editing the piece for the following morning. A few days later, an article ran in the Sunday paper in which we were labelled 'irresponsible'. It also featured an interview with the petrol station attendant, who said he had been distressed by the incident, as he was afraid there was actually someone in the boot about to be killed.

Did it affect ratings? Who knows? Could we have found a way to create publicity without causing anyone distress? Probably. Could we have been charged with some sort of offence? Definitely. Did I learn anything from it? I'm not sure.

But you can guarantee right now, somewhere in the world there is a radio DJ climbing into the boot of a car with a mobile phone, to replicate a stunt he read about on the internet.

Sick Kids

Even the best of us have the capacity to do bad things. Especially under pressure. Especially when your job is on the line. I just wanted to say that. You'll find out why in a few moments.

We were sitting in the Programme Director's office for our daily aircheck meeting. It entailed listening back to the show with the ads and music taken out, and discussing whether or not we were any good. Trust me when I say that the word 'aircheck' will always send a shiver down the spine of anyone that has ever worked in radio.

The last thing you want to do after coming off air at 9 a.m. when you've been awake since half past three is to listen to everything you just said, and analyse exactly how funny it was. Often we'd be joined by a variety of "experts" – including interstate programmers and international consultants. They'd give suggestions on what we could have said better, we would hear replays of what we said wrong, and we would be constantly reminded to 'hook people through the ad breaks'. Always promote what's coming up after the ads, so that the listeners don't change the station.

Sometimes the PD was busy at 9 a.m., and we'd have to wait around until midday before rehashing the day's show like a sick dog sniffing its own vomit.

Add to this a promotions meeting once a week, a daily planning meeting for the next day's show, and a weekly announcers' meeting, and you'll understand why I once suggested publicly that SAFM stood for Shit, Another Fucking Meeting.

Anyway, it was in one of our daily airchecks that one of the 'experts' had a brainwave. Let's call him 'Rick'.

'We're gonna raise money for a sick kid.'

'A great idea. Who is the kid?'

'I dunno. We haven't found one yet.'

'What?'

Rick went on to explain that our sister station in Brisbane had spent the entire morning show raising money for a young girl who needed an operation. The station devoted the rest of the day to the appeal and raised in the vicinity of $40,000, enabling her to have the life-saving operation. More importantly, the show had received the highest ratings of any station in Brisbane.

'I want you guys to do the same thing,' Rick exhorted us.

Again we queried who the child would be, to which Rick responded, 'I don't care. Go and find one.'

Now, I'm all for helping a child raise money for a life-saving operation, but I was getting the impression that Rick's motives were less than altruistic. It seemed to me that a genuinely ill child was about to be exploited in the name of ratings, and that made me bristle.

'What do you want us to do?' I started. 'Go down to the hospital and walk through the wards, shouting, "Who needs an operation?"'

'If you have to,' shot Rick, without a hint of irony.

I suggested that perhaps we should raise money for Canteen, a charity that helped teenagers deal with cancer. As major sponsors of the cause, it seemed only right that they should benefit from the station's listeners.

Rick replied that we needed to raise the money for a specific person, rather than a charity, because it creates a personal connection for the listeners. I then suggested that we contact Canteen, ask them which teenager was in need of treatment, and donate the money to them.

'Nah, cancer kids are no good,' he retorted without emotion. 'They're gonna die anyway. We need to find someone who has a chance of living, otherwise we'll never hook people through the ad breaks.'

It was the harshest thing I have ever heard someone say, and it sat me back in my chair in slack-jawed amazement. I mulled over what I had just heard, and tried to formulate the appropriate response.

Then I said, 'Rick, one day I'm going to write a movie about my time in radio. And in that movie there'll be a character based on you.'

He smiled.

'And everything that has been said here today will be in that movie. And you know what, in the final scene of that movie, I just decided that your character will find out he has cancer.'

His face dropped.

I don't remember much of the rest of the meeting. I remember my own anger, some mutterings about me keeping my mouth shut, and someone offering to find a sick kid. I also recall Rick's face. He was so honestly taken aback by what I said, in fact he looked mortally offended.

I don't think he considered for a second that what he said was in any way out of order, and he was hurt and saddened by my opinion that he basically deserved cancer. Although technically I wasn't wishing cancer on Rick, I was just suggesting that it would be a karmically appropriate outcome for a movie character based on him.

A week later, I happened across a memo regarding the 'sick kid'. It read something like this:

MEMO TO: Rick
RE: Sick kid

I have contacted the Women's and Children's Hospital and found two kids that may be suitable. The results are as follows.

Kid number one: Has leukaemia and needs a total
blood transfusion.
Pros: Will sound great on air. Is a serious disease.
Cons: Operation may not necessarily keep him alive.
There is a chance he will die, therefore no happy
ending.

Kid number two: Needs a voicebox operation.
Pros: Fairly simple operation. Should be successful.
Cons: Not life threatening. He can't speak, and there-
fore we lose the chance to chat to him on-air.

Let me know what you wanna do.
Derek.

Thankfully the whole thing never happened, but it sickens
me now to think that a child's illness could be analysed so
selfishly. It sickens me to know that for the sake of a few
ratings points a human being's compassion can disappear
completely. And it sickens me to know that, given the chance,
I would probably have gone through with the scam.

Like I said, when your job's on the line, it is very easy to
blur the line between right and wrong. Sure, at the end of the
day a child and his family might have benefited from the
procedure, but does that still make it right? What about the
children that could have done with a life-saving operation,
but were turned down because they didn't fit the demographic
survey of the audience. Or because their condition was too
depressing to 'hook the listeners through'.

I'm just glad I never had to make the moral decision.

A few months after all this happened, I walked into the
toilets to find Rick staring into the mirror, ashen-faced. He

told me he had just had a scan, and that there was some sort of cloud on his lungs.

I did the only thing I could do – put my hand on his shoulder, and told him I hoped he was going to be OK.

I am very, very happy to say that it turned out to be nothing, and that Rick is still alive today.

Whatever Life Throws Up

Although I was permanently employed at the radio station, and on quite a good salary for your average twenty-three-year-old, I kept performing stand-up every chance I got. I didn't want to lose the comic edge, the fear of dying in front of a roomful of strangers that forces you to find the funny. I also didn't want to lose the joy that came from performing to a live audience, which radio simply couldn't replicate. Even on my first ever night in Adelaide, having flown into a new town and about to start a whole new life, my first task was to visit a stand-up comedy club.

Often on a Friday I would do the breakfast show, stay at the station until three in the afternoon, head home, get changed, have an hour's sleep, then head to the comedy club to perform a gig. On at least three occasions I arrived home at 4.40 a.m. on a Saturday, having been awake since 4.40 a.m. on the Friday.

As I write this, I'm having a warm flashback to my childhood, when I'd come home from school to find that my dad, the Qantas flight service director, had arrived back from a trip overseas. He would often regale us with how little sleep he'd had. I thought my dad was the coolest person in the world when, at three in the afternoon, he'd say, 'I've been awake since seven o'clock last night.'

As a treat, Dad would sometimes take my brother and I on a flight with him – usually it was a trip to Melbourne and back in a day – and Brad and I thought he was famous because he made the inflight announcements.

'That's Dad!' we'd say, nudging each other as he kindly asked the passengers to return their tray tables to the upright positions.

As far as I was concerned, my dad's job was to fly around the world and talk to people on a microphone.

Is it any wonder I do what I do now?

Anyway, it was with a total disregard for sleep and a need to do a live gig that I accepted a slot as the support act for Stevie Starr, aka the Regurgitator.

Stevie's act consisted of him swallowing a variety of objects, and bringing them up again on demand. One trick involved swallowing an audience member's engagement ring which had been secured into a padlock. He then swallowed the key and after thirty seconds of internal wrangling brought up the ring, the now opened padlock, and the key – separately.

Unfortunately, the gig was in Whyalla, a small town which is (in keeping with the Australian tradition of measuring distance between places by the amount of time it takes to get there) a four-hour drive from Adelaide. So it was that I set off from Adelaide at around one on that fateful Friday afternoon to drive north across the South Australian countryside, to be the support act for a man that regurgitates inanimate objects for a living.

I stopped on the outskirts of the city to top up both the petrol tank and the radiator, the latter at my mother's urging on a phone call earlier that day.

(You know the way mothers urge. 'Make sure you check the radiator.' 'I checked it last week.' 'I know, but check it again, you never know what might happen.' It is an urging born of love and concern, but still and all, an urging only a child knows. 'Don't spend too much time writing in parentheses.' 'Mum, I know what I'm doing, OK?' 'I know, but you know how carried away you sometimes get.' Actually she's right, I have spent far too much time in these parentheses, but there's no way I'll admit it to her.)

An hour later I was lost in a driver's reverie, staring dreamily at the road ahead while occasionally glancing sideways at the beauty of the passing flora and fauna, when there came a loud bang from the engine, followed by a sudden loss of revs, and an accompanying loss of power. The engine shut down, and the car glided (glud?) to a halt on the crunching roadside gravel.

I immediately exited the car, popped the bonnet, and did what every guy in the history of roadside breakdowns has ever done – I stared at the engine as if I knew what I was looking for.

I managed to maintain this charade for a good ten minutes or so, fooling the passing traffic into believing I could locate and rectify the problem, before doing the second thing that every guy does in this roadside situation – I tried to flag down a car.

Eventually a good Samaritan stopped, however not before at least twenty devil worshippers sailed blithely past, ignoring the panting pleas of my open bonnet, and the steamy sighs of the exasperated engine. (Ooh, I got all metaphoric then, and slightly alliterative. Yes, Mum, I remember what you said about the parentheses.)

Trouble was, I had no idea where I was, nor where the next town might be. I asked the Samaritan to start driving, and to drop me at the first garage we encountered.

Turned out my car had expired exactly five minutes from a town called Lochiel. Now when I say town, I mean it in the sense that only Aussies will recognise. There was, in order of appearance – a service station/trucking company, a pub, and seven houses. Two of the houses were derelict.

I was jettisoned at the service station/trucking company and dutifully informed that 'the boss' was 'in town' at 'the pub' and would take me to my car as soon as he returned. Twenty minutes later he weaved his way into the yard, grabbed the keys to the tow-truck, and headed back towards my prone vehicle. I'm sure if Mum had thought to, she would have urged me not to enter a tow-truck with a stranger in a stained singlet smelling of Victoria Bitter. I guess she forgot that one.

We made it to my car without any major incidents, where-upon he informed me that I had 'cracked the heads'. This was caused by the 'radiator overheating'. This had happened because 'someone had forgotten to put the radiator cap back on after checking the water'.

Hey, give me a break, I had been up since 4 a.m.

The boss kindly towed my car back to the garage, where I arranged, for a fee, for the car to be towed back to Adelaide and deposited at the same service station from which I had purchased the petrol, not two hours previously.

I was still stranded in a no-horse town, however, hours from Whyalla, and with no way of getting there. I called my agent Ingrid (who had left the Comedy Store and set up her own management company) and explained the situation, fully expecting her to say, 'Oh you poor thing. Listen, don't worry about the gig, just head back to Adelaide with the car and have the night off.'

Anyone who has an agent will know that wasn't her response. If Ingrid could deal with a roomful of drunken stags, she could handle a forgetful comedian in the contryside. Fifteen minutes passed, and she called back.

'Here's the plan – the woman in charge of the gig will come and get you and take you back to Whyalla. However, the gig starts in a few hours' time, and she doesn't have time to do a full round trip. What I've suggested is this: she will meet you at the Shell petrol station on the outskirts of Snowtown. It will then take an hour for you to get back to Whyalla from there. All you have to do is find a way to get to that petrol station.'

The lads at the garage, who I'm sure were highly amused by the panicky performer who couldn't even check the radiator properly, got on the two-way and asked if there were any trucks in the area that were on their way north. A response came in the affirmative, and half an hour later, I boarded the cabin of a sheep-laden semi-trailer for the two-hour ride to Snowtown.

It was about five-thirty when I alighted at the Snowtown Shell, and in all honesty it wasn't a bad journey. Sure the cabin carried the stench of the dozens of sheep crammed behind us, but I wound up spending most of the time chatting away to the driver, who seemed happy for some company.

I can't recollect exactly what a sheep-carrying truck driver and a radio-announcing stand-up comic found in common to chat about, but it was one of those unexpectedly pleasing experiences that come only when you stop worrying about the situation you've found yourself in, and 'go with whatever happens'.

As you can probably imagine, the men's toilet of the

Snowtown Shell is not the best place to have a shave. Shave I did, though, and exactly half an hour later the woman who ran the show arrived, looking a little flustered but in high spirits, and once again we chatted for the entire journey.

I think at this point the whole thing started to become an adventure for me – a broken-down car, a drunk tow-truck driver, riding in a big rig with a load of sheep behind us. Neither rain nor snow nor sleepy radiator-related mishaps would stop this show from going on.

We arrived at the theatre, well, more a town hall, exactly five minutes before the show was to start. I ran backstage, introduced myself to Stevie, changed my clothes, ran on stage, and did my allotted twenty minutes.

Later that night, as I sat in the back seat of the Stevie Starr tour van, I heard Stevie remark that he needed a toilet break. The van slowed, searching for a town and a pub, and once again the roadside gravel crunched as we approached (you guessed it) the Lochiel pub.

Needing a break myself, I followed Stevie sheepishly into the establishment, and was met by the cheers of the assorted locals, not to mention 'the boss' and his lads. It seems the story of the forgetful stand-up comic had done the rounds, and now the prodigal sump had returned.

There was only one thing I could do – I bought them all a round of drinks. Stevie and his manager, who had already been regaled with my day's events, joined in the fun, until one of the locals turned to Stevie and enquired, 'So what kind of act do you do?'

Within thirty seconds Stevie had swallowed two fifty-cent pieces, two twenties and a ten, and was asking the assembled mob which one they'd like him to bring up first.

'The twenty-cent piece,' came the response, to which Stevie replied 'Which one? The coin from 1982, or the one from 1985?' He regurgitated each coin, on request, by year of minting, and we exited the bar to a round of applause.

I learned a lot that day. I learned to go with the flow, to never give up on a gig, and to trust in the kindness of strangers. But most importantly, I learned to listen to your mother's urgings. If I hadn't, I would probably have made it to Whyalla on time with no hitches whatsoever. And where would be the fun in that?

Big Yin and I (Part Two)

The second time I met Billy Connolly, he was absolutely brilliant. Gregarious, generous, funny and inspiring. What he said to me that night has stayed with me for my career, and influenced one of the best decisions of my professional life.

SAFM was promoting his Adelaide concert, and ran a competition giving six people the chance to go to the show, and meet the Big Yin afterwards. In an act of kindness I had learned not to expect in radio, the programme director asked me if I'd like to chaperone the winners backstage.

I say this was an act of kindness, because at that point my star status at the station was dimming to say the least. I was no longer the breakfast announcer, and therefore behind another four or five people in the 'getting to meet a star' stakes. However, the PD knew I would be the person to appreciate the opportunity the most, so he took me aside and discreetly asked if I'd like to meet Billy Connolly. Bear? Woods? Shit?

As I stood backstage with the six competition winners, I

made the decision to let them have the attention. Personally, I wanted to elbow them all out of the way, take Billy out for a coffee and chat about the good old days. You know, that time I met him in front of the Sydney Opera House and he said I could take any joke I liked. Professionally, however, I thought it best to let the 'winners' have their 'prize'.

Billy's manager came out first, and politely asked that we not refer to anyone as 'winners', or indeed refer to the competition at all, as it made Billy feel uneasy – as if he were suddenly the meat tray at a raffle. We agreed, but still I promised myself to show restraint.

The moment came, and into the room strode the big man, full of adrenaline from the gig, and radiating charm.

'Wellll?' he boomed. 'Who's going to talk first?' His manager introduced the 'listeners-formerly-known-as-winners', all of whom managed to squeak a 'hello', before clamming shut through nerves.

Since I had been introduced as being from the station, Billy politely thanked me for all the publicity he had received. After attempting conversation again with the now awe-struck listeners – each one ending in a conversation cul-de-sac, he turned to me and asked, 'So how is radio treating you?' I responded that it was all going well, but that, 'I'm not really a DJ, I'm actually a stand-up comic.'

Oh my God. It was as if I had suddenly said the Secret Word. Polite banter was dropped, all pretence went out the window, and for a split second it was just him and me in the room.

'Really?' he enthused, genuinely excited, before asking, 'What did you think of the show?'

Billy Connolly, the Big Yin, the man I had listened to since the age of twelve, was asking my opinion of his show. I replied that it was like sitting in the back row of a comedy lecture, that I spent the entire show making mental notes on how to do comedy, learning from his every move.

He took a step towards me, threw one arm around my shoulder and said, 'I'll tell you a secret – it gets easier as you go along.' For a whole ten minutes, Billy stood with his arm around me giving me pearls of comedy wisdom.

'Silence is your best friend. Too many comics think they have to get a laugh every second, and if they aren't laughing they must hate you. That's not trooo. If they're silent they're still with you, and they'll wait as long as you ask them to for a laugh.

'You'll find your own style without even realising it. People used to say to me, "I love the way you start a story and then go off on a tangent," and I'd be thinking, Christ, I never even knew I did that.'

I asked for a photo opportunity, and he obliged, arm around me waiting for the flash to warm up. 'Oh, the amount of time you'll spend, standing next to a punter waiting for their flash to come on.' I remember thinking, he just assumes that I'm going to be famous.

More than anything, I was struck by the instant bond that seemed to be formed by the fact we were both comics. I had encountered this in various interviews with comedians, and had learned to tell them up front that I was also a stand-up, thus relaxing them on air. This was the same.

By far the best piece of advice Billy gave me was: 'Just do it. It's the best job in the world. You'll hate it, but you'll fucking love it. A lot of comedians will tell you to get a stable job, but I won't. There should be more comedians in the world and less soldiers. Just do it. Fucking do it.'

At this point he was called away to sign autographs, and actually apologised that he had to go, but by this stage I was floating. As he bade farewell to the assembled mob, he again shook my hand and said, 'Just do it.' I promised that I would and he strode down the hallway to the dressing room, pausing only to turn, raise his fist to me and boom, 'Just fuckin do it!'

I Did It

Two weeks after Billy Connolly told me to 'just do it', I took his advice and quit my radio job, although it did take a little pushing.

A new programme director had been appointed to the station, and he in turn needed to find a new breakfast team, as the old team had disbanded (mainly because one of them got a better job offer from the sister station in Melbourne).

We sat down and chatted, the new boss and I, and he told me I'd be filling in for the breakfast show over the holidays, and that I had three weeks to impress him.

After two weeks of more 4 a.m. starts, and 8 p.m. bedtimes, I received a call from a network station in Newcastle. They were looking for a new breakfast announcer, and were wondering if I'd be interested in the job.

I told them that even if I didn't get the Adelaide breakfast gig, I was quite happy doing the nine-till-midday shift, and being that Adelaide was a bigger city than Newcastle, I was happy where I was.

The following day, a fellow announcer called me into the studio while he was on air, and we chatted between the songs.

'So,' he began, 'are you gonna take the Newcastle job?'

I told him I was happy where I was.

'I think you should take it,' he said, to which I asked why.

'Because they've already found a replacement for you here, and he starts next week.'

Not only had the PD already found a new breakfast team, he had also given my morning job to someone else.

'Are you sure?'

'Yep,' he replied, 'I know the guy. He told me about it this morning.'

Armed with this knowledge, I returned to the PD's office, where he asked what I was going to do about the Newcastle job.

I told him I didn't want it, that I was happy in Adelaide, even if it meant doing the morning shift. I didn't want to leave my friends, uproot my life, and besides, there was a comedy festival coming to town, and I had started to prepare my first one-man show.

He suggested I take the job. I asked why. He said it would be a better career move. I disagreed and said I was happy in Adelaide. He said it would be better if I moved. I said I wanted to stay at the station.

Then he said, 'Well, I don't want you to stay at the station.'

I knew then that it was true, he had already found a replacement.

I told him I wanted to stay so I could perform at the upcoming Adelaide Comedy Festival, to which he replied, 'Listen. Sooner or later you're gonna have to choose between radio and stand-up. At the moment you can do both, but eventually you're going to have to choose.'

So I chose. With the words of Billy Connolly ringing in my ears, I quit radio for good. I guess all I really needed was an ultimatum, and when it came down to a choice between stand-up and radio – there was only ever going to be one winner.

'Just do it.'

I left the station with no hard feelings, and my departure, and that of the breakfast team, made front-page news. As I drove home that day, the banner headlines in front of the newsagents yelled at me: RADIO STARS IN SHOCK DEPARTURE. I still have that headline at home.

I have bumped into that programme director a few times since, and each time he apologises for not giving me the breakfast gig. And each time I tell him not to give it a moment's thought, that it was the best thing he could have done for me, and that if he had given me that job, I wouldn't have ended up travelling the world, doing what I do today.

Besides, I wasn't really the best DJ in the world. One morning I managed to introduce a song that I had forgotten to put into the CD player. As I calmly wrapped up my spiel, I hit the 'on' button, but nothing happened.

I frantically searched for the CD (Alanis Morissette, if memory serves me), found it, and put it in the player, all the while desperately filling for time on air. Eventually I hit the 'on' button and the track kicked in.

Livid at myself, I sat back as the music started and yelled, 'Oh, for fuck's sake, Adam.' I then looked down and realised I'd left the microphone on.

A few months after leaving SAFM, I found myself back at the Sydney Comedy Store, among old mates. Jim Burnett, the man who had advised me a few years earlier to 'talk about what you know', asked why I had left radio.

I told him of the offer to move to Newcastle, and said, 'If I'd loved radio, I would have moved.'

'No, darling,' he replied. 'If you had loved radio, they wouldn't have asked you to move.'

My Mum's advice was just as comforting: 'You'll be ok. You always land on your feet'. I'm not sure if the pun was intended, but it was a sentiment she has often repeated, and I've come to believe.

A year later, after returning home from my first Edinburgh Fringe Festival, I was called back to the station and offered my old job back, at double the salary. I shocked the network when I said no. Every top brass exec came to Adelaide to persuade me to take it, but I held firm.

As I tried to explain my reasoning, one director, by the name of Rob Logan, put words to it.

'Listen to me,' he said. 'As a network director, I think you should take the job. It'll be good for you, and good for the network.' I gulped.

'As a friend, though, and a friend who has seen you on stage, I think you should do what you love. You're a great stand-up comic, and you've just had an amazing experience at the Edinburgh Festival. I can see it in your eyes: you've seen Everest, and now you want to climb it.'

And that's exactly what I did.

Thanks Rob, thanks Jim, thanks Mum, and thanks Billy.

Part Three

Late Nights

Life Is Good

The Adelaide Fringe Festival is the world's second-largest arts festival, behind the Edinburgh Fringe. Until 2006 it was bi-annual, and 1997 was an off-year. Thus the inaugural Adelaide Comedy Festival was held.

A whole bunch of acts were shipped over from the UK and Ireland, including Richard Herring and Stewart Lee, Hattie Hayridge (from *Red Dwarf*) and Michael Smiley. Adelaide locals were invited to do their own shows, so I cobbled together all the material I had at that point, and added a few more bits to bring it up to an hour.

I called the show 'Stand Up and Deliver' and came up with a poster featuring me as an Adam Ant-esque highwayman. The venue was an upstairs room at Boltz Café on Rundle Street, where a group of us had begun performing on a Thursday night. Much like the Sydney Comedy Store days, a family of comedians had formed that included Justin Hamilton, Mickey D, Lehmo, Jodi J. Hill, Dave Williams, Alex Collins, Jo Coventry, Jack Smith and Pete Monaghan.

We encouraged each other to be creative, and offered up jokes that we thought would fit into each others' acts. I felt at home at Boltz, and while the bar held only about a hundred people, it had the low ceiling and wooden floors that made for a great comedy room. It was the perfect place to perform my first solo show.

I learnt very quickly that being on breakfast radio doesn't necessarily guarantee you an audience. Why would someone who wakes up to the sound of my voice every morning, want to come see me on stage at night?

Besides, what was I gonna do on stage for an hour? Make prank calls and introduce songs? It was clear I had to re-establish myself as a stand-up comic.

The festival gave me an insight into what it took to make it on the international circuit, and also what happened when a bunch of international comedians were away from home for the first time.

The opening night gala was particularly illuminating. Held at the famous Thebarton Theatre, the backstage area was like a Bacchanalian stag night. Booze flowed a little too freely, and each act got progressively drunk. What made things worse was that we could all watch the show on a big-screen TV, so everyone heckled everyone else's act.

'Watch this, fuckers, I'll show you how it's done,' one act yelled to the room, before going on stage and bombing worse than a twenty-year-old comedian at a christening.

Throughout it all, one performer kept quiet – a tall, charismatic Yorkshireman called Boothby Graffoe. He even slept in his chair. As his stage time approached, he softly stood up, strapped on his guitar, and headed to the stage with no fanfare whatsoever.

By this time the show had run over, and the audience clearly wanted to go home, but Boothby calmly, and subtly stormed it. He didn't even seem to try that hard, but he received the best response of the night by a mile.

I marvelled when he came backstage and immediately rushed over to him.

'All these egos,' I said, 'all these over-the-top preening egos bombed. But you kept to yourself, didn't show off, and had the best gig of the night.'

'Ah yes,' he replied. 'That's because I have the biggest ego of them all.'

I became good friends with Boothby, and by the end of the festival he gave me the advice that convinced me to have a crack at the Edinburgh Fringe Festival.

'Go to Edinburgh,' he said, 'because even if you die on your arse every night for the month, you'll still be a better comedian at the end of it.'

From Australia I applied for a venue, organised someone to distribute the posters, found accommodation, and took out some ads. My 'fuck you money' was already coming in handy.

One of the other acts at the Adelaide Comedy Festival, a genial Geordie by the name of Dave Johns, had offered to help get me some gigs in the UK, so I arrived a few weeks before the Fringe to take him up on the offer.

True to his word, Dave took me along to a gig in Colchester, where I was introduced on stage for my five-minute spot by a young lad I was told would be huge, a fella called Ross Noble. The following weekend Dave organised for me to do a couple more spots at the Glee Club in Birmingham, as long as I could get myself there and sort out some hotel accommodation (more 'fuck you money').

Those spots went well enough that the venue owners told me to let them know the next time I was in the UK, and they'd book me as a professional.

I'll always be indebted to Dave Johns for taking me under his wing, in an act of kindness I've seen him repeat to other comedians as well. That generosity is why every act on the circuit, to a person, was genuinely chuffed when Dave became a film star in the movie *I, Daniel Blake*.

Comedians can be a pretty jealous and cynical bunch, but when Dave made it big, we all agreed it couldn't have happened to a nicer bloke.

My first trip to the Edinburgh Festival consisted of at least three hours a day handing out flyers and free tickets to my show, doing whatever I could to raise an audience. Along with every other performer at the Fringe, I'd trudge the city streets and bars, descending on groups of friendly looking people with a sales pitch and a few free tickets.

My venue was an underground cellar with stone walls called the Honeycomb, and it held about eighty people. My show was at 5.15 p.m., so I'd hit the streets at one, hoping to catch some lunching workers, who might fancy an early show when they knocked off for the night.

It can be quite disheartening work, as people look at the flyer, look at you and comment, 'He can't be that good if he's handing out his own flyers.' Others, however, would see that as a personal touch, and if I could entertain them for a few minutes, would be more likely to come to the show.

I couldn't even count on my countrymen coming to see me, as I once overheard one of them look at my flyer and remark, 'Why do I wanna fly halfway around the world to go watch another Aussie?'

I soon learned that on a sunny summer's day, in a city not known for buildings equipped for the heat, I could entice a few punters in purely with the phrase, 'It's one of the only venues in Edinburgh with air conditioning.'

Some days I'd hand out thirty free tickets, only to have an audience of twenty-five people. This meant that I not only had no paying customers, but that five people didn't even want to see me for free. Still, I'd get a few laughs by recognising someone from the street, and enquiring how their meal was.

Eventually, those that saw the show and enjoyed it would tell their friends, and by the end of the run I was starting to attract semi-decent sized crowds, although not on the night my parents came to the show.

They flew from the other side of the world to see their university-educated son, who had turned his back on a burgeoning radio career, perform to fourteen people in a dank cellar.

I received a three-star review that described my comedy as 'sun-drenched, celebratory humour' that left the audience 'stumbling and smiling into the street, suffused with goodwill'.

It reminded me of the advice Billy Connolly had said to me backstage at his show in Adelaide: 'You won't know what your style of comedy is, but other people will tell you. You'll read a review and think "that's interesting, I never knew I did that".'

That review was the first time my comedy had been described as 'celebratory'.

The route from my rented apartment to the city took about fifteen minutes to walk, and brought me along an underpass at Buccleuch Street, where a daily assortment of elderly winos would gather, drinking Tennant's Special Brew, and entertaining each other in broad Scottish accents.

Every day I would walk towards these grey, grizzled men, and every day I would look directly at my boots, avoiding eye contact at all costs in case they asked me for change. They never did. Day after day, the ritual was in place – head down, eyes down, walk straight past, keep my change.

Then one sunny afternoon I found myself in the centre of the city, strolling the Royal Mile, being approached by a well-dressed young chap and his friends. It seems they had found themselves short of change for a parking meter, and asked if I could help them out. Without hesitation, I reached into my pocket and produced a fifty pence piece.

It was only as I left them to attend to the meter that I realised my hypocrisy. I was quite happy to spare some loose change for a group of well-dressed, brogues-and-tweed Daddy's boys, who had brought the BMW up to bonnie Scotland for the weekend, but I wouldn't even make eye contact with an elderly wino who could probably do with a few quid, and yet who never once asked me for money.

It occurred to me that perhaps I should at least show a bit of compassion to the man I passed every morning.

The next day at approximately 11 a.m., I approached the motley crew of, let's not say winos, let's say 'alcoholically enhanced non-homeowners', determined I would make an effort to be friendly. As I neared the pack, I made eye contact with the man I had previously ignored.

He had a face that only a Scotsman could possess. As red and tarnished as a freshly scrubbed beetroot, with more lines than a Shakespearean sonnet. With a shock of grey hair and a bushy beard, it looked a little like Santa had fallen on hard times. All this was neatly capped off by a Sherlock Holmes-style hat, lovingly resting on his noggin.

'Hiya,' I offered tentatively.

'Hello,' he returned gruffly.

'How are you going?' I asked, doing my best not to look like I was trying too hard.

At this, his face lit up. 'Life is good,' he beamed. 'I've got a beer in my hand, the sun on my face, and my best friend beside me. Life is Good.'

It was not what I was expecting. I had prepared myself for a hard-luck story, a tale of woe, intrigue, betrayal, and heartbreak. I was expecting to hear a tirade against the government, and a plea for a bit of spare change, but instead I charged head on into the most positive attitude I had ever encountered.

'Good on you,' I smiled.

'Aye, life goes on y'know. Ob la di, ob la da.'

I couldn't help but laugh with him.

'Who sang that?' he suddenly quizzed.

'The Beatles.'

'Aye,' he said, grinning, 'but who sang it in Scotland?'

I replied that I had no idea.

'Marmalade,' he rejoiced. 'And it went to number one!'

He fixed me with a glint in his eye and started to sing, 'Ob la di, ob la da, life goes on, bra! Na na, how the life goes on.'

And there, beside an underpass on the edge of Edinburgh's Old Town, I joined in.

For the remainder of the festival, whenever I passed by, I would always stop and ask how he was doing. And each time he would remind me that 'Life is good.'

A few months later, when the din of the festival had quietened, I decided that my next show would be called 'Life Is Good' and that I would tell the story of the man beside the underpass who made my day, and my festival.

I also decided that I would always try to uplift people, make them feel good, and remind them that life is good at every opportunity. Or as my review said – use my 'sun-drenched celebratory humour' to leave people 'laughing and stumbling into the street'.

The following year I returned to Edinburgh with my second solo show, entitled 'Life Is Good'. I made it my mission to find that same old bloke and invite him along, but alas he was nowhere to be found. I checked the underpass every day, but there was no sign of him or his mates.

Maybe he found a hostel, maybe he found Jesus, maybe he went to God, I'll never know. But his spirit stays with me, and I still do my best to remind others, but more importantly myself, that life is indeed good.

Ob la di, ob la da, my friend, wherever you are.

Uncorked

I returned from the Edinburgh Fringe and found that I was indeed a better comedian. Although I didn't feel any different, I did notice that I was getting a better response from the audience. The jokes I'd been doing for years were now getting better laughs. The new jokes I was writing were slightly better than the old ones.

I immediately set to coming up with a new show, and decided to head back to London earlier to do more gigs. Thankfully I had a family friend, 'Auntie' Carol, who offered me a spare room. Unfortunately, Carol lived out past Heathrow, which meant that it often cost me twenty pounds in train fares to do an unpaid five-minute spot. If I missed the last train home, it cost another ninety pounds in a taxi.

My years of experience in Australia meant that most of the try-out spots I did went well, and once again I'd be offered a paid slot for the next time I was in the UK. I made sure to keep everyone's numbers.

The year after that I decided to base myself in Dublin, where one of my ex-radio colleagues from Adelaide, a lady by the name of Carolyn Lee (Flee to her friends) had started a comedy agency.

As my 'fuck you money' began to dwindle, Flee gave me some invaluable advice: 'Think of it as investing in a company, except that the company is you. Eventually it'll pay dividends.'

She was right, too, as my second Edinburgh season did substantially better than the first. I lost only four thousand pounds in 1998, as opposed to five thousand in 1997. That was close to twenty thousand Australian dollars in two years.

It took me until 2000 to finally make a profit at the Edinburgh Fringe, and even then it was around five hundred pounds. I had left radio with enough money to buy an apartment in Adelaide, and within four years I was down to my last few hundred dollars.

Just when things were starting to look a little worrying, the universe stepped in. It was the 2001 Melbourne Comedy Festival, and Johnny Vegas had pulled out of a three-hundred-seat venue. I was asked if I would take his spot, which was a massive step up from my sixty-seater. I took a punt, and thankfully by the end of the season I was selling out. My bank balance was saved – in the nick of time.

I returned to Dublin and a booming comedy scene, and once again found myself part of an extended comedy family. This time it was the Comedy Lounge that became the central focus for us all – an old converted cinema with a giant brick wall behind the performer where the screen used to be, and a long red carpet leading from the stage to the bar at the back of the room.

A posse began to form that included Deirdre O'Kane, Eddie Bannon, David O'Doherty, Des Bishop, and Dara O'Briain. Once again we'd all spur each other on and, because Flee was now managing us all, we would live together in a shared house during the Edinburgh Fringe. I think Dara and I racked up three consecutive Fringes together.

On Mondays I'd also join the Dublin Comedy Improv in a tiny room above the International Bar on Wicklow Street. How small was it? There was no microphone. How small was it? It held fifty people at a stretch. How small was it? If you jumped up in the air while on stage, you hit your head on the ceiling.

My year took on a pretty familiar schedule – I'd try bits and pieces, jokes and stories at every comedy club I could find from October to December, go home to Australia for Christmas, then turn it all into a brand-new show at the Adelaide Fringe Festival in February and March, and on to the Melbourne Comedy Festival for all of April.

A few more gigs around Australia, then back to the UK and Ireland for June, where I'd spend two months previewing the show before the Edinburgh Fringe Festival in August. I'd then sit on the couch for a month to recover from the Fringe, and start the process all over again in October.

Ireland became my new home for half the year, and I loved it. I performed from Limerick to Kinsale to the eventual Holy Grail – the Kilkenny Cat Laughs Comedy Festival – and relished the chance to prove myself to a new audience, and new colleagues.

One particular night at a Festival in Galway, a group of us had a candlelit pre-show meal in a restaurant that was experiencing a blackout. After the gig, one of my dining companions, a gently spoken but incessantly funny comedian called Barry Murphy approached me.

'I enjoyed your set tonight,' he said softly.

'Thank you,' I replied.

'I'm glad I enjoyed your set,' he continued. 'Because I quite liked your company at dinner, but if you'd been shite on stage I would never have talked to you again.'

Two of the best comedy rooms on the planet were The GPO in Galway, and City Limits in Cork – another underground cellar, built into a hillside. It was literally under someone's house, and when the woman who lived above the venue flushed her toilet, you could hear the water rush through the pipes above the stage.

That club saved me one night.

When Flee offered me a gig at a stag night in Cork, my first response was to turn it down. If only I had listened to my inner voice. 'Whaddya crazy?' it pleaded. 'Stag nights are always death.' And it was right.

A group of drunken males, celebrating one last night away from the missus, all vying to be the alpha male, do not want to hand over the spotlight to a comedian, unless he tells the kind of jokes that would make a wharfie blush.

I took the gig for a couple of reasons: firstly, I had the night off anyway and had nothing planned, and secondly, it would be £400 Irish for twenty minutes' work. Eight hundred Aussie dollars for twenty minutes of hell. How bad could it be? I said yes.

At this time I should let you know that I am aware £400 is a lot of money for twenty minutes' work. But bear in mind, it's not an easy job. Twenty minutes of solid, original material to forty-odd blokes. I know it averages out at about £20 per minute, but when you take into account the years of working clubs and so on to get to this point, plus the fact that it's not the best audience in the world, well, who's to say if it's fair. Either way, it was around the going rate.

A week later, I'm standing in Flee's office, confirming the details. Cork Golf Club, accommodation and travel paid for, and a twenty-minute set? 'Hang on,' she replied, 'I'll call and check.' The next few minutes told me what kind of hell I was in for.

'Yes, I'm just confirming the details for Adam Hills this Friday. He'll arrive at 9 o'clock, do a twenty-minute set, and you've organised a hotel, right?'

(*Pause*)

'That's right, twenty minutes.'

(*Pause*)

'Well, that's what we agreed.'

(*Pause*)

'Yes, for £400.'

(*Pause*)

'Well, that's how much a comedian costs.'

(*Pause*)

'It's not a case of how much that is per minute, it's more that . . .'

(*Pause, more pausing, big pause*)

'I'll have to get back to you.'

She hung up and informed me that 'the lads' were coming over from England, and had hoped that I would compere the entire weekend. See, they were having a round of golf on Saturday, and they thought I could run the stag night, do some comedy, and keep them entertained on the golf course and at dinner the next day.

I could think of no worse form of punishment. There are probably millions of people who would gladly accept $800 Aussie to play a few rounds of golf, get drunk, and tell a few jokes, even if it is with a group of strangers. I'm sure there are various holiday-resort entertainment directors who do exactly that every day. But I didn't want to.

I agreed to do forty minutes of comedy, for the original fee, but no more. I secretly hoped they would baulk at even that and cancel the whole thing. They didn't. I had to go.

It's a funny thing, the human body. If it really doesn't want to do something, it will find a way not to. The day of the gig, I lost my voice.

And I mean, really lost my voice. I'm talking unable to make a sound, everything comes out as a whisper, couldn't shout if a shark bit me, lost my voice. I should have cancelled the gig, I really should have, but for some masochistic reason I took the train to Cork, checked into my hotel (through a combination of sign language and written notes) and started gargling.

I was still convinced my voice would return when the taxi pulled into the golf club car park, and revealed a scene that made me shudder. It was as if some deranged cinematographer was projecting *Caddyshack* and *Bachelor Party* on the same screen. Men in varying states of undress were swilling beer, smoking cigarettes and wearing women's underwear on their heads.

As I approached the clubhouse, I heard the following conversation.

'He looks like the comedian.'

'No, he doesn't. He looks like a cunt.'

I was dutifully offered a puff on a joint, which I declined, and pointed in the direction of the party. As the sounds of a drinking game emanated from the main room, I was informed by the venue manager that there was no spotlight, no mic stand, and no speakers. I'd be using an old hand-held microphone (prone to cutting out at any time), and the sound would come through the in-house, club room speakers. He suggested that to avoid distortion through the speakers, I should try not to talk too loudly. There was little chance of that happening.

After a few more drinking games, all of which ended with someone being covered in beer, I was ushered into the main room, introduced as 'the comedian', and promptly died on my sorry arse.

I opened with a few solid observations about Ireland and got nothing, not even a titter. I moved on to some stronger material, and got even less. Sweating now, I decided to pull out the big guns – the Guinness poo joke – always a killer. Nothing.

Every comedian knows that feeling. When you've just thrown your best gag at them and received no reaction whatsoever. It's all downhill from here, folks.

I tried ad-libbing with the lads. 'What's your name, where are you from, what do you do?' and although the lads did laugh, it was mainly at each other's jokes. I headed back into material, and after seven brutal minutes of croaking, one of the stags politely raised his hand.

Like a substitute teacher reassessing their career choice, I motioned to him to speak, and he spoke thusly.

'Listen mate, it's not going well, is it? I mean, you got the stag to shut up, and that's more than we've managed to do.

Tell you what, give it a couple more minutes, and if it's not working out, we'll call it quits.'

It was possibly the most polite, eloquent and cutting heckle I've ever received. He stated his case, gave an ultimatum, and even paid me a compliment. I continued in vain, with no confidence, no material, and no voice, until the stag arose.

Through bleary eyes, he raised two pints of Guinness, and also raised the stakes.

'Right, we're all agreed this is shit, so here's the deal. If you can drink your pint faster than me, we'll pay you. If not, you have to come out drinking with us for the rest of the night.'

How could I say no to that? I downed the pint a good few seconds slower than the man-of-the-hour, after which it was decided I would come out drinking with the lads. Thinking on my foot, I suggested a compromise. I'd head back to the hotel, change out of my lovely suit and into more suitable drinking attire, and I'd meet them at the next nightclub.

'It's a deal,' the stag agreed. 'But if you're not there, we'll come looking for you. We're all staying in the same hotel, and we know you're in room sixteen.'

I shook hands on the deal, quietly aware that I was in fact staying in room twelve, and left the venue with promises of 'catching you all at the club in half an hour.'

Five hours later, I was huddled over my toilet bowl, regretting the copious amounts of Guinness, whiskey and tequila it had taken me to cheer myself up. I didn't meet up with the lads, instead I went to the City Limits comedy club, and bemoaned my evening with whoever was on the bill. I think it was Reginald D. Hunter, and he had in turn, plied me with alcohol.

As I curled up on the toilet floor, afraid to leave my friend Mr Cistern, I berated myself for taking a gig purely for the money, for not listening to my inner voice, and for dying so comprehensibly.

An hour later I was woken by the sound of seven drunken stags, banging violently on the door . . . of room sixteen. I smiled to myself, and fell back to sleep on the cold, cold bathroom tiles.

I never did get paid for that gig.

A Noble Profession

Ross Noble is undoubtedly one of the world's best comedians. Born and raised just outside Newcastle in the north of England, he is a master of improvisation, often ad-libbing up to three-quarters of a two-and-a-half-hour show. He has released CDs and DVDs, regularly plays sold out theatres to thousands of people a night, and has set a new standard for comedians – both as a performer and as a businessman.

As a friend, he is equally inspiring, with a constant sense of adventure and a playful attitude to the world that never seems to wane. I am proud to say that Ross has become one of my best friends, and I in turn became best man at his wedding. And it all started with one simple road trip.

The year was 2000, and the Adelaide Fringe Festival was coming to an end. I had met Ross a few times, and worked with him as well, and we had always gotten along well. On the final night of the festival, he approached me and asked me (1) where I was headed next and (2) how I was getting there.

The answers of Sydney and driving were exactly what he was hoping for. He had been asked to appear on a TV show in Sydney, and rather than booking a flight, was hoping I'd have a spare seat in the car.

Luckily I was taking some belongings from my old house in Adelaide to my parents' place in Sydney, and the best way to do that was by car. I told Ross that he was more than welcome to take the passenger seat, but I also warned him that it was quite a long trip, fully aware that he came from a country that could be traversed in a working day, including a lunch break.

'How long is it gonna take?' he asked, in that unmistakeable Geordie accent.

'About fourteen hours,' I replied. 'We'll probably split it up over two days.'

Ross's face lit up. 'Brilliant! Can we wear cowboy hats and listen to Kris Kristofferson tapes?'

Now how could I say no to that? Two comedy outlaws, crossing the wide, brown Australian land, armed only with stetsons and country music.

Ross paused for a second, then asked one more question.

'How good is your car?'

I told him not to worry, that it was only seven years old, and was more than capable of taking us the required distance in comfort and, unless I forgot to replace the radiator cap after checking the water, with no danger of breaking down.

'No, no. What I mean is, is it an old enough car that we could cut the roof off with a chainsaw and turn it into an open top?'

Within the blink of an eye we had gone from two comedy cowboys riding the open range, to a commercial for feminine hygiene products. I informed Ross that my 1993 Ford Laser would probably not increase in value were we to hack the roof off with a chainsaw. He was visibly disappointed, and I began to wonder what kind of trip I was in for.

The following day, Ross arrived at the pick-up point on Pirie Street, wearing a bright yellow long-sleeved shirt and red shorts, and sporting a bright pink shock of shoulder-length hair. He was also carrying an orange backpack, a blue sports bag and as promised, two straw cowboy hats and a cassette tape of 'Country Classics' (apparently Kris Kristofferson albums are hard to come by in central Adelaide).

And so it was that three hours later, two comedians (one Geordie, one Aussie) were cruising through the South Australian countryside, both wearing cowboy hats, one with pink hair, one with one leg, in a dark blue Ford Laser, singing 'Rhinestone Cowboy' at the top of their lungs.

I once heard a theory that there are two types of comedian – the ones who are naturally funny and the ones that funny things seem to happen to. I think that day we constituted both.

After a few hours of driving, singing, and a meaningful discussion of comedy, we made it to Mildura and pulled into a McDonald's for some lunch. Every head turned as we entered the store, and they all turned towards Ross.

It was only after a few minutes that we realised why. Who is the one man that regularly enters McDonald's stores dressed in a yellow long-sleeved shirt, with red shorts and a mad wind-blown shock of pink hair? Ronald!!!

All the kids watched as we made our way to the counter to order some food, as it gradually dawned on them that this was either not Ronald, or Ronald on his day off. Ross approached the front of the queue and tried to make light of the situation.

'It's all right, I'm not here for a spot check. I just want to order some food.'

The assistant stared at him as if he had just broken wind. So he continued.

'I'd like a veggie burger, please.'

This time she stared at him as if *she* had broken wind. So he reiterated.

'I'd like a veggie burger, please.'

'A what?'

'A veggie burger.'

'A widgie burger?' she replied, obviously unable to fathom his accent.

'No, no. A veggie burger.'

Now we all looked as if we had just broken wind.

'Hold on. I'll call the manager.'

A slightly older, but no more comprehending, woman approached and feigned politeness.

'Can I be of some help, sir?'

'Yes, I'm wondering if you make veggie burgers?' Ross persisted.

'Veggie burgers?' she repeated quizzingly.

'You know,' said Ross. 'A burger made of vegetables.'

'Oh!' exclaimed the manager, as if the penny had finally dropped. 'Of course, sir. All our burgers have salad on them.'

Turns out the penny fell into the wrong slot.

'No, no. What I want is a burger that doesn't have any meat on it. Do you have that?'

Both the women turned to scan the menu board behind them, and after what seemed an inordinate amount of time, the manager turned to Ross and offered the following solution: 'We've got a chicken burger.'

Ross and I looked at each other. The kids were still looking at Ross. The manager looked at the assistant, then back to us. Then Ross looked back to the manager and calmly said, 'Chicken's a type of meat, isn't it?'

Ross eventually settled for a large fries and a small fries, an order which somehow sent the manager scurrying to the

One of the few family photos my mum didn't take. This was just after I was born, and well before selfies were invented.

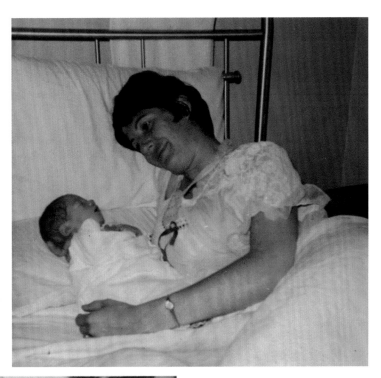

With my dad in the backyard, learning to stand on my own one-and-a-half feet.

On the back balcony at home. Dapper. Bound for laughs.

This may be the Aussiest photo ever. On my dad's shoulders, at the beach, with my Uncle Chris. Made more Aussie by Dad's bathers and Chris' moustache.

Wearing my beloved South Sydney jersey, looking nothing like a Rugby League player.

This *would* be the Aussiest photo ever if the kangaroo was ours. Sadly, it was at a local wildlife park. And I think it's a wallaby. Note the matching t-shirts on Brad and me.

Everything you need to know about my family is in this photo. My grandfather and I at my graduation. The Napoleonic pose was his idea.

My dad as he appeared in a Qantas ad. Look at that jacket, look at the sparkle in his eyes, look at that hair.

The first photo taken of me on stage. Look at that shirt, look at the sparkle in the eyes, look at that hair.

The face that launched a thousand shops.

Crouching alongside Alice Cooper so that our heads were the same height.

It's the law in Australia that everyone must have a photo with
John Farnham. Here's mine (with Toni Tenaglia).

My brother, Brad, and me in our signature pose (that we
stole from the TV Show *Night Court*).

Toni and I with Aussie rock legend Jimmy Barnes. Toni, Hillsy and Barnesy.

No laughing matter for SAFM as stars depart

By SIMON YEAMAN

Steve Bedwell   Adam Hills

Radio SAFM has been rocked by the resignation of two of its top-rating stars.

Steve Bedwell, 32, and Adam Hills, 26, are leaving to pursue careers elsewhere.

Bedwell, the station's breakfast show host, will host a mid-morning shift at Triple M in Melbourne, and Hills, the mid-morning host, is to become a full-time comedian.

Hills, who will present his last show today, will remain in Adelaide but aims to tour nationally.

"Comedy's what I love to do . . . I'm just following my heart," he said, after declining an interstate promotion with SAFM's Austereo network.

"I'll still be doing 'Gotcha' links (joke calls to listeners) for SAFM."

Hills, who joined the station in 1993, began his stand-up career at the Sydney Comedy Club, working alongside Jimeoin and Steady Eddie.

He has appeared on several TV shows and was also an audience warm-up man for Channel 7's Wheel of Fortune.

Bedwell, also a stand-up comedian and former head writer for the TV shows Tonight Live and Full Frontal, joined SAFM in 1994.

He said the Melbourne offer was one "I couldn't say no to". "I enjoyed my time in Adelaide and will be maintaining a presence on SAFM out of loyalty to the listeners," he said.

"I look forward to coming back as often as I can, doing stand-up."

SAFM's program director, Mr Simon Mumford, said the station wished Bedwell and Hills "all the best".

"The sad thing is Steve loves Adelaide, but it's good for his career," he said.

"Adam's a great talent, we'd welcome him back with open arms."

Mr Mumford said SAFM was introducing new talent, including Leigh Towler, who will partner Craig Bruce, retired State cricketer James Brayshaw and newsreader Skye Murtagh in the breakfast shift.

Former Perth disc jockey Mitch Braund will replace Hills.

Either I was a star or it was a slow news day. Regardless, my resignation made the paper.

My first Edinburgh Fringe flyer. Can you tell I was obsessed with Adam Ant?

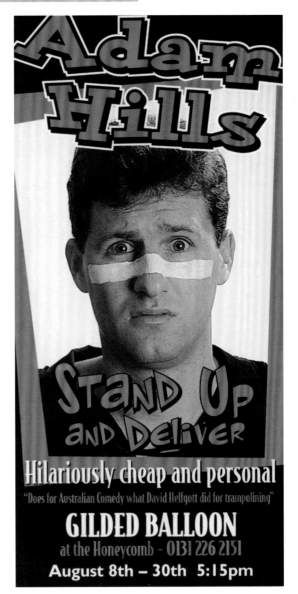

Publicity shot for my first solo show – *Stand Up and Deliver*.
This was taken in the Adelaide Parklands, which means I
probably wasn't the only person carrying a weapon.

McManual to see whether that was possible, and we made our way further into the Australian countryside.

A few more hours passed, consisting of more singing (this time to Dolly Parton) and a few stops at some of Australia's famous 'big' icons – the Big Orange at Berri being one of them – and as the sun made its way to bed and snuggled under the covers, we pulled into a small town for the night.

From memory the town was Hay, and I daresay the owner of the motel beside the highway had never seen the likes of us. Two young blokes, one with an artificial limb, the other with bright pink hair, both in cowboy hats, wandered into his motel and asked for a double room for the night. I don't think he thought we were gay, but he may have assumed we were aliens.

We found a room, loaded our stuff in, then paused as I surveyed my prized possession in the back seat, the one I was transporting to my parents' house for safe keeping. It was a framed artist's contract from 1974, signed by Groucho Marx. I had bought it at auction for two and a half thousand dollars, although it was probably worth four times that amount.

I couldn't leave it in the car overnight (in all honesty, the contract was probably worth more than the Laser) so we decided to take it inside. Once inside, however, it seemed a shame not to hang it, so we removed the standard hotel-issue painting of a ship on the high seas and replaced it with Groucho Marx's contract.

We spent the night eating hot chips from the local takeaway (we didn't dare ask for a veggie burger) and watching a documentary about Hollywood. As we prepared for sleep, Ross added one final cherry to the day's cake.

'Oh, now I should warn you. I do talk in me sleep.'

I wasn't too worried. Anyone that has slept over at a mate's house as a kid knows that there's always one guy who talks in his sleep.

'No, no. I really talk in me sleep. Proper conversations and all. Just don't get too alarmed if you wake up in the night and I'm standing on a table holding a mirror above me head, trying to focus a laser across the room.'

When I awoke the next morning, I recalled waking a few times in the night to the sound of Ross's conversations, but could only remember one sentence he had come out with in his sleep.

At one point, in the middle of the night, Ross had sat bolt upright and exclaimed, 'Helloo lovely ladies!'

When I told him this the next day, Ross said, 'Well, that's just great. Even in my own dreams I'm still a sleazy bastard.'

Like I said, sometimes a comedian is just a person that funny stuff happens to.

Drifting the Night Away

When my mate Dave Smiedt said we were to be joined at dinner by the Drifters, I erroneously thought he meant the 1960s Aussie doo wop band The Deltones. Sure, the idea of dining alongside Peewee Wilson (will we ever stop giving tall people the nickname 'Pee Wee'?) was enticing, but my excitement didn't seem to match Dave's.

The lack of enthusiasm in my response prompted him to follow up, 'You know – the Drifters! "Saturday Night at the Movies", "Save The Last Dance For Me;', "Under The Boardwalk" . . . The Drifters.'

'Oh, the Drifters,' I brightened, the penny not so much dropping as crashing through the floorboards. 'Brilliant!' That was more like it.

Dave had just published a history of Australian comedy with his and my mate Rob Johnson, called *Boom – Boom! A Century of Australian Comedy* (available where all good books are sold) and had invited me to a celebratory dinner. His publicist happened to be working on the Drifters' Australian tour, and was bringing along a couple of the guys.

An hour later we sat overlooking the Yarra River, at a table that featured Dave, myself, our university pal and now singer Miguel Ayesa, a few publicists, and two of the Drifters. To be fair they weren't the original Drifters. One had been part of the touring Drifters for about five years, while the other was originally a member of the Coasters, and was responsible for singing the immortal line, 'Yakkety yak, don't talk back.' Oh yeah, we were in heaven.

Once the perfunctory chat and niceties were done with, Dave began to ask about their show.

'So what songs do you guys do?'

'Ah, to tell the truth I can't actually remember,' replied the Coaster.

Seeing the disappointment in our eyes, he explained, 'Sorry, boys, I don't mean to be rude. But I'm so used to doin' it night after night, I'm on auto pilot. Right now, right here at dinner, I couldn't tell you what songs we do.'

'Well, what song do you start with?' Dave persisted.

'Man, I couldn't even tell you that. I'm serious, man. Every night I walk to the same spot on the stage, take the same pose, and wait for the music to start. Once that music starts, I know exactly what to do, and the whole show just flows from there, but for the life of me I have no idea what that song is.'

Strangely enough, I know how he feels. Once I'm up and running in an extended season such as the twenty-five nights in a row of the Edinburgh Festival, I get into such a rhythm with a show that I can't remember certain jokes without the five minutes of material that leads up to it.

Unfortunately, I can't recall *that* material unless I've done the ten minutes that leads up to that, and before I know it, I can't do one joke from the show without doing the whole thing. To be honest, if I've written the show with a consistent flow, I need only remember the first joke, and the rest follows naturally. I once saw a cartoon of a stand-up comic looking over the script for his act. All that was written on the page were the words, 'Good evening, Ladies and Gentlemen . . . etc.'

Back to the Drifters, and Dave was searching for a conversation. We were both fans of Sixties music, and often spent the hour-long car journeys to university singing along to Ben E. King, Sam and Dave, and of course, the Drifters. In fact, with the right encouragement at the right piano bar, Dave had been known to belt out a cracking rendition of 'Stand by Me'.

'Do you do "Saturday Night at the Movies?"' Dave quizzed.

'Yeah, I think so,' replied Coaster, waning slightly.

'Do you do any Sam and Dave songs?' Dave asked, his voice almost cracking with desperation.

Coaster eyed us both. 'Whaddyou boys know of Sam and Dave?'

I jumped in, kinda cocky, 'I've got a couple of Sam and Dave albums.'

'Oh yeah,' he warmed. 'You tell me one Sam and Dave song, and I don't mean "Soul Man" or "Hold On I'm Comin", cos everybody know them.'

I rose to the challenge. 'How about "You Got Me Hummin?"'

Coaster was astounded. 'Shit. How's that go?'

This was getting fun. I sang a few lines from 'You Got Me Hummin' – which, to be fair, consisted of 'You got me humming, yeah, you got me humming, hmmm'.

Coaster boomed at his co-singer across the table. 'Wayne! Wayne! The man knows Sam and Dave!' He turned back to me. 'Do another one.'

I didn't have to rack my brain too hard. I used to listen to that album over and over while studying.

'How about "You Don't Know Like I Know"?'

Again, 'Ooh, how's that one go?'

As before, I launched into the song, without stopping to consider that I was attempting to sing in front of the Drifters. This time, however, they joined in with me.

'You don't know like I know, what that woman has done for me. In the morning she's my water, in the evening she's my cup of tea . . .' They even did the harmonies. Each time we sang as much of the song as we could remember, and after each one, Coaster prompted, 'Do another one.'

Eventually we all launched into a rendition of 'When Something Is Wrong with My Baby', a song familiar to the entire table, as it had recently been covered by Jimmy Barnes and John Farnham, or as they soon became known, Barnesy and Farnesy.

As Dave, Miguel, a Drifter, an ex-Coaster and I hit full stride, Wayne halted the song and turned to me with mock aggression. 'Hey, man. You doing my harmony. Back off.'

I would have backed off, too, if only I had known what harmony I was doing, how to find an alternative harmony, and what a harmony was.

I reckon we spent half an hour banging out Sam and Dave tunes, each one starting with gusto, ending in a taper, and followed by laughter and applause. We had found a common ground, and before long the guys were regaling us with stories of gigs, touring and other performers. I told a story I once heard about James Brown, Wayne told us his brother was good friends with James Brown, and often dined at his house. Touché.

As the dinner wound to a close, Dave took a moment to express how the three of us were feeling. 'Listen,' he started, 'this has been a real thrill for us. We used to listen to your stuff all the time, and I just wanna say that—'

'Man,' the Coaster cut him short. 'None of that matters.' He surveyed the table.

'Right here, right now, we all just a bunch of guys that like the same music. And that's all there is to it.'

Stumped

I knew he'd be there, of course he would – he was the director. But still . . . Mel Smith! One half of *Alas Smith and Jones*, director of *Bean: The Movie*, the albino from *The Princess Bride* (one of my all-time favourite films). I was about to audition for a role in a film, not just a film but an Ealing Comedy, not just an Ealing Comedy but an Ealing Comedy directed by one of my comedic heroes.

What do you say in this situation? I've heard that even people like Tom Cruise get flustered when they first audition for, say, Steven Spielberg. But lil' ole me. In front of Mel Smith.

I had learned my lines (as an Australian lawn bowler) and tried to adopt a demeanour that looked as if I wasn't trying to adopt a demeanour. I took a deep breath, entered the room and awaited his direction. What happened next was the most inappropriate, unexpected and hilarious sentence I have ever heard. But first, let's backtrack.

About a year before all of this, I had been staying at Ross Noble's place in Walthamstow. The doorbell rang at 3 a.m., and I stumbled out of bed (sans artificial foot) to find Australian comedian Brendon Burns outside the front door. He was there to pick up his girlfriend, who had been watching videos with Ross's girlfriend. He claims my next words were the most Aussie thing he has ever heard, 'Hang on, mate, I'll just put me foot on.'

Having 'footed up', I opened the door and allowed him in, only to face a barrage of questions about the stump. These questions continued over the ensuing weeks, and included the following car conversations:

7.15 p.m. (On the way to a gig)
Burnsy: 'So has a woman ever asked you to put it in her?'
Hillsy: 'No.'
Burnsy: 'Never?'
Hillsy: 'Never.'

12.38 a.m. (On way home from gig)
Burnsy: 'So you've never put it in a woman?'
Hillsy: (Attempting to shock) 'Ah now, that wasn't what you asked me.'
Burnsy: (After a pause) 'Ohhhhhh. Nooooooo. You stump women! I don't believe it! You stump women!'

For the record, I was joking.

Now Brendon has never been known for his powers of subtlety. For the next year I received phone messages, emails and texts, I read comedy message boards, and received heckles both off-stage and on, from Brendon simply repeating the one phrase, 'You stump women.' He even mentioned it in his act, for God's sake!

Flash forward to a small, unremarkable audition room in Ealing. My head was filled with the following simultaneous thoughts: Oh my God, that's Mel Smith . . . I really want this role . . . whatever you do, don't make a dick of yourself. My heart was pounding, my head was swimming, and the butterflies in my stomach were having epileptic seizures. He shook my hand, and motioned me to sit.

He took a moment to study my biog and photo, then without looking up from his page uttered the following words. 'Now Adam, before we start the audition, something has just come to my attention that I have to ask you about.' (Long pause for effect.) 'Apparently you stump women.'

As I laughed embarrassingly loudly for a casting call, I can't tell you who was more relieved – me, for the fact that Mel Smith broke the tension with a joke, or him, for the fact that I didn't leave the room in disgust.

'Where did this come from?' I eventually managed to ask. His response: 'Brendon Burns auditioned for the same role half an hour ago. He made me say that to you.'

He even made Mel rehearse it!

I will bet any amount right here and now that the next sentence has never before in the history of the English language been written in print, and if it has, I will gladly pay up – here goes.

So there I was, auditioning for a role in an Ealing Comedy, directed by a member of *Not the Nine O'Clock News*, when the albino from *The Princess Bride* announced that I apparently stump women.

In case you're wondering, I didn't get the role, but as I left the room, Mel said, 'I'm glad you laughed at my joke.'

Better Late 'n' Live Than Never

Any comedian that has spent any time at all at the Edinburgh Fringe will shudder at the words 'Late 'n' Live'. Any comedian that has actually played it may well drop into the foetal position and cry like a baby.

Late 'n' Live is one of the most notorious gigs on the planet. It starts at 1 a.m., in a four-hundred-seat venue, filled by some of the drunkest people you will ever meet. Air conditioning is redundant, smoking was encouraged, and heckling is virtually mandatory.

It is billed as 'the abattoir that has slaughtered a hundred comics' and was often attended by punters wanting to see a comedian 'die', much like those who attend car racing to see a crash. Whenever a new comic took to the stage, the doorways to the gig would be crammed by other comics, who had gravitated from the bar. I'm told that when I made my first Late 'n' Live appearance, someone was heard to comment, 'Look at all the sharks, circling for the kill.'

I actually quite enjoyed the Late 'n' Live experience. I guess it reminded me of the early days at the Sydney Comedy Store, watching the previous act be booed off the stage while Ingrid commented that I was having kittens in the corner – a belief confirmed backstage one night when the Aussie comedy duo, The Umbilical Brothers walked in.

'How's it lookin' tonight?' they enquired.

'Rowdy as all hell,' I responded. 'They've already shouted one act off stage, and I think a fight's gonna break out any second.'

'Right.' They looked at each other, 'So a regular Saturday night at the Store then.'

My first two Late 'n' Live appearances were uneventful. I got up, banged out fifteen minutes, and got off. My third gig I will never forget.

Most audiences are dubious about a performer until they get their first laugh. You can almost see faces in the crowd thinking: This guy better be good. I've paid good money to watch this. If he's shit, he'll be shit for twenty minutes. Uh oh, here comes the first joke. (*Big Laugh*). Phew. Thank God he's not shit. I can relax now.

The Late 'n' Live audience internal-monologue went something like: If this guy's shit, we're gonna kill him. Here comes the first joke. (*Big laugh*). Not bad. Do it again. (*Second big laugh*). Hmmm, two in a row. Do it again. (*Third big laugh*). Alright then. He's not shit. But we could still turn at any minute.

My third Late 'n' Live gig was compered by the very lovely Stephen K. Amos, a highly respected comic and one of the best MCs in the business. I can't recollect who the first two acts were, but I do recall they were less than a hit. Not horrible deaths, nor were they a storming success.

As the second act wound up his set, to a less than riotous response, Steve turned to me and said, 'I'll just do a quick bit, then I'll put you on.' Famous last words, my friend. It was the equivalent of Nelson Mandela saying, 'Yeah, but with good behaviour, I'll be out in five years.'

As Stephen took to the stage, and back announced the previous act, an inebriated voice in the second row piped up, 'The first two acts were shit.'

He was followed by a more vehement voice in the third row who noted, 'Yeah. And this guy's the same colour.'

I should point out that Stephen is black.

I don't need to tell you the many ways in which this was considered offensive. The audience quite rightly booed the offending felon, and sided with Stephen as he launched a tirade of abuse against the yob. However, Steve's tirade soon became a tidal wave, which became a tsunami, and pretty soon he had spent five whole minutes castigating this offensive and defenceless sod, invoking references to his education, upbringing and maternal influences.

The audience didn't know how to react. Sure the guy had been well out of line, but this attack from the stage was relentless and vicious. Before long the entire room had boiled over, like a kettle that had been forgotten about, and abuse was flowing in every direction.

Steve yelled at the yob, the yob yelled at Steve, some of the crowd yelled at the yob, some yelled at Steve, the yob yelled at the crowd . . . and I was the next act on.

To Steve's credit, he realised that this wasn't entirely the best atmosphere in which to introduce an act, so he decided to calm things down with a singalong, a Calypso song. Somehow it soothed the masses slightly, and after a 'quick bit' had become twenty minutes of near-bloodshed, I was introduced to a room that was still simmering with tension.

With a calm appearance, masking a heartbeat like a Burundi drummer, I took the mic.

'Good evening,' I said, 'and welcome to *Mississippi Burning*.'

A friend of mine was recording the show that night, and I have since listened back to the tape. There was at least three seconds of silence following that line. That may not sound like a lot to you, but during those three seconds I reminded myself of the emergency exits from the venue, in particular those nearest the stage, questioned my choice of an opening line, and wondered if I should have perhaps followed my mother's advice and become a journalist instead.

When the three seconds were up, the crowd applauded. The next twenty minutes was solid without being outstanding, and in the light of the previous twenty minutes, was a decent way to finish the show.

But oh my God, those three seconds nearly killed me.

*   *   *

To this day I've never been as terrified as when I compered Late 'n' Live. The few minutes directly before the gig, from when the stage manager would inform me that we were about to start to when he had made it back to his booth to introduce me on stage, were pure hell. Even as I write this paragraph, the memory of it has caused my stomach to tie itself in more knots than an obsessive-compulsive's shoelaces.

During those horrifying minutes I would stare at the floor, often kicking a wall with the tips of my shoes, asking aloud why the hell I was putting myself through this. The full extent of the panic would truly hit when I heard the intro music start up, a raucous and violent Marilyn Manson track called 'Beautiful People'. If you have the track, listen to the first thirty seconds or so, and imagine yourself about to face four hundred drunken punters at 1 a.m.

As soon as my name was announced, however, a bizarre calm would settle upon me. Friends of mine who have suffered near-death experiences (particularly car accidents) have described a quiet sense of inevitability about it. A feeling of, oh well, it's out of my hands now. That's kinda how I felt once my name was announced. Oh well, I can't get out of it now, they've said my name.

One particularly memorable evening, I opened the show, and after fifteen minutes of bantering, 'What's your name/ where are you from?' I was ready to put the first act on, an impossibly charismatic young up-and-comer by the name of Russell Brand.

The minute Russell walked backstage, I knew he was going to die. Just how badly I had no idea. I have since learn that he was in the middle of the 'drug stage' of his life. That would explain the amazing amount of confidence exuded by the man that I had never met, as he strode into the dressing room, announced that he had been out of comedy for a while, but now he was back. He then strode out of the dressing room, leaving me perplexed as to who this overly assured man was, why he'd been out of comedy, and who actually cared that he was back.

I followed him into the men's toilets to find him naked from the waist up, gaffer-taping a plastic bag filled with tomato sauce to his stomach. He told me it was all part of the act, that he wanted to try something new, and to put him on stage as soon as I could. I asked what kind of introduction he would like. 'Just tell them that I've been out of comedy for a while, but that now I'm back.' Oh God.

I introduced him as requested, and returned to the dark, dank concrete corridor that led from the back corner of the stage to the dressing room. From what I could make out,

Russell goaded the crowd by calling them 'a bunch of Scottish pussies', then proceeded to commit harakiri by smashing a beer glass and plunging it into his shirt front, thus piercing the now-concealed bag of tomato sauce.

All of this was fascinating to watch. The chemicals in Russell's body were telling him that he was the funniest man on the planet, while the hecklers in the crowd were telling him the exact opposite. I scurried backstage to warn the next act, Alice Springs mother-of-five Fiona O'Loughlin, that she might be on stage a little earlier than expected.

She accompanied me to my side-of-stage vantage point, just in time to hear four hundred people booing mercilessly. Russell shouted a few more obscenities, called them all names and left the stage. I passed him mid-stage, stood at the mic and waited for the booing to subside. Which it did.

I was about to assume some sort of control, when a lone voice piped up, laden with sarcasm, 'More!'

He was joined by a few others, and gradually by the whole crowd, all of them laughing at the irony of calling for an encore from such a diabolical act. I laughed and said something to the effect of 'I don't think so', at which point they all booed me, good naturedly I might add, and continued calling for more.

'All right then, you fuckers,' I said. 'If you want more, I'll give you more.' I looked off-stage for Russell, saw him peering on from the shadows, and asked him if he wanted to do more. To his credit, he saw the joke, and agreed.

'Ladies and Gentlemen, welcome back on stage, Russell Brand.'

I returned to the dank corridor, perched next to Fiona, and apologised to her for the false start. There's nothing worse than getting yourself all hyped up for your spot, nerves a-jangling and pulse a-racing, only to have it forestalled for some reason. No one likes a case of Comicus Interruptus.

However, I also took a punt that Russell's on-stage death would help Fiona to have a better gig. Often when a performer really dies, the crowd will like the next act, purely to spite them.

I was reassuring Fiona of this, when I heard Russell scream, 'Come on Late 'n' Live, I thought you were supposed to be violent. I dare someone to throw a glass at me.'

At which point he mounted a stool and began to belt out a defiant rendition of 'God Save the Queen', pausing only to yell, 'Come on, you weak Scottish cunts. I'll take you all.'

Of course, this had the desired effect, and the audience immediately became a boiling pot of venom. The same people that had called for an encore were now screaming at him to 'Get off', while those that didn't want him there in the first place were almost violent in their heckling.

Then Russell informed them that 'I'm not leaving the stage until someone throws a glass at me.' Oh God.

Surprisingly enough, there was a genuine hesitance amongst the crowd to throw anything, let alone a beer glass. It is one thing to yell at a performer, but it's another to hurl a danger-ous object in a public place, even in the city that inspired the movie *Trainspotting*.

Russell was relentless, though, egging them on. 'I mean it. If you want me to leave the stage, you'll have to throw a glass at me.'

Eventually a large, Scottish man stood up, and with a reluc-tant shrug of his shoulders hurled an empty pint glass at the stage. It was an act borne more of pity than hate, a genuine desire to put us all out of our misery – the comedic equivalent of clubbing a terminally injured bunny to death, rather than watch it suffer.

So merciful was the punter that he even aimed to miss. His glass sailed diagonally across the stage, missing Russell by a good few metres, thus satisfying his request while sparing him a lasting injury.

Unfortunately, after missing Russell, the twirling pint glass continued across the stage and directly into the corridor that led to the dressing room, hitting the wall less than a foot away from Fiona and me, shattering upon impact and showering us both with glass.

Shaken and stirred, we retreated to the dressing room, and examined ourselves for injuries. None were found, and after ensuring that Fiona was not only alright, but still wanted to do the gig (and full credit to her, she didn't back down) I returned to the stage as Russell was leaving it.

I said it to him as he left and I'll say it again now – well done, that was brilliant.

If you're gonna die at Late 'n' Live, then you're better off going down in flames. A mediocre death leaves the audience feeling somewhat lethargic, but a proper balls 'n' all, kami-kaze crash 'n' burn at least leaves some energy in the room. And as I said before, it often makes the audience more receptive to the next act.

The first thing I did was to remind the audience that they were responsible for what had just happened, after all, they called for an encore. It was a kind of power play between them and me and I had to let them know I was in control – fuck with me and I'll fuck with you right back.

The next thing I did was to find the appropriate way to introduce Fiona, and between you and me, I'm a little proud of what I came up with.

'Ladies and Gentlemen, as an Aussie there are certain things that make you homesick, depending upon where you're from. When people from Melbourne see an episode of *Neighbours*, they form a quiet tear in their eyes. I'm from Sydney – whenever I see a photo of the Harbour Bridge I get all sentimental. The next act is from Alice Springs. When that beer glass shattered on a wall next to her, she turned to me and said, 'Ohhh, it's just like being at home.' Please welcome on stage, Fiona O'Loghlin!'

Fiona was magnificent. I'm sure she was shaking with fear on the inside, but to those watching she was calm, composed, and completely unruffled. She regaled the crowd with stories of Alice Springs, and won them over with a routine about being a mother of five – and then did one of the best things I have ever seen on a comedy stage.

Ten minutes into her act, Fiona paused, glanced downwards and exclaimed, 'Oh my God.' She then proceeded to pull a shard of glass out of her leg. I'll say that again – she pulled a shard of glass out of her leg. I'll even put it in capitals: SHE PULLED A SHARD OF GLASS OUT OF HER LEG.

'Well, that's a good pair of trousers ruined,' she ruminated, then returned to her act.

Just like that. How many people do you know could stand on stage at two in the morning, in front of four hundred drunken idiots, and casually pull a piece of glass from themselves, then continue to entertain?

It says a lot about the power of adrenalin, the commitment of a performer, and the attitude of Australians, but more than anything it says something about mothers. When you've got five kids, nothing fazes you.

The rest of the show featured Daniel Kitson, Johnny Vegas and Sean Hughes commandeering the stage for something they called 'Three stages of Perrier', and finished with an act called the Happy Sideshow (also from Australia), who performed such feats as snapping dingo traps on their arms, and using an angle grinder on their own metallic codpieces, thus showering the crowd with sparks.

It was sensational, spectacular, and bordered at all times on being completely out of control. In other words, it was a true Late 'n' Live night.

But the highlight of it all was when an Alice Springs mother of five pulled a shard of glass from her own leg.

Second-Best Foot Forward

Remember when I said you wouldn't read about my right foot for a while? Well, time's up.

Two things happened in the space of a few weeks that made me decide it was time to talk about my lack of toes.

The first came at the end of August 2001, when I was nominated for the Perrier Award at the Edinburgh Fringe Festival.

Now known as the Edinburgh Comedy Award, the Perrier was the biggest award in British comedy – not that I knew it when I first came to the Fringe.

In my first year at the festival, a publicist for the venue asked how my show had gone one night. I replied that it had been OK, but not one of my best.

She said, 'Too bad, you had a judge in tonight.'

'A judge! For what??'

'The Perrier Best Newcomer Award.'

I didn't even know there was such a thing!

I had no idea how big a deal was the main prize, which had been won in the past by Frank Skinner, Lee Evans, Lano and Woodley, and the Cambridge Footlights, featuring Emma Thompson, Stephen Fry and Hugh Laurie. The year of my debut, it was presented to an up-and-coming sketch group called League of Gentlemen.

Four years later, I was nominated for the show I wrote to stop me taking myself too seriously, *Go You Big Red Fire Engine*.

The nominees that year were Jason Byrne, Daniel Kitson, Dan Antopolski and the eventual winner, a comedy play called *Garth Marenghi's Netherhead*, co-written by Richard Ayoade.

Any comedian who has been nominated will tell you it's a double-edged sword, as the nomination guarantees sell-out crowds, but those crowds suddenly have very high expectations, because you're supposedly one of the best shows in Edinburgh.

Plus, all the judges who have seen your show individually throughout the Fringe, now return to cast a second eye over it. Often on the same night.

Which means you are now doing your show to a highly judgmental audience, and ten even more judgmental judges.

Nonetheless, I walked away with a lovely nominee's trophy. For some reason, that bottle of fizzy water, enclosed in a solid glass case, proved to me that I knew what I was doing. At least a bit.

In an industry in which there are no degrees, no diplomas, and no concrete proof that you have learnt any type of skill whatsoever – one nominee trophy can make a difference. It shouldn't, but it did.

One of my first gigs after the Fringe that year was a corporate event in Birmingham for a gaming company. I was accompanied by my pal Ross Noble and an Irish comedian by the name of Eddie Bannon, also a pal.

Eddie and I were due to fly to Dublin the next day, but I managed to leave my passport in the hotel, so I had to take a later flight.

As my cab pulled into Birmingham Airport for the second time that day, I heard a news item about a plane flying into a building in New York City. Like many, I pictured a light aircraft mistakenly clipping a skyscraper, then plummeting to the ground.

No further details were to hand, said the newsreader, and that was that.

All checked in, and with passport safely in hand, I headed to a café in the departures area, and started sending a few texts.

The first was to one of my best mates, the comedian Dave Gorman, whom I had last seen at the Fringe a few weeks prior, drunkenly shouting, 'It's always a winner,' at any cheesy joke either of us cracked.

Smiling at the memory of that night, I texted him the words, 'It's always a winner!' and waited for the reply.

Almost immediately he responded: 'Yeah, it's awful. I'm watching it now. Hard to believe.'

Wait, what?

I tapped the buttons again. 'Watching what? I'm in Birmingham Airport.'

My phone rang. Dave's name appeared.

And he explained the events of 9/11 to me over the phone, live, while I sat in an airport café. I made him describe the first tower coming down at least four times, because I simply couldn't fathom what he was trying to tell me.

By the time the flight boarded, everyone knew what was happening in New York. I scanned my fellow passengers to see if anyone looked shifty, and immediately suspected the guy carrying the 'Dubai Duty Free' shopping bag. I later wrote a joke about it: 'I'm pretty sure no one flew out of Dubai airport thinking, "Death to the West! Death to the infidels! Ooh, Hugo Boss, half price!"'

It was a tense yet uneventful flight to Dublin, where I sat glued to a TV set for three days straight.

Then, on 14 September, I flew to Paris to do some shows. I assumed those shows would be called off, either for safety concerns, or due to flights being cancelled. But no, the show must go on.

Unfortunately, I had to go via Heathrow, which meant two lots of security checks. If you've seen my stand-up, you'll know what comes next, but I want you to know the story I tell on stage is exactly how it went down.

You see, ever since I first took to the skies, my prosthetic foot has set off metal detectors. The foot itself is made of titanium (you know, like the Sia song), but there are also metal bits and pieces that hold everything in place.

Until 11 September 2001, I would simply tell a security guard, 'It's an artificial foot,' and they would happily wave me through. I expected all that to change after 9/11.

Loath as I am to reinforce Irish stereotypes, I have to report that the Irish security guards could not have been more laid back about the whole affair.

As expected, my foot set off the metal detector. As usual, they asked why. As per normal I explained it was a prosthetic foot, and as casual as you like, they said, 'Well, that's okay then,' and waved me through without checking.

When I got to London though, things were slightly different.

Once again, the tell-tale beep alerted Security to some metal on my person. This time they took me aside in a very officious manner, and began padding me down. When their hands reached my fake foot, eyebrows, suspicions and hackles were all raised.

Another security guard joined the first, and they stepped back and eyed me up and down very carefully.

'What's going on down there, then?' the first guard asked.

'It's an artificial foot,' I replied meekly.

His reaction became the reason I talk about my foot on stage.

Horrified that he may have said the wrong thing, he recoiled and said, 'Oh, I'm so sorry, mate. Just go through.'

What? No! Some arseholes in America just hijacked a bunch of planes with knives, the least you could do is check I'm not trying to do the same.

The second guard looked as embarrassed as the first, and added, 'You're right, mate, go through.'

I was shocked.

Firstly, I'd have had absolutely no problem with someone checking under my jeans to make sure I was indeed wearing a prosthetic foot, and not carrying a dangerous object.

Secondly, scary times call for extra prevention, and even if I was offended, I'd have to suck it up for the safety of us all.

It made me think of all the times in my life I'd been asked, 'What happened to your leg?', and the awkward, embarrassed stammering that would come once people found out it was a prosthetic.

As far as I was concerned, there is absolutely no offence in asking what happened. And yet people would crumble, apologise profusely, and break out into a sweat, when they learned the truth.

Why? Why is a prosthetic more awkward to talk about than a broken ankle, for example?

I thought back a couple months to the Edinburgh Festival, when Scottish comedian Phil Kay first learnt I had one foot. All he wanted to know was, 'Are you okay with it?'

I wanted people to know it's okay to talk about it. It's okay to ask about it. And that I'm okay with it.

And that it's certainly okay to check that I'm not hiding a knife down there.

I remembered the advice I received way back in the early days of the Sydney Comedy Store: 'Wait till you get really good at this shit. Wait till you find a reason to talk about it.'

Well, I had a glass-encased bottle of fizzy water that suggested I might indeed be good at this shit. And now I had a reason.

The time seemed right. I was lack-toes tolerant.

I remembered the only joke I had ever told about my missing foot. You know the one, about the woman who asked, 'Can you still have sex?'

Then a punchline came to me.

'Of course I can still have sex. What does *your* boyfriend do? Does he take a run up?'

And there it was. The difference thirteen years of comedy could make.

A few days later, back in Dublin, I told the story of the security guards. I spoke of the suspicion with which they regarded me, and the shift to utter helplessness as they waved me through. I tried to find a line that would convey how ridiculous it felt to me, to be more worried about my reaction than an actual terror threat.

The line I came up with to describe the security guard's reaction, sums up why I talk about my foot on stage: 'He looked at me with a face that said, "I don't care if the plane goes down, I don't want to offend a spastic."'

P.S. (Prosthetic Script)

I know how offensive the word 'spastic' is to a lot of people, but for me it is integral to the routine. It suggests someone who is so desperate not to offend, that he accidentally uses the word that offends the most.

Years later, I performed that routine on an American talk show, *The Late Late Show with Craig Ferguson*. I had filmed myself on stage doing the bit, and had submitted a script as well.

The day before the show, I got a call from one of the producers, whom I had met a few times in Montreal.

I should point out now that he is a lovely, lovely man, and there was absolutely no offence taken by me at this call. But I did find it funny.

Here's how it went:

PRODUCER: 'I'm sorry, Adam, you can't say spastic on
the show.'
ME: 'Why not? Is it too offensive?'

PRODUCER: 'No. We just don't call people like you spastics here.'

ME: 'What do you call us?'

PRODUCER: 'Cripples.'

ME: 'I'm not gonna refer to myself as a cripple.'

PRODUCER: 'Oh.'

ME: 'How about retard?'

PRODUCER: 'You can't say retard.'

ME: 'Why not?'

PRODUCER: 'Cos a retard is a mental thing, and yours is physical.'

ME: 'So if I can't say spastic, or retard, what can I say?'

PRODUCER: (*Pause*) 'How about gimp?'

I went with cripple.

Part Four

Strange Days Indeed

Notes from a Diary, Pt 1

I have a confession to make. I actually started writing this book in 2003.

While circumnavigating the globe doing stand-up comedy, I began compiling most of the stories you've read thus far. I guess I thought that maybe someone, somewhere would fancy reading the tales of a lone stand-up comic with a very minor profile. And if they didn't, maybe one day I'd become better known, and they would.

While remembering my past adventures, though, I was also having new ones, so for a couple of years I kept a diary as well.

What follows are a few selections from it.

29 January 2003

I'm sitting in my hotel room in Dubai, as a gale of what seems like biblical proportions muddies the sky outside. I've been informed it is a sandstorm, and is quite common. Shakira is on the television – is there anywhere in the world she isn't? – and my head is slightly fuzzy. How can I possibly describe yesterday to you? Let's see, it all began with a trip to the beach.

We met a woman at the gig the night before who managed a string of hotels in the Middle East, including the Ritz

Carlton in Dubai. 'Why don't you come to the beach club?' she had asked. 'I'll make sure you're looked after.'

'Ohhh. You'll love the beach club,' echoed those around us, like a Foster's-fuelled Greek Chorus, 'that's where Mariah Carey stays.'

So it was that at midday yesterday, two comedians – a one-legged, ex-tennis coach (me) and an entirely black-clad, death metal drummer sporting a goatee and a crew cut (Steve Hughes) strolled casually through the lobby of one of the world's zhoozhiest hotels. That's right – zhoozhiest. The appropriate names were dropped at the appropriate times, and *voilà*, we were directed past the patently wealthy businessmen and discreetly wealthy sheikhs, towards the beach.

But this was no ordinary beach. Beautifully vibrant gardens surrounded painfully manicured lawns – crimsons, yellows, and lush greens that shouldn't be seen this close to a beach, let alone a beach in the Persian Gulf. Palm trees led to pristine sand, unnaturally smooth, soiled only by sporadic footprints that made one feel as if one was the first ever to traverse this hitherto unexplored paradise.

It was so posh it made one start referring to oneself as 'one', and use words like 'hitherto' and 'traverse'.

We felt like two slugs in a bowl of potpourri. I approached the beach hut and addressed the impossibly good-looking South African man. 'Hi, we're guests of Alison, we're just wondering what the protocol here is.' I figured saying 'guests' and 'protocol' would be less of a giveaway than, 'G'day. Whaddaweefuckendoo?'

'Well, sir, if you'd like to take a sunbed, I'll bring some towels over for you,' he dutifully replied. I asked if there was

somewhere we could take in a quick snack before the sun.
'Certainly, sir, I'll have someone bring some menus to you.'
What about sunscreen? I'm gonna need some sunscreen. 'Not
a problem, sir, I'll track some down for you.'

Twenty minutes later we were laying on Ritz Carlton towels,
spread over Ritz Carlton sunbeds, under Ritz Carlton umbrel-
las, drinking piña coladas, and picking at two exquisitely cut
club sandwiches, accompanied by their own individual,
miniature jars of mayonnaise.

Before us was truly a scene from *Lifestyles of the Rich and
Famous*. Jetskis buzzed, Hobie catamarans graced the breezes
with their presence, and dangerously tanned men strolled
with impeccably shaped women, followed by their joyously
happy children. A gracefully middle-aged woman sat under a
sunshade, casually painting the scene before her, while chilled
hand towels were distributed to a stylish Swedish couple. And
all the while Steve and I giggled like Homer Simpson chasing
a dog with a puffy tail.

As a man in a Ritz Carlton uniform approached us carrying
a silver tray of chilled strawberries and sliced coconut, I
reflected on the fact that only a few hundred miles away, on
this very body of water, American warships were amassing,
circling like sharks at the verdict of UN weapons inspectors.
It reminded me of something we had been told last night at
the Aussie Legends Bar, a hotbed of political gossip and crick-
eting memorabilia.

Along with such guests as Mariah Carey, and no doubt
Shakira – who, by the way, has just made her second appearance on my television – the Ritz Carlton also plays host to
American generals, in particular General Tommy Franks,
who uses it as a base from which to direct the Iraq War.

Between us, Steve and I conjured an image of a war-hardened US General in a swimsuit barking orders into a CB radio.

'I want three hundred tanks outside Baghdad, I want a missile attack on the Communications Centre, and I want forty F-18s in the air now!' (*Places hand over receiver and turns to waiter politely.*) 'I'd also like two daiquiris and some chicken goujons, please. Oh, and sunscreen. I'm gonna need some sunscreen.'

After three ridiculously short hours of sun, sea and incessant silliness, Steve and I promised never to take any of this for granted. We compared our diaries for the upcoming week. He was scheduled to play the Magnet Leisure Centre in Maidenhead, and in exactly one week I was due in Norwich. In seven days' time, we would each be on separate trains in the English countryside, receiving an explanation by a clearly bored rail assistant over an outdated Tannoy, as to why we've been stopped in the middle of a field for the past thirty-five minutes.

And that's the thing about this job. One week you're on a pristine beach overlooking the Persian Gulf spending forty dollars (I'm not kidding) on a bottle of sunscreen delivered to your seaside sunbed, the next you're shelling out five pounds for a cheese sandwich and a coffee on a grey railway station in Loughborough.

I sincerely hope I never take these good times for granted. In comedy as in life, the rough days remind you to enjoy the good days, and the good days make it all worthwhile. The day that a man approaching me on an Arabian beach offering a chilled hand towel while I drink a piña colada on a sunbed ceases to make me giggle with joy, is the day that I have lost all perspective on life. Until then, however – let the show go on.

4 February 2003

Billy Connolly came to the show on Saturday night. It's taken me a few days to make sense of it all, and come down from the buzz of performing in front of my, and most comics', all-time hero, but I now feel calm enough to describe what happened.

The London Comedy Store is undoubtedly one of the world's best venues. Downstairs, low ceiling, four hundred people all crammed together to face the stage – it is always a joy to play. It has seen the likes of Ben Elton, Eddie Izzard, and Mike Myers, and audience spottings include Ewan McGregor and Paul McCartney.

Dara O'Briain went on first, had a killer, then ran off to do another gig in Tufnell Park. He was followed by a forty-something housewife, who had written to a new TV show asking to have a wish granted; in this case she wanted her son to win a trip to Memphis to visit Graceland. All she had to do to ensure his holiday was perform a five-minute set at the Store. With a few killer lines that were written for her, she had a cracker. John Linehan followed with a bit of comedy mind-reading (I still don't know how he did it) and we went to the break.

It was during the interval that our esteemed compere, and one of the best comics in the business, Sean Meo, visited the bar. He returned three minutes later and casually announced to the room, 'Billy Connolly's just walked in.' My heart almost exploded. I cannot explain to you the sudden rush of adrenalin that took hold of my system. I'm not afraid to say I had imagined this moment.

Ever since my backstage encounter with Billy in Adelaide eight years before, his 'Just Do It' mantra, and my subsequent decision to quit radio for stand-up comedy, I had literally dreamt of meeting him again. In fact, as I'm writing, I realise that I have had dreams in which I'd been at one of his shows, and been presented with the chance to say thank you. In the most recent one, he smiled and thanked me, always gracious, then wandered off, and I remember waking up feeling slightly unsatisfied.

Now my dreams were in every sense coming true. Seven thousand different thoughts went through my head, but the one that came out was, 'Does he want to go on?' Even in that moment of madness, I still thought of him as I would any comic in the world.

'Dunno,' replied Sean nonchalantly. 'I think he just wants to watch the show.' At the time I was struck with how relaxed Sean was, but in retrospect I think he was as panicked as the rest of us, possibly more so, since he was the compere and therefore in charge of the ship, but didn't want to let on.

'Where is he?' I quizzed. 'Front row of the back section. You can't miss him, he's surrounded by punters,' said Sean. 'It looks like Father Christmas just arrived.' I wandered casually out into the audience, and quietly surveyed the room. Sean was right. There he was. Yoda. The man who once told me to 'Do it' was chatting to complete strangers with more generosity than anyone I'd ever seen, and was about to see me perform. I suddenly knew what I must do, and it made my heart beat faster than I had ever felt it.

Now here's the thing. As I've mentioned, comics generally don't laugh at other comics. This is for two reasons. Firstly, we know the tricks. We know how to construct a joke, where to place the emphasis, how to hide the gag, and we can usually see a punchline coming well before it's been told. Secondly, when someone does surprise us with a killer line, there's just a wee little part of us that gets a wee little bit jealous. It's hard to laugh out loud when your first reaction is 'Bastard!'

There's also a funny thing that happens when a celebrity, and especially a comic celebrity, is in an audience. Everyone looks to see if they're laughing. In spite of this, or maybe because of it, Billy smiled, laughed, and applauded every act on stage. He genuinely enjoyed himself. Sean Meo was on fire, and as Mickey Flanagan finished one of the best sets I'd ever seen at the Store, I headed backstage. Mandy Muden performed a ten-minute open spot of magic, then it was my turn.

I cannot describe to you how nervous I felt. At one point I demonstrated something with my hand, and noticed that it was ever so slightly shaking, which of course made me more nervous. If I was to be over critical, I rushed a little, and stumbled over one or two words, but somehow managed to get everything out in order, but to be honest, it was a cracking gig. I talked about the British weather, Aboriginal Australia, the Bali bombings, and the importance of telling the people you love that you love them. I offered the thought that whenever I try to express my love for my friends, 'I end up saying something really naff, like – you rock.' My final line got a round of applause, and as I placed the microphone back in the stand, there was only one more thing to do.

'Ladies and gentlemen, before I go I want to tell you a quick story. Eight years ago, I was a radio announcer in Adelaide. The station was sponsoring a gig by this international comedian, and I got to go backstage and meet him. I said, 'Hi, I'm Adam,' and he went, 'Hellooo.' (*Applause.*)

I went on to tell the rest of the story. Of Billy's advice, his arm around my shoulder, and his war cry of 'Just Do It'. I told them of my boss's suggestion that I'd have to choose between stand-up and radio, and that as Billy's words rang in my head, I told him, 'You can stick your job up your ass.' An embellishment, perhaps, but the sentiment was there.

'And now, eight and a half years later, on the first night he has ever been to the London Comedy Store, I'm closing the show. I've never had a chance to thank him, so if you'll bear with me, ladies and gentlemen, I just want to say – Billy, you rock.'

Through the glare of the spotlight, I could just make out a fluffy beard, framing a broad grin, and a pair of hands above his head, applauding. 'Thank you, and good night.' I didn't notice it at the time, but as I left the stage, a few audience members rose to their feet and turned to face him, while still clapping.

Sean closed the show, and I sat backstage – shaking, buzzing, and laughing. Hyped up and full of wee. The backstage door flew open, and he strode in. There was the briefest of moments in which I wondered how he would take all that; was it weird, did I look like a nervous fan (which I was), would he just shake my hand politely and say well done?

Nope, he gave me a bear hug. A proper, man-to-man, in the moment bear hug, all the while exhorting, 'You did it! You did it!' It was one of those moments that are so good, you can only laugh.

And for the next hour and a half, Billy Connolly stood backstage, chatting. He introduced himself to every comic on the bill, and told him or her how good they were. Except Dara, of course, who was off at his gig – man, I still feel for him, but I also know he'll have his chance to meet Billy one day. He absolutely loved Mickey Flanagan (bastard!), and told Mandy Muden, 'You're gonna be huge.' I thought she was going to cry. Even the forty-something housewife got a kiss.

He had photos taken with all of us, swapped comedy stories, and reminisced about the old times. We talked about Adelaide and Australian bands; he told stories about his wife, about Steve Martin, about Judy Davis. He told tales of his films, wished he could do magic, and reaffirmed our thoughts that this truly is the best job in the world.

Eventually it was time for the late show to start, and Billy bade us adieu. As he slipped through the late-show audience, I had one more thought. I grabbed my mobile phone, and dialled my girlfriend's number. She's back home in Australia, but I really wanted to share the moment with her.

By the time I got to Billy, he was on the stairs.

'Billy, I hate to do this to you. Would you say hello to my girlfriend in Sydney?' 'Of course I will.' (*Takes phone.*) 'Hello, I'm very busy. Who is this? What do you want?' I felt like such a tool, but I had to do it. I wanted her to share this moment with me, even if she was on the other side of the planet. 'I'll hand you back to your boyfriend.'

As the phone was returned to me, one of my best mates, Miguel Ayesa (with whom I sang Drifters songs) descended the stairs. To complete the coincidences, he had been perform-ing in *Rent*, across the road. I had mentioned him in conversa-tion a few minutes earlier, which now prompted Billy to shout, 'You must be the guy in *Rent*.' Stunned, Miggy could only nod and smile, jaw agape.

I think Miguel's presence put the magnitude of the situa-tion into perspective. There we were, both performing in the

West End of London, doing what we loved, standing in a stairwell with Billy Connolly.

As he reached the top of the stairs, there was the loveliest of moments as Billy turned back to me, appropriately silhouetted in the doorway, and with the broadest of smiles, raised one fist in the air. 'We did it,' he yelled. 'We did it!'

Like I said. The best job in the world.

7 February 2003

It is times like these that I stop feeling guilty about being paid to do what I do.

It's day one of my tour and I'm sitting on a train in Glasgow Central Station. I am looking ahead at three hours of travel to Whitehaven on the north-west coast of England, to open a tour that for all I know may draw thirty-five people and three dogs.

Last night I appeared on *The Live Floor Show* for BBC 2, which despite the name goes to air tomorrow night, alongside Ed Byrne, Al Murray, and the host, Dara O'Briain. The set went well – I talked about America, Bush's War on Terror, and my artificial foot – and was particularly appreciated by one of the guest bands called the Polyphonic Spree.

Now I'm sitting in seat 20B, wondering what the next six weeks have in store for me. Twenty-one gigs around the country; from Cumbria to Norwich, Colchester, Bournemouth, Leicester, Swindon, Coventry, Birmingham, and finishing back in Glasgow on 22 March – the day before my brother's thirtieth birthday, which I will miss.

Having a dad that worked for Qantas meant we were kinda used to celebrating birthdays without the whole family around, but I really wanted to be there for his thirtieth. Comedy used to bring our family together. Now it's keeping me apart from them.

The day before yesterday, my girlfriend phoned to tell me (a) she won't be able to make it to the UK in time for Valentine's Day, which we had planned to spend in Paris, and (b) she won't be able to make it to the UK any time at all in the next six weeks, as we had also planned. Six weeks! We've already been apart for two. Needless to say, there were tears on both sides.

Right now I'm really wondering why I do this job. Why do I travel to the other side of the planet, leaving behind my family, friends and loved ones, to do a job that entails days of endless travel, nights in strange hotel beds, and nerves that often induce diarrhoea? Is it really worth it for an hour of nightly self-indulgence in front of a roomful of strangers? I guess I'm about to find out.

Twelve Hours Later

I had the best time on stage tonight! Forty-five minutes in the first half, an hour and ten in the second, an encore, and by the end of the show there were people on their feet.

It all started when I arrived at the hotel. My agent, Flee, bless her soul, decided to call ahead and organise a fruit basket to be delivered to my room as a 'Good luck with the tour' gift. Apparently not a straightforward task in Whitehaven. I arrived to find the largest box of fruit I have ever seen. My mum never brought that much fruit home from her weekly shopping, and we were an Australian family of four.

I didn't take a complete inventory, but I think there were two melons, five bananas, six oranges, two bunches of grapes, half a dozen strawberries, four apples, four tangerines, a mango, a dozen peanuts, four plums, a pineapple, a grapefruit and a packet of dates. I had to call a taxi so I could get it to the gig.

Why would I take it to the gig, I hear you cry? Obviously, to show to the audience. After fifteen minutes of gags, I outlined what I like about Whitehaven. From various local half-statues, to the lovely La Venue café (both of which I discovered during the afternoon) and eventually to what constitutes a basket of fruit in this town.

I brought the box out from backstage and gave various pieces of fruit to audience members, who then entered into the spirit by hiding the box during the interval, leaving me a half-peeled banana and two strawberries as some sort of fruit genitalia. No prizes for guessing what the dates represented.

The line of the night even went to an audience member. After finding a guy in the front row that hailed from a town called Cockermouth, I rattled off a number of single-entendres: 'What's the neighbouring town – Fingerinarse? It's an out of the way place, but the men seem to like it.'

I then wondered what the town motto was, and suggested, 'Cockermouth: For God's sake swallow', but was topped by a lone voice: 'How about "Cockermouth: Come again".'

To be honest, I don't think I could ever capture in print why I loved the gig. It just worked. It was one of those nights during which I was totally and utterly swept up in the moment. A one-off, truly unique show that I now have to try and replicate for another twenty nights.

Put simply, I had a ball, and as I walked out of the venue and into the night air, I felt like a proper comedian. No support, no compere, just me, on the road, in a theatre, doing a two-hour show. I could imagine myself doing this for the rest of my life.

I called Flee, who was in hysterics about the basket of fruit. Turns out, the people hardly spoke English, asked for a cheque to be sent, and forgot to give an address. I wandered off to find a late-night takeaway and met a couple of audience members strolling home, who pointed me to the nearest Chinese. As they headed off, they told me that the locals have their own nickname for Cockermouth – 'Nobagob'.

* * *

25 July 2003

Monday night was Latino night at the Laugh Factory on Sunset Strip, and I was the first act on.

Why?

Well, it began a few months ago, when my Australian agent, Kevin called me and said, 'There's no delicate way to put this. The head of casting at NBC wants to meet you. His name is Marc Hirschfeld, and he's the guy who cast *Friends* and *Seinfeld*.

'Apparently he's seen you a few times at the Edinburgh Fringe, and just found out you're going to be in Montreal next year for the Just for Laughs Comedy Festival. So he wants to fly you to LA afterwards, to do a showcase for some NBC executives.

'Even if nothing comes of it,' he said, 'you'll still walk away with an LA story, and everyone should have one of those.

Plus, did I mention you'll be picked up at the airport by a limo?'

Oh yes, my friend, a limo at LA airport. More importantly – a driver holding a sign with my name on it. A jet-black, tinted-windows, air-conditioned, sweets and magazines in the back-seat limo took my girlfriend and me to the Hilton Hotel Universal City (opposite Universal Studios), where we were led to a corner King Suite with views over the northern stretches of Los Angeles. Dinner for my lady's birthday at Spago in Beverly Hills (and a possible sighting of Sidney Poitier), before a day of preparation for the following night's gig.

I've spent a lot of time away from her this year, so I had begged and pleaded with her to come to LA with me. To be fair, I didn't have to beg and plead too hard.

In the morning, Kev called and outlined the plan. 'The show will be at the Laugh Factory on Sunset Strip. There'll be about twelve or so NBC executives, they're going to film it, and they want to have a casting meeting with you the next day. They already love what you do, and asked if you were interested in being in a sitcom.'

Two hours later, he called me again. 'I just phoned the club. You'll be on at eight-fifteen, for a fifteen-minute spot. I'll meet you in the hotel lobby at seven-thirty. Oh, and by the way – it's Latino Night tonight.'

Latino Night!!?! How in the name of Gloria Estefan am I going to relate to a Latino audience? I am a thirty-three-year-old white Australian from the southern suburbs of Sydney. The only contact I'd ever had with anyone vaguely Latino was a poster of female tennis player Gigi Fernández blue-tacked to my wall, and that was hardly due to the rich Latin culture.

I arrived at the club early and watched the audience enter. Sweetest Jesus, I had never seen so much hair product in my life. Dark swarthy features as far as the eye could see, and not a single blonde eyebrow in sight. My only saving thought was that perhaps despite the audience, the comics would be doing material that would appeal to all nationalities. Let's see how the compere begins the show.

'Hey, Laugh Factory, welcome to Latino Night. How many Latinas are in the house toniiiight?' Two hundred people went ballistic. I sweated a bullet.

'How many non-Latinos are in the house?' Three hands went up. 'Boy, are you in the wrong place.' I shat a pellet.

The MC then launched into fifteen minutes of jokes that began with, 'Hey, isn't it funny the way Latino women do . . .', and, 'Have you ever noticed that Latino men . . .' The audience were in fits of nodding, tear-induced, it's-funny-cos-it's-true hysterics, and I stood bemused, confused, and wondering what exactly two hundred Latinos would find funny about me.

It came time to be introduced. 'Ladies and gentlemen, welcome on stage your first act, she's had her own TV special, she's absolutely brilliant, put your hands together for (some woman's name).' I gave birth to kittens.

The MC left the stage and came towards us, wondering why no one had approached the mic. The manager went into palpitations, and quickly pointed at the running order. The woman who was introduced looked confused. The MC swore, ran back to the stage and re-introduced me.

'Ah, the running order was changed. Please welcome on stage, a Laugh Factory regular, Adam Hill.' There was nothing left to excrete.

'Hello,' I smiled at the unfamiliar audience before me. 'I just arrived from Australia (*OK, a bit of a fib*), came to the first club I found and asked if I could do a spot. I only just found out it's Latino night.' (*Audience laughs*). 'I'm so not Latino.' (*Big laugh*).

And we're off.

I then launched into my standard material about the Crocodile Hunter and my artificial foot and received a fairly strong response. It wasn't until I launched into some jokes about Eighties music with the line, 'You Latinos are so lucky – you have all the best music. White music is so shit,' that they really came alive.

I left the stage, and the club, to a round of back-slapping from a bunch of NBC executives I had never met, all of whom were apparently meeting with me the next day. 'We just loved what you did. We'll see you tomorrow.' I later found out that the talent bookers for *The Tonight Show with Jay Leno* were amongst them.

Dinner at an Argentinian Steakhouse on Sunset Strip while impossibly well-built men drove home from dates with surgically enhanced women in Humvees, a stroll past the Chateau Marmont, and a possible sighting of Mötley Crüe – I couldn't be more Hollywood.

* * *

I awoke at four-thirty the next morning with a strange feeling in my stomach. It wasn't nerves, it wasn't excitement, it was . . . food poisoning. I ran to the bathroom, emptied the contents of my churning guts, and returned to bed, hoping not to repeat the process. But repeat it I did, over and over and over . . . and over and over and oh my God it's diarrhoea as well, and I'm not sure which end to deal with first.

This whole procedure continued until about ten o'clock, when my girlfriend phoned the hotel doctor, the lovely Dr Oppenheim, who came and administered me with an injection for the vomiting, which 'may make you a little drowsy'. I won't lie to you, at one point I managed to soil my pants while spewing.

I don't need to tell you I never made it to the meeting. I had never felt so pathetic in my entire life. I'm in LA, about to have a meeting with some of the most important TV execs in, well, the world and I'm vomiting so intensely I can't get out the door. Was I doing this to myself? (Very possibly.) Was it bad luck? (Probably.) Had a rival network drugged my food? (I really doubt it.)

I spent the rest of the day in bed, as Kev phoned the network execs and made his apologies, and a day later I boarded a flight back to London – still a little ill, slightly jet-lagged, and feeling very, very fragile. Kev was right: at the end of it all I walked away with an LA story, and everyone should have one of those.

* * *

AUTHOR'S NOTE

In Edinburgh, two weeks later, I bumped into Lou Viola from NBC New York, who had been one of my most vocal fans and who knew all about the aborted meeting. His words of advice? 'Eat good food, and you'll have a long career.'

Notes from a Diary, Pt 2

15 August 2003

I had afternoon tea in Edinburgh with Marc Hirschfeld today, the man who organised the LA trip. He said he hoped I felt better. He also said he wanted me to be in a sitcom.

'We're making a spin-off of *Friends* in which Joey moves to LA to follow his dreams. You'd be great as his best friend, who has also moved to LA to be a stand-up comic. Would you be interested in something like that?'

Well now, Marc, I'm not sure I could get along with Joey, I'm more of a Ross fan as a matter of . . . ARE YOU KIDDING ME? OF COURSE, I'D BE INTERESTED! PUT ME ON A PLANE NOW!

'OK, well we'll stay in touch, and maybe in the new year we'll get you back to LA for some auditions.'

I left the meeting thinking (1) What a truly lovely guy, (2) How much would I love to be Joey's best mate? and, (3) How much of all that did he really mean? I mean, this Hollywood bullshit happens every day of the week, right? I'll probably never hear from him again.

Two weeks later, I received an international call on my mobile phone.

'Adam. Marc Hirschfeld at NBC. I'm just calling to congratulate you on your nomination for the Perrier Award. Everybody here at NBC is crossing their fingers for you.'

Now, that's gotta be a good thing.

1 September 2003

I haven't left the couch for a week.

The Edinburgh Fringe Festival ended seven days ago and I have spent that time playing computer games, catching up on emails, and watching crap television. I have slept until at least 1 p.m. every day, and generally been in bed by 3 a.m. every night. Holy sweetest Jesus, what a month that was.

In the twenty-seven days of the Edinburgh Fringe I did approximately sixty performances. Twenty-nine of those were my one-man show *Cut Loose*, including three added matinees. Twelve were as host of *Best of the Fest*, a late-night combination of the best acts from the Fringe. The rest were made up of various late-night spots at clubs around town, and two improv shows put on at the last minute to cover for a performer whose wife was taken to hospital.

While the comedian in question rushed home to be by his wife's side, two of his friends – Ross Noble and Dave Johns – put the call out for anyone willing to help keep his venue full, and his pockets less empty.

Within a few hours a makeshift improv troupe was formed, comprising myself, Ross, Dave, Ian Coppinger and my guitarist and comedy buddy Pete Monaghan. A few signs were posted around the venue to announce the line-up and lo and behold, it sold out.

We had a ball, and I think it's fair to say a cracking show, and everyone offered their services should they be required again. The following night we *were* needed again – this time the line-up was Bill Bailey, Ross Noble, Andy Smart (from the Comedy Store players), Dave Johns, Pete Monaghan and myself.

Word got out again, and once more we sold it out. Sadly, the show itself didn't live up to the night before. Sure, there were a few lovely moments, but Dave's closing remarks to the audience were, 'For God's sake, don't tell anyone what you saw here tonight.'

It didn't matter, though. We helped out a mate, gave the audience something special, and had fun doing it – and for that I felt a little proud of us. Later that night, Dave encountered an American theatre producer, who had bought a ticket to the show after seeing the names on the line-up.

His words pretty much summed up the show: 'All I kept thinkin' was – what a waste of talent.'

I received at least twenty reviews over the Fringe, ranging from 'Five stars. Hills is in amazing form' to 'Two stars. If this is Adam Hills Cut Loose, I'd hate to see him tied down.' Ouch.

One night I chatted to a heavily pregnant woman who was in the front row of my show with her husband. Two nights later my stage manager stopped the show to give me a message. The woman formerly known as 'heavily pregnant' had given birth, and her husband's first thought was to call the box office and let me know.

I also hosted *Four at the Fringe* for Radio Four, featuring myself and three comics doing ten minutes each. The shows were recorded at 11 a.m., which meant each of us had about four hours' sleep under our belts. It also meant that the audience were quite, um, varied.

In my happy place. Onstage at *Late 'n' Live* with Ross Noble and Daniel Kitson.

The night Billy Connolly just dropped in to the London Comedy Store. With Mandy Muden, Micky Flanagan, and Murray Fahey in the background.

A typical night backstage at *Best of the Fest* in Edinburgh – Rich Hall, Jeff Green, Dara Ó Briain, Cecilia Noel, Owen O'Neill, Ingrid (my first ever manager), Eddie Izzard, and me.

Career goal ticked off: we made the cover of the Rolling Stone.

Alan, Myf and I on an Eighties-themed episode of *Spicks and Specks*. Still with the Adam Ant obsession.

Oh you know, just hangin' out backstage with the Prime Minister of Australia, Julia Gillard. No biggie.

This one time I was in Hobart and my photographer friend, Wombat, said "Hey, I've got a car, a nun's habit, and an idea. Fancy a day trip?"

The night I introduced my dad to tennis legend Rod Laver. No jokes, just joy.

Wiping the sweat off my hand as the Queen met Lady Gaga. It's against the law to report what Her Majesty said to me, so whatever you do, don't read the chapter titled *Happy and Glorious*.

The exact moment I met the Dalai Lama. Not sure who was the bigger kid.

With Kermit the Frog. Not sure who was the bigger Muppet.

Obsession complete.

At the 2012 Paralympics with Jonnie Peacock. Who knew I'd go on to host multiple series of *The Last Leg*, and that he'd become a successful dancer?

The cake I received for my 45th birthday. Sometimes my workmates can be so cruel.

The cake we received for our one hundredth-ish episode. Sometimes my workmates can be lovely.

Oh you know, with the Deputy Prime Minister of the United Kingdom, on our way to a Prince gig. No biggie. (See, I *was* wearing a purple shirt!)

With Josh and Alex at the Royal Television Society Awards. The night that inspired the nickname "Slosh Widdicombe".

Playing Disability Rugby League for the Warrington Wolves.
Finally, I look like a Rugby League player.

My favourite all time photo of me. At the Superhero Series disability
sports event, cycling alongside my teammate, Danielle.

I walked out to host the final episode, and was met by an elderly woman in the front row dressed, as they say, to the nines. I asked her name, to which she proudly replied, 'I'm Mrs Armstrong.' Brilliant.

I asked her to stand up to show off her attire to the audience.

'I'm eighty-three years old, dear,' she countered. 'I can't just hop up whenever I want, you know.' I spent my entire stage time (all fifteen minutes of it) chatting to lovely Mrs Armstrong and her friends, creating lurid stories of a life spent flitting between Edinburgh and Monte Carlo (the only other place she had ever lived).

Everything I said was then repeated to an even older woman alongside her, who was apparently deaf. One of the most beautiful things I've ever seen was that of a perfectly coiffed octogenarian turning to a partially deaf grandmother to say, 'He just called us "a posse of bitches".'

On the last Wednesday of the Fringe, at about 1.30 p.m., I was nominated for the Perrier Award, for the third year in a row.

The following day I was announced as the bookies' favourite. Ladbrokes the betting agency had me at evens to win – as if I was a horse and there was anything I could actually do about it. The day after the nominations, each nominee was to be interviewed by Sky News live on air.

Hee, hee, hee. Me, being interviewed live on Sky News, because I told a few funny jokes. I arrived for the interview, in a local bar, and stood alongside the journalist, waiting to be interviewed 'live on Sky News'. The same people I had been watching all year for coverage of the Gulf War were now about to throw to an interview with me. Hee, hee.

With thirty seconds to go before we were 'live to air', the journo turned, held his hand to his earpiece, and muttered into his microphone.

'Yeah, I'm here . . . uh huh . . . uh huh . . . OK . . . No problems . . .'

He turned to me, 'I'm sorry, we're gonna have to pre-record the interview. Kofi Annan has decided to give a speech for the UN.'

Hee friggin' hee! My interview is being postponed because Kofi Annan wants to give a speech for the United Nations? I thought that was hilarious. I imagined the conversation back in the Sky News control room.

'Nigel, Kofi Annan's about to give his response to the bombing of the UN Headquarters in Baghdad. Do we run with the feed, or go live to Adam Hills instead?'

Even now, I'd love to think the director paused, just for a millisecond before giving his answer, 'Well, it *is* his third nomination.'

As it happened, New Yorker Demetri Martin 'beat the odds-on favourite', and a folk parody duo from New Zealand called Flight of the Conchords, to take out the award. And for the record, he deserved it. What I saw of his stand-up I loved, and he was undoubtedly one of the most genuine people I've met on the circuit for years.

He later told me that his 'live interview' was also postponed. The reason he was given: 'The cease-fire in the Middle East has just been broken.'

* * *

When my agent asked me to play the comedy tent (in fact, the Alternative Stage) at the Reading Festival on the final Friday of the Fringe, I originally said no. It would mean getting up at 7.30 a.m. (after performing until 2 a.m. the night before), flying from Edinburgh to Heathrow, then being driven an hour to Reading. I would then perform a forty-five-minute set at around 3 p.m., be driven back to Heathrow for a 5.15 p.m. flight, arrive in Edinburgh at 6.30 p.m., take a taxi to the venue and be on stage at 8.30 p.m.

My agent, and also the gig's booker, pleaded, begged, and assured me that the promoters had asked for me especially and would bill me as the headline act. I still said no. The thought of being able to say, 'I headlined the Reading Festival' was tempting, but I knew that by the end of the festival I'd be knackered.

A week later my agent phoned back, saying, 'They'll double your fee.' I said yes. So it was that on the final Friday of the Fringe, I woke after a refreshing three-hour sleep, and began the most rock-and-roll day of my life.

I boarded the flight with only a backpack, was asleep before we took off, and spent the next hour drifting in and out of consciousness, trying desperately not to snore or talk in my sleep. As I walked into the arrivals hall, I glanced to my left and saw rapper Ice-T with his entourage. They had performed in Edinburgh the night before, and had arrived on the same flight. As they looked around vaguely for the lifts, I was met by my agents and chauffeured away to my gig.

I say 'chauffeured' – I was bundled into the back of a Ford hatchback, and we made the trek down the M4 to Reading. An hour later I was confronted by the backstage manager, who asked me if there was anything I needed in the dressing room. Half asleep and in need of some pep, I replied politely, 'As much Coke as you can rustle up, please.' There was a pause as nervous glances were exchanged by all and sundry, before I added, 'Coca Cola, please.'

An hour to kill – so it was off to the hospitality tent to redeem my Artist's Lunch Voucher. As I passed ponytailed roadies, shaven-headed security guards, and semi-trailers of sound equipment being unloaded, I noticed a sign: 'This Area for Linkin Park ONLY'.

Loving every moment, but still feeling very out of place, I suddenly recognised a friendly face. I had made an appearance on a musical game show called *Never Mind the Buzzcocks* earlier in the year with Eighties chanteuse Sam Brown and a guy called Jaret Von Erich – the lead singer of US rock band Bowling for Soup.

I heard them finishing their set as I arrived, and was hoping I'd at least get the chance to say 'G'day'. After a brief chat, they generously allowed me to join the band for lunch. The conversation was an off-putting mix of proper rock 'n' roll band-speak, tempered by the sensible attitudes of thirty-something married men and their wives. For example:

Guitarist: 'Did you see the girl with her boobs out?'

Jaret: 'Oh man, I didn't see them. Were they good boobs?'

Jaret's wife: 'Oh, they were good boobs.'

Guitarist's wife: 'Not as good as the boobs in Dallas, though.'

Jaret's wife: 'Oh, I remember those boobs.'

In all honesty, they were the loveliest bunch of strangers I've ever had lunch with. They chatted to me about comedy, about mutual friends we had that were comics, and promised to come see my spot at the comedy tent.

As I left the table, I took note as a spiky, multi-colour-haired rock singer in a sleeveless shirt, and wearing studded leather bracelets, turned to a tattooed, twenty-something-stone guitarist and remark, 'Man those meatballs were spicy. I'm gonna be feeling that later.'

At three o'clock precisely, I took to the stage of the comedy tent before about a thousand people and ripped off a lovely forty-five-minute set. Now it's hard enough to remember your act, listen to the audience's reaction, be mindful of how long you've done, and make sure everyone's getting into your set. It's harder when the audience are sitting on the grass of an enormous marquee in the middle of the day, and are separated from you by a three-foot-high security fence, and five security guards.

They gave me security guards! I performed to a thousand smiling faces, and the backs of five shaven-headed Glaswegian bouncers. The audience got right into it, the bouncers didn't even crack a grin – or if they did, they kept looking at the crowd the entire time.

It's even more difficult to do comedy when you're only a few hundred yards away from two other stages, featuring some of the world's biggest, and loudest bands. Normally you ask for a light to be flashed when you come to the end of your set. I knew I had fifteen minutes left when the Datsuns started playing. I finished the last fifteen with the Datsuns playing 'Sittin' Pretty' in one ear, and Alien Ant Farm playing 'Just Like the Movies' in another.

To give them credit, the crowd were amazing. In amongst this cacophony of noise they were attentive, polite, and very giving in their laughter and applause. Possibly the most bizarre moment of this entire scene took place as I informed the audience that I had an artificial leg.

Before I could even rip off the first joke about it, there was a scream of joy from the back of the tent. I looked at the raised platform that held four people, one of whom was a woman in a wheelchair, and exclaimed, 'Holy sweetest Jesus!'

The audience turned as one to see what I could see – the woman in the wheelchair had removed her artificial leg and was waving it over her head. A cheer went up from the room, and I dared her to crowd-surf it around the tent. Sadly, she declined, but it did give me the opportunity to yell, 'Come on, party people – wave your leg in the air like you just don't care!'

I left the stage to a rousing round of applause, picked up a can of Coke, and walked straight into the passenger seat of the waiting car. As we left the car park, still wearing my Access All Areas pass, I heard the Datsuns kick in to one of my favourite songs, 'Motherfucker from Hell'. Could I be more rock 'n' roll?

*   *   *

AUTHOR'S NOTE
Over time I worked out that the best way to play comedy tents at music festivals was to throw the act out the window and do something, big, nuts and memorable.

I also learnt that the crowd is generally made up of three different types of audience member:

1. *Comedy fans who have come specifically to see you perform. They make up the majority of the tent. They will sit politely, lap up the act, and generally have a good time.*
2. *People with a hangover so bad it would show up on a photograph. They have had a huge night, very little rest, and the comedy tent is the quietest place they can find. They barely react to your set, and often fall asleep during it.*

3. *Ravers who are still high on whatever they took the night before. They're not entirely sure where they are, or what you're saying, and look at you with a glassy-eyed confusion. There's no telling how they'll react, which I now know is why there are security guards.*

When I performed at the Leeds Festival, I told the story of the woman who refused to crowd-surf her leg, prompting someone in the audience to shout at me to crowd-surf mine.

So I did.

I took off the prosthetic, threw it to someone in the front row, and implored them not to run off with it. The foot made it to the back of the tent, then back to the stage.

The next time I performed at Reading, I told the same story and the woman in question yelled out from the back of the tent, 'I'm here again!'

'I wanna come and give you a hug,' I shouted.

'Might be tough,' she replied. 'I've got no arms.'

But, but . . . how did she wave her leg over her head the first time? Was someone else waving it for her? Was she originally wearing prosthetic arms?

I didn't think to ask any of these questions. Instead, I crowd-surfed all the way to her, gave her a hug, and crowd-surfed my way back to the stage.

As I righted myself in front of the microphone, I glimpsed someone a few rows back waving something in the air.

'Oi,' he shouted, 'you dropped your Oyster card.'

Only in England.

11 January 2004

I'm so incredibly jet-lagged.

On Wednesday I flew from London to LA, spent five hours in the transit lounge, then flew from LA to Melbourne, arriving at 9 a.m. Friday morning.

Thirty-six hours of travel to be best man at Ross Noble's wedding, which took place on Saturday. Ross met me at the airport, but I was so tired and travel sick I had to ask him to pull the car over on the way home, so I could throw up by the side of the road.

We spent Friday night eating pizza and composing our respective wedding speeches, which is a surprisingly tricky proposition when you're a comedian. Ross summed it up thus: 'If I don't make jokes, people are gonna wonder why. And if I do, my wife's gonna say I turned our wedding into a gig.'

I had similar qualms. Half the room would be comedians, who are harsh judges even if they are your friends.

After a good hour of mulling it over, I finally said, 'Listen. Most guests expect a wedding speech to be heartfelt, but they're blown away if it happens to be funny. We're the opposite. Most people will expect us to be funny, but they'll love it if we happen to be heartfelt. So let's be genuine, with a little bit of funny.'

I stayed at the wedding until 1 a.m., then managed three hours sleep before taking a 9 a.m. flight from Melbourne to LA, via Auckland. I arrived in LA at 7.45 this morning, and spent the day hanging out with my agent.

We're staying at the Standard Hotel on Sunset Boulevard, West Hollywood – that for some reason has a half-naked woman lying in a fish tank above the hotel reception desk.

I'm not sure why.

Sometimes she reads, sometimes she sleeps, sometimes it's a different woman. It's Hollywood, so I'm just gonna accept it.

After my previously aborted attempt to crack LA, my guardian angel at NBC, Marc Hirschfeld, has lined up a week of meetings for me with the heads of casting for Warner Brothers, Universal, Sony and Paramount. I also have a meeting with an LA manager, and a possible audition for a sitcom.

My Australian manager Kevin has flown in to accompany me, and he said that according to one email, the woman at Warner Brothers 'would LOVE to meet Adam'. Not just 'love', but 'LOVE'. That can't be a bad thing. And now that I'm writing all this, I'm hoping I'm not jinxing myself at the same time. Can you unjinx yourself by expressing your fear of jinxing yourself? Has the jet-lag completely taken over now? Very possibly.

This could be the week that changes my life, depresses me forever, makes me a star, changes nothing, leaves me broke, or is just a helluva lot of fun.

17 January 2004

Well that was a helluva lot of fun.

We LOVED the woman at Warner Brothers, as well as the woman at Universal. Both were chatty, friendly, genuine, and somehow wrapped their meetings up after exactly an hour, despite never glancing at their watches.

We also spotted Nicolas Cage at dinner.

I auditioned for a role in a new sitcom, in which a slacker brother moves in with his businesslike younger sister . . . with hilarious consequences. Apparently, and you didn't hear this from me, the sister may be played by Alyson Hannigan, aka Willow from *Buffy the Vampire Slayer*, aka Michelle, from band camp in the *American Pie* movies.

The only feedback I got was that my American accent was 'flawless'. Good thing, too, after I spent forty-five minutes (and a hundred and fifty US dollars) on the phone with a dialect coach trying to iron out my Aussie twang. Apparently we have a tendency to go up at the end of every sentence. Who knew?

Also, as I pulled onto the lot for the audition, Will Smith drove in alongside me. And I saw British actor Rufus Sewell at breakfast.

I had a meeting with a woman at Sony Television, who informed me, 'I don't shake hands', and another meeting with the man who cast the sitcom *Cheers*. He ate sushi as we talked, and wrapped up our chat with the words, 'Sorry to rush you, I'm due on the set of *Frasier* for a read-through.'

That night we saw Avril Lavigne in the lobby of my hotel.

The week ended with me meeting the people who cast *Scrubs* (they also didn't shake hands, apparently there's a really bad flu going around), and the woman who cast one of my favourite sitcoms of all time, *Mad About You*.

She asked how long I was in town, and expressed genuine regret that I was flying home at the end of the week, because 'we have a guest spot for something that needs filling next week.'

Her sister, who is about to cast the movie *Ocean's Twelve*, was also in the meeting, and she asked me if I could speak Dutch, Italian or French.

I said I could learn really quickly.

Now I find myself back on a plane, trying to take stock of it all. Before this week I was reluctant to take the step towards Hollywood, especially towards a sitcom. Now, however, I'm starting to come around to the idea.

I don't know whether it was the thrill of the audition, the lights of Hollywood, or the fact that it suddenly all seems so achievable. Maybe it was because everyone was so damn friendly.

Having said that, I am fully aware that may have all been Marc Hirschfeld's influence. I can't imagine how tough it would have been had we just landed in LA and attempted to garner the same meetings off our own bats.

Even while sitting here, I've been watching the inflight comedy channel, recognising the names at the credits of the sitcoms. *Frasier*, *Scrubs*, *Will and Grace*. I met the people behind these shows.

And then a name popped up that really stood out – the people responsible for casting one of my other favourite sitcoms, *The Drew Carey Show* – Zane/Pillsbury Casting. Debra and Bonnie Zane were the two sisters I met on my final day, along with Gayle Pillsbury.

I had a sudden pang. I wonder if that was the guest spot they needed filling on Wednesday. Had I just blown a big chance?

I guess now I sit back, play it cool, and hope a few Hollywood offers come my way.

Notes from a Diary, Pt 3

16 July 2004

Nothing came of my LA meetings. Not a jot. Not a single call. And I didn't hear back from the audition.

I should have known.

A few weeks after the trip, I had lunch with my Irish acting agent, Richard. He's au fait with the Hollywood way, having also represented Colin Farrell and Cillian Murphy.

I gushed for at least fifteen minutes about how it all went, the offers I got, the people I met. He told me not to get too excited, because that happens to everyone.

'I know,' I countered, 'but a few of them said they had roles in the next few weeks that I'd have been perfect for.'

'Did they tell you that before or after they knew you were only in town for a few days?' he queried.

I thought for a second, and replied, 'After.'

Bugger.

But there is a glimmer of light.

For years I've been mulling over the idea of a film about my time in radio. After my trip to LA, I started to wonder if the same idea could be slightly moulded to fit a sitcom format.

At the Melbourne Comedy Festival earlier this year, I approached a US comedian by the name of Maria Bamford to see if she'd be interested in being the co-star. She jumped, I jumped, and a week later we found a late-night venue in which to perform an episode.

Well, not so much perform, as improvise around an idea.

The basic premise was that I was an Australian radio DJ, who winds up in a small-town radio station in America – 'after an hilarious mix up'.

Maria was the station receptionist, but also doubled as the head of sales, and the station manager's assistant – adopting different voices for each on the phone.

Our characters bond and eventually become an on-air duo.

We told both of our regular audiences about the show, emphasising that it was free, and at midnight we had assembled a few hundred people in front of us to see whether we had 'it'.

From all reports, and our sensory organs, we did indeed have 'it', so I began to work on a few story ideas. After a few more weeks, and a few rough drafts, I sent Marc an email with an extremely rough and very vague outline. I didn't want to give him too much information all at once.

Three weeks later, I received an email from a woman called Lisa Leingang at NBC, which read something like, 'I have a producing deal at NBC. Marc forwarded me your idea. I'd love to meet up with you in Montreal to talk about it.'

Hello.

In two days' time I'll be heading back to the Montreal comedy festival to host the 'Late Night Down Under' show, and to have a meeting with Lisa about the sitcom idea. This, by the way, was exactly the plan my agent and I had set out in LA in January.

The lovely part about it all is this: it doesn't matter whether or not my sitcom is made, whether or not I sign a development deal for an obscene sum of money, or whether I become a star. I'm giving it a damn good shake – and that's all I can ask of myself.

29 July 2004

It was a point of national pride to make the first ever Australia/New Zealand show at the Just for Laughs Comedy Festival in Montreal the best show we possibly could. We never realised quite how good it was going to be.

The Montreal comedy festival is one of the big four in the world – the others being Edinburgh, Melbourne, and recently Aspen. It is the place where producers from across the world mingle with the head honchos of Hollywood to discover the 'next big thing'.

Montreal claims to have discovered Jerry Seinfeld, Drew Carey, Jim Carrey, and in a famous story, Tim Allen was offered his own sitcom deal purely on the basis of his seven-minute spot at the Gala. Accordingly, every show is a 'showcase' – a two-hour show in which a dozen or more comics are paraded on stage to perform a seven, twelve, or if they're really lucky, fifteen-minute set.

The audience for said routine comprises Montreal locals, a few tourists, and a wall of industry bods, ranging from the Hollywood heavies to the Minnesota lightweights. Often the shows start late, awaiting the arrival of the 'industry', who are shuttled in last minute, so as to avoid having to actually queue up with the great unwashed. Said industry then take their seats in a roped-off area, and take notes throughout the show, using pens with inbuilt lights. From the stage it looks like the back row is made up entirely of fireflies.

I performed at the New Faces show last year, and was given these instructions beforehand: 'If a joke dies, it doesn't matter. If you bomb, no one cares. These people are not here to book you for a comedy tour; they are here to put you in a sitcom, where someone else will write the jokes for you.'

I find it very hard to do comedy when no one cares if you're funny or not. That said, there were some very inexperienced acts on that show, for whom the pre-show pep talk probably worked wonders.

It was in amongst this melange of business that I was asked to host the first ever 'Late Night Down Under' shows, 'spotlighting the best of Australia and New Zealand comedy'. For some reason, I took this very seriously. Some sense of blatant Aussie patriotism (sparked I'm sure by a prolonged absence from the wide brown land) mixed with a very Aussie desire to 'stick it to the industry'.

The line-up was announced as Wil Anderson, Carl Barron, Cal Wilson, Flight of the Conchords, Benjamin Crellin and ex-Men at Work lead singer Colin Hay, all hosted by yours truly. I was so excited by the prospects of working with Colin Hay, I immediately bought a Best of Men at Work album, to get myself in the mood.

The sound check gave me goose bumps. Standing in an empty comedy room, surrounded by only the bar and venue staff, as that inimitable voice began to sing, it was truly exhilarating. I looked around me, and everyone in the place had stopped what they were doing and was transfixed. After each song Colin received a round of applause, and when the flute sounded at the start of 'Down Under', I wondered if the show could possibly top this feeling. It did.

The show began with Colin Hay singing 'Who Can It Be Now', and then introducing me as compere. Each night, I walked on stage buzzing. 'The man responsible for "Down Under" just introduced me on stage,' I told the audience. 'For the Americans in the room, that's like Bruce Springsteen playing "Born in the USA", then bringing you on stage. For the Canadians, it's like . . . Anne Murray singing "Songbird".'

Every act was brilliant. Each one of us took to the stage to give the best show we possibly could, and the audience knew it. Three hundred or so punters, and a few executives from NBC and Warner Brothers, saw the best that Australia and New Zealand had to offer.

The third act (after Benjamin Crellin and Carl Barron both had great sets) was a return appearance by Colin Hay to tell a few stories and sing a few songs. He told tales of growing up in Scotland, making it big in Australia, and being hassled by every movie producer for the rights to use 'Down Under', then he sang 'Overkill' and a couple of new songs.

He closed the set with 'Down Under' and as in rehearsal, when the flute started, I jumped. Standing by the kitchen door, I sang my little Aussie heart out, as did the entire crowd, regardless of nationality, and halfway through the song the strangest thing happened. I got all teary.

I guess the emotion of the moment got to me; being ten thousand miles away from home, missing my friends and family, and yet knowing that if I was back in Australia, I wouldn't be having this amazing experience. I hadn't felt like this since I saw Paul Kelly in Edinburgh in 1999, an experience I also shared with Wil Anderson. It was all I could do to pull myself together to back announce Colin and announce an interval.

The atmosphere backstage was brilliant. Normally in a Montreal showcase, the green room is deadly quiet, as nervous comedians and expectant managers pace, check their watches and rehearse material. This time there was raucous laughter, constant chatting, and a general hubbub so loud it could occasionally be heard from the audience. Wil chatted to Carl and Benjamin, I chatted to Cal, and we all planned a surprise finale with Colin Hay and the Conchords.

The second half was as good as the first, as Cal and Wil both stormed the crowd, and Flight of the Conchords were their usual deadpan, amazing selves. As they came to the end of their set, they announced that they would be accompanied on their final song by Colin Hay, with whom they had written the lyrics when they worked together in a stationery store. Colin played along with the joke, and then the song, which led up to a rousing chorus of, 'Brown paper, white paper. Stick 'em together, with sellotape of love.'

On cue, the rest of us took to the stage, arm in arm, and swayed as we joined in the chorus, in a faux 'We Are the World' moment. Cal wrapped herself and me up in gaffer tape, Wil handed his camera to audience members to record the moment, Carl ad-libbed his own lyrics, and I thanked the audience for coming, and wrapped up the show.

And they gave us a standing ovation.

Three hundred people leapt to their feet, and stayed there with their hands above their heads, banging out their approval.

In my previous fifteen years of comedy, I had only ever received two full-on standing ovations, and as a true Aussie, I'm a little shy about recalling them. I would certainly never write about them as I have this one. I guess that's because I'm not really one to blow my own horn.

However, in this case I'm quite happy to blow everyone else's horn. It was such a magical feeling to be on stage in the middle of it all, such a team event, and such a proud day for Down Under comedy, that I want my compadres to share the glory. And I know they felt it, too, because I could feel Cal's heart beating when she taped us together, and it was going even faster than mine. We did what we set out to achieve, which was to give them one hell of a show.

The remainder of my week in Montreal consisted of pitching my sitcom idea to the NBC exec (who said she loved it and wanted to take it further), signing on with an LA manager (who said he loved me and wanted to take me further), and seeing a live script-reading of my favourite TV show, *Family Guy*.

It was all brilliant, but none of it matched the moment when I stood on stage with Wil Anderson, Carl Barron, Benjamin Crellin, Cal Wilson, Flight of the Conchords and Colin Hay, and received a standing ovation for the first ever Down Under show at the Montreal comedy festival.

All together now: 'He just smiled and gave me a vegemite sandwich . . .'

* * *

AUTHOR'S NOTE
According to my biog, I have now performed at the Just for Laughs festival on more occasions than any other Australian. Some of my best comedy moments have happened there, including sitting in a dressing room with Craig Ferguson and Danny Bhoy as they discussed the ins and outs of buying a Scottish castle.

The first year I was there, I actually dreamt that I was at the Montreal comedy festival, then woke up and found that I was.

I got to meet so many of my comedy idols, including Don Rickles, Nathan Lane and Chevy Chase, with whom I discussed the pros and cons of a Western grip when hitting a forehand in tennis.

One year I was booked to perform at the Gala, but arrived late due to a scheduling mix-up and a traffic jam. Sweating, flustered, and in a mild panic, I rushed to my dressing room, only to find Martin Short outside my door. He recognised me from a previous festival and asked if I was OK.

Panting, I told him how late I was, and how stressed I now felt about my spot.

Like a comedy Buddha, he placed a hand on my shoulder and said: 'There's no need to worry, Adam. I just know you're gonna kill.'

Nothing else mattered after that.

30 October 2004

I bumped into my friend Gretel Killeen last year and congratulated her on becoming a big star as the new host and presenter of the *Big Brother Australia* series.

'Thanks, but you know how it is in this industry. You have a hundred different projects on the go at the same time, hoping one of them will pay off. And then something you don't expect comes along and makes you a star.'

Right now, I can relate to the first part of that answer. As I write this, I have three different opportunities on the go – any or all of which could be something that takes me to the next level of my career.

Remember when Marc Hirschfeld, the guy from NBC, flew me to LA for meetings, after which I wrote my own sitcom that I then sent to Marc, who forwarded it to Lisa Leingang at NBC, who met with me in Montreal and liked the idea?

Well, Lisa and I met up in Edinburgh, then did some more work over the phone, and then arranged a conference call for me to pitch the idea to the NBC Universal Studios execs. They liked it enough to suggest a pitch to the network, which again entailed a conference call between the network execs in LA, Marc and Lisa in New York, and me in a hotel in Brighton.

As it stands now, I am awaiting a final response – that could entail anything from 'Yes, we want to make a pilot episode' to 'No, but keep in touch'. It has been three weeks since the last pitch, and I don't know whether no news is good or bad news.

Two weeks ago, I also had a meeting with a TV production company and the host of *The Weakest Link*, Anne Robinson, to discuss a topical panel-type comedy show that she was hosting and for which I was being considered as a regular guest. Plus, Channel Nine in Australia are currently looking over a proposal for a travel/comedy show that would see me traversing the globe doing stand-up comedy.

So . . . an NBC Sitcom, a BBC comedy chat show, and a Channel Nine travel series. The waiting is killing me.

The irony is, as Gretel pointed out, it could well be something unexpected that comes along and makes me famous yet. Meanwhile I'm doing my second ever UK tour, and tapping away at these diary entries hoping someone, someday, may want to put them in a book.

Sooner or later, something's gotta give. Surely.

19 November 2004

It is as if the universe was listening to me, but then, when does it not? The BBC comedy chat show said, 'Thanks, but no thanks,' and the Channel Nine travel series is still on hold.

Meanwhile I have received no word whatsoever from NBC about the sitcom. Seriously, not one message. I remember my agent telling me, 'No one in Hollywood says no, even when they mean no,' and now I see what he meant. No one has actually told me that they won't be making my sitcom, but even Lisa, who was championing my cause like a prize fighter, isn't returning my emails.

Three irons in the fire, three eggs in separate baskets, three chickens ready to hatch. Three cold irons, three smashed eggs, three unborn chickens (probably because someone smashed the eggs).

And then, as Gretel predicted, along came something unexpected – an offer to host a music/comedy/quiz show on the ABC in Australia. Not only would it give me the chance to gain experience in front of the camera, it would allow me to be funny (which is after all, what I do), while talking about music (which is after all, what I love). To cap it all off, they reckon they can film a year's worth of episodes in six months, thus allowing me to spend some quality time in Australia, while still being able to tour the world for the other six months.

Plus, to place the Neneh Cherry on top of My Friend the Chocolate Cake, I'll only be filming two days per fortnight, recording two shows per day, which means I can use the rest of my time to write a new show for next year's festivals. It will mean bigger audiences in Australia, a year-round presence on Australian TV, even when I'm touring the UK – and it will give me a chance to see my friends and loved ones, while also satis-fying my girlfriend's desire to spend more time in Australia.

Finally, at the Living End of the Green Day, it will be fun. And hey, isn't that what it's all about? TV experience, Australian profile, time at home with family, and a whole lot of fun. I haven't said yes yet, but I think I might.

AUTHOR'S NOTE
The girlfriend referred to in these diary pieces is no longer my girlfriend, and she didn't become my wife. Turns out, the choice of either staying at home while I travelled the world, or coming with me while I vomited in hotel rooms wasn't an attractive one. There was more to it than that of course, but the time away from each other and the unsocia-ble hours of a stand-up comic (not to mention my single-minded obsession with comedy itself) put a huge strain on the relationship.

She once told me if we ever had children, the only way I'd notice them is if we named them 'laughter' and 'applause'. I pretended to be offended, but deep down all I could think was 'I wonder if I can use that line one day.'

We're still friends now, and I'll be forever grateful she supported me through these crazy times.

9 January 2005

So here I am again – on a Qantas flight, approaching the Australian coastline, anticipating that moment when I am at last above the wide brown land of Oz. I have taken a break from my reading to take stock of where I am.

I said yes to the ABC TV project.

The advice that tipped me over the edge came from my UK manager Joe. That's right, I now have an Australian, an Irish and a British manager. If they all walked into a bar together, not only would something funny happen, they'd sell tickets to watch it, and take commission on the profits.

Joe had said simply, 'Go home, make your mistakes on Australian television, then when you know how to do it, come back to England.'

At the present moment in time I have no idea what the show will be called, and have yet to scan the document outlining the segments. All I know is that I arrive in Sydney in five hours' time, spend a night with my parents, then head down to Melbourne to start at the ABC the following day. It has been eight years since I left my radio job at SAFM, and I am kinda excited by the prospect of turning up for work at an actual office, with actual people whom I'll be seeing every day.

I'm also excited by the prospect of working at the ABC. The network that has been home to such Australian comedy greats as Andrew Denton, Norman Gunston, Aunty Jack, Roy and HG . . . and of course the international genius of Tony Hancock.

Interestingly, I have also been invited to perform at the very exclusive Aspen comedy festival in Colorado in February. It is a five-day festival, favoured by the US network executives, and this year will see a live read through of the TV show *Arrested Development*, and a one-man play starring Christopher Lloyd (aka the Doc in *Back To The Future*). Other shows will feature stand-up bills including Eddie Izzard, myself, two of my best Irish mates in David O'Doherty and Des Bishop, plus UK comic Stewart Lee, and New Zealand's finest in Flight of the Conchords.

As well as my stand-up duties, I have also been asked to take part in a late-night chat show, live on stage. It seems that the network honchos are running low on potential *Tonight Show* hosts in the States, so the festival programmers are instituting a series of performances designed to showcase the next Lettermans and Lenos – and they have asked me to host the first show. Over the next few weeks I will be receiving a list of possible guests, from which I am to draft a dream team. Hmmm, TV experience in Australia, plus a showcase spot in front of Hollywood's biggest producers. Could the universe be leading me somewhere?

A quick glance at the seat-back map has told me that we are all but above the Western Australian coastline, and a look out the window confirms as much.

A quick glance at my career path tells me I have a burgeoning career in the UK, a few nibbles in the States, and a chance to take the next step in the Australian TV industry.

Who knows what will happen from here?

Maybe the next time I put pen to paper, or at least finger to keyboard, I'll have a compendium of gossip, brushes with fame, and celebrity tattle to dispense.

I have enjoyed every minute of the last fifteen years, from that first exhilarating but forgettable open mic night, through my days in radio, and up to my most recent performance in Lisburn, Northern Ireland – a show I had to pause while a stomach virus forced me off-stage to vomit.

It's time to start a new chapter.

*   *   *

AUTHOR'S NOTE
Literally.

Part Five
Hey Days

Spicks and Specks

There is no formula to getting on TV.

Some people write their own shows, film it, and take it to a channel. Others audition for role after role until one sticks. I had done both and nothing had come of them.

I'd also been offered a few hosting gigs, but none of them felt quite right. Did I really want to break into America as the host of *The Guinness Book of World Record Pet Tricks*? (Not a joke, I was actually offered that one.)

The offer to host the music quiz show *Spicks and Specks* came from appearing on a variety of other panel shows as a guest, and doing a good-enough job that the right people remembered me. In the end it's actually quite simple – try to be really, really good at every job you do. No matter what that job is.

The first episode of *Spicks and Specks* attracted around 660,000 viewers. The next week it dropped to around 600,000. The following week it jumped to 770,000.

I didn't find any of this out until episode three, and it's probably just as well. I'd have been gutted to have known we dropped sixty thousand viewers after the first episode.

I know now that often happens.

People tune in on the first night to see what this new show is gonna be. It stands to reason that whatever the show is, it won't be for everyone, so the people who don't want to keep watching a panel-based music quiz show don't tune in the following week.

Meanwhile, as the show finds its feet, word slowly starts to travel among people who are partial to a bit of casual music trivia and even more casual jokes, and gradually your audience builds itself.

It helped that our second show featured a rebelliously funny Ross Noble, who went off on flights of fancy, disrupted the script, and generally did his own thing.

I knew the format was strong though, when he apologised afterwards for not being funny in the final segment. 'Sorry mate, I was too focused on trying to win the game.'

That's exactly the type of TV show you want to make. One in which the guests forget they're on a TV show.

The name of the show came from a Bee Gees song – 'Spicks and Specks' – the first of theirs to hit number one in Australia. Years later, the fearless US comedian Joan Rivers would baulk at reading out the word *'Spicks'* at an Australian TV Awards Ceremony, despite having just dropped the F-Bomb twice on live TV. The games were developed by a crack team of producers, and by the time I came on board, a few test episodes had already been shot with a different host and team captains.

We filmed a couple more test episodes, with a couple more team captains. One was a New Zealand-born comedian and actor, whom I knew well from the comedy scene, Alan Brough. He had an encyclopedic knowledge of music, having once worked in a record store, and was also very funny off the cuff.

One of the other possible captains was a diminutive, raven-haired DJ from radio station Triple J, called Myf Warhurst.

She'd never been on TV before, and had no comedy experience, but she had something more important – she was
genuine.

There was absolutely no artifice about Myf, which meant
there was nothing blocking the audience's view of her heart.
She was real, and that's rare on television.

Alan, Myf and I made a good team. The very funny music
nerd on one side, the gorgeous and fun music lover on the
other, and the guy in the middle holding it all together.

Cleverly, each round was named after a song – Know Your
Product (the opening round, in which each team were quizzed
on their chosen musical topic), Look What They've Done To
My Song Ma (where well-known songs were played in an
unusual way, say by a klezmer band, and the teams had to
identify the songs), and The Final Countdown (a rapid-fire
set of questions to end the show).

One in particular made me laugh out loud when I read it in
the proposal for the show – Substitute.

One team member had to sing songs for their team-mates,
but using the words of a completely unrelated book. Their
team-mates had to work out what the songs were. For example, one might have to sing Abba's 'Mamma Mia', using the
words of the *1974 Ford Corona Owner's Manual*.

Try it yourself with the next few paragraphs. I'm going to
write them to fit 'Mamma Mia':

It's surprisingly hard just to change all the words,
Cos your brain has to do different things at once.
Try it right now, go on have a go, give it a crack, and
   you'll find you can make it work. But it's hard and
   you have to think.

One more sentence and you're just about there, keep on
   going and the chorus is here (woah woah).
Now you've done it, yes, you really did. My my, I didn't
   think you'd get there.
Yes, you did it, and I'm proud of you, why why, did you
   keep on going?
Yessss, we should stop this right now, but, I don't really
   know how.
My, my, I am gonna end it now.

That round aside, it was a proper quiz, and was actually more
fun to watch when we took it seriously, rather than going for
the gags. We came to that realisation early on, when one show
seemed to lack energy. Upon watching it back, I saw that we
were trying too hard to be funny.

Comedians are more likely to crack a joke when everyone
else is trying to be serious. So it stood to reason that if we
tried our hardest to win, the jokes would not only come thick
and fast, but more naturally.

I had three bits of advice to everyone who came on the
show: Talk lots. Don't talk over each other. Try to win.

It's important on a pre-recorded show to say lots. You
never know what's going to be funny, or helpful, so you
may as well put it all out there. If it doesn't work, it'll be
edited out. If it does, you'll look great. You can always edit
a sentence out of a show, but you can't edit one in
afterwards.

It's also vitally important not to talk over other people. In
normal conversation it's OK, because the ear can distinguish
the loudest voice, or separate one voice from another. But on
TV, when all the voices are fed through the same mixing desk,

and out of the one TV speaker – they all mash together and become indecipherable.

Also, gaps mean you can edit. I knew from my old days in radio that if there's half a second of silence on either end of a sentence, the whole thing can be cut out. Over time I learned to assess what should be taken out while recording an interview, and leave gaps for myself to edit it later.

I did the same thing when we made *Spicks and Specks*. Say, for instance, someone gave an answer while being talked over by someone else. I knew that the viewers wouldn't be able to hear the answer correctly, so I'd pause, leaving an edit point, then ask them to repeat the answer, knowing that the second attempt would be the one edited into the show.

The same would go for a joke that might be inappropriate, or heaven forbid, didn't get a laugh. I'd pause, remember what I was doing before the joke, return to that position, then pick up with whatever was next in the script. Sometimes it looked as though I was blanking someone's joke, but I was actually leaving a bit of silence to make the edit easier.

I took it as a point of pride that our producer one day joked he was going to put a Sudoku puzzle on my desk, to see if I could host the show, read the questions, respond to the guests, read the autocue, edit as we went, and do the Sudoku all at once.

So the three main secrets – talk lots, don't talk over each other, play to win.

In truth, though, everything I learned about hosting a TV show came from one man, by the name of Peter Faiman.

Pete was in his fifties when I met him, although he was one of those people who could have been any age. Wearing a baseball cap at all times, dressed casually, grey hair and glasses, he had the air of a Hollywood producer who is also a mad billionaire.

Pete's pedigree was astounding. He had worked with Paul Hogan on his sketch show that appeared on both Aussie and British TV, and was the director of *Crocodile Dundee*.

That should be enough for a reference, but before all that, Pete oversaw the most successful entertainment shows on Australian TV: *The Graham Kennedy Show* (the first ever variety/talk show on Australian TV), *The Don Lane Show*, and *The Bert Newton Show*.

These names may not mean much to international readers, but to Australians, they were the Letterman, Leno and Carson of our industry. In fact, Pete did spend some time in Hollywood, where he turned down the chance to direct a talk show starring Chevy Chase.

I owe everything I know about TV hosting to Pete, as he dished out constant gems. The first was how to prepare a script for autocue.

'You need to know every word that's in the script,' he told me. 'You don't want to be reading off an autocue and taken by surprise by what the next words are. Don't let anyone else write your script, cos it won't be in your words. Make sure you are the one writing your own words, otherwise they won't sound natural.

'Underline the important words in each sentence, because when you read off an autocue, there are only two or three words per line. In a book, your eye naturally scans ahead to see what's coming, but you can't do that on an autocue. So underline the words that need emphasising, that way you'll hit them properly even if you don't know why.'

To this day I write my own scripts, underline the important words, and <u>nobody</u> is allowed to add anything without me knowing what it is.

Pete taught me to focus less on the one-hundred-and-fifty live audience members, and more on the hundreds of thousands watching through the lens. This was counterintuitive to a stand-up comic, whose priority is always to the living, breathing humans in the room.

He taught me to explain the rules of every game clearly, and even made me put them in bold on the script, so that I would remember to emphasise them lucidly and slowly.

After one particularly shaky run-through of the show, Pete approached me.

'I don't know who the fuck any of you are talking about,' he said bluntly.

'What do you mean?' I asked.

'What the fuck is a Limp Biscuit?'

'Well,' I started, 'it's a late-Nineties, heavy-rock band, known for their on-stage aggression.'

'Well, tell me that,' he responded.

He continued, 'The audience aren't gonna know every single band you talk about, so you have to explain who they are. Not a lot, just enough to put them into context. If someone knows who Perry Como is, they may not know who Britney Spears is. And just because they know Britney, doesn't mean they know Madonna.'

The trick was to describe each artist in a way that wouldn't make those who knew them feel patronised.

'Don't assume the audience know who you're talking about,' Pete would say, 'but don't presume they don't.'

So, if for example we were asking what those three artists

had in common (in a game called Common People), I'd word the question like this: 'What do the following three people have in common – Fifties crooner Perry Como, Nineties "Queen of Pop" Madonna, and modern-day pop princess Britney Spears?'

That way at least everyone at home had a little bit of context. It was a stroke of TV genius on Pete's behalf.

Many years later we'd get people approach us on the street and say, 'I had no idea who you were talking about, but I loved watching you all have fun together.' Little did they know that Pete was the one who kept them all watching.

Another tip came when one panel member referred to something called 'kway'. I later found out 'kway' is a nick-name for the style of singing favoured by certain Nineties grunge bands, in which every third word sounds like 'kwayyyy'.

At the time though, I had no idea what was being talked about, so I kept my mouth shut, rather than look stupid.

'What the fuck is kway?' asked Pete in exasperation after the show.

'To be honest, Pete, I don't know.'

'Then ask!' he commanded. 'If you don't know, then the viewers probably don't know either. You have to ask on their behalf. It's better that you ask and feel a little foolish, than you don't and the audience feel left out.'

It was a lot to take in.

'Look,' said Pete, sensing my stress levels. 'You've gotta treat this show like a dinner party, where the viewer has turned up late. They don't know who the other guests are, or what the conversation is about. Your job is to introduce the viewer to the guests, explain who they are, and tell the viewer what's going on. If you think the guests are talking about someone the viewer doesn't know, you've got to explain it to the viewer.'

It is the single best piece of TV advice I have ever been given.

Unfortunately, I now have a habit at dinner parties of over-explaining everything to anyone seated next to me.

I can't emphasise enough (even if I underline the words), how instrumental Peter Faiman was to me making the transition from stand-up comic to TV host. I was sure to thank him when I won a Logie Award for Most Popular Presenter on Australian TV, and even threatened to do a nudie run at the following year's ceremony if he didn't receive a lifetime achievement award.

(He didn't. And I didn't.)

It was a rigorous training schedule, and sometimes between takes I would dread the sight of Pete heading towards me, as he offered yet another gem of advice. But they were always valuable.

Even when I was asked to present some backstage interviews with American TV stars at Australian television's night of nights, the Logie Awards, Pete asked me what I intended to ask them.

'I thought I'd start with – how do the Logies compare to the American awards shows?'

'Who gives a fuck?' replied Pete, with characteristic nuance. 'I couldn't care less how we compare to the American shows. Why do we need to compare ourselves to them anyway?'

(I should point out that Peter Faiman has one of the calmest, gentlest voices I've heard; so even when he swears, you still feel somehow soothed by it.)

He continued, 'How many questions are you gonna ask them?'

I had about three or four questions per celebrity.

'Fuck that,' he said, again, somehow managing to command me and destress me at the same time. 'Just get one bit of gold out of them, then get off.'

When the night came, I asked one, maybe two questions of each celebrity, designed to get the best possible answer from them as quickly as possible, then signed off. Pete was beside me the entire time, and as much as he could be blunt before going to air, he was unfailingly complimentary afterwards.

Actually, Pete's best piece of advice came directly before we filmed the first ever episode of *Spicks and Specks*.

After weeks of writing, rewriting, rehearsing, re-rehearsing, learning and re-learning every lesson I could, I returned to the dressing room for some last-minute quiet time before hosting my first ever TV show.

I opened the door to find Pete lounging on my couch, baseball hat on his head, sneakers on his feet, and his feet on my coffee table.

He must have seen my shoulders drop.

I had so many lessons, bits of advice and reminders of what to do going through my head, I honestly didn't think I could take one more in. It was like the file marked 'TV Host' was full, and one more piece of information would cause the whole system to crash.

Nevertheless, I steeled myself, took a deep breath, and said, 'Alright, Pete, what are you gonna tell me now?'

'The most important thing of all,' said Pete, as he took to his sneakered feet, and put his arms out to the side with a beaming smile.

'It's only fuckin' television. No one's gonna die out there.'
Best. Advice. Ever.

Snow Bunny (or Rabbitting on)

As the first episode of *Spicks and Specks* went to air in Australia, I was at the US Comedy Arts Festival in Aspen. Nestled in the heart of the Colorado Mountains, it is where anyone who can buy or sell anyone comes to play. Picture-perfect streets lined with snow, inhabited by picture-perfect people with no lines on their faces. Remember the movie *Dumb and Dumber*? They went to Aspen.

In a country dominated by the entertainment industry, the reasons for holding a festival in Aspen are simple – that's where the industry go on holidays. The Melbourne, Montreal and Edinburgh festivals draw producers to them, to scout for the next big thing. In Aspen, the festival was taken to the producers.

Therefore the US Comedy Arts Festival in Aspen was one of the most prestigious festivals in the world. The Monty Python reunion in which Graham Chapman's ashes were 'accidentally' knocked over the carpet happened in Aspen. Steve Martin, Billy Connolly, Robin Williams? All performed in Aspen.

The assembled players of 2005 included a cast reunion of the film *Waiting for Guffman* (Christopher Guest, Eugene Levy, Catherine O'Hara and Fred Willard), a reunion show featuring Cheech and Chong, and a lifetime achievement award presented to Jim Carrey.

Aspen was also the only festival in the world in which oxygen bottles are provided backstage, due to the altitude sickness from being in the Colorado mountains. At first it seems laughable, but trust me, after three days of vagueness and headaches, I was suckin' back the O2 like there was no tomorrow.

I compered a couple of nights, and hosted a late-night chat show accompanied by David O'Doherty, Janeane Garofalo and Sam Seder from Air America Radio, as well as the man who co-wrote the book *He's Just Not That Into You*, Greg Behrendt, and New Zealand's fourth most popular folk-parody duo – Flight of the Conchords.

I was also booked to perform in the 'Experts Only' shows, featuring Dane Cook, Greg Behrendt, Colin Quinn, Paula Poundstone, and Patton Oswalt. It was pretty hot company, some of the best stand-ups in America, which is why I was more than a little surprised one night when the stage manager informed me that a rabbit was 'doing five minutes' before me.

'Surely you mean a guy in a rabbit suit?' I pondered.

'Nope,' came the reply, 'it's a live rabbit.'

'Well, what's he gonna do?' I pondered again.

'Stand-up comedy, I guess.'

Now, I often watch the acts on before me. For one thing it gives me an idea of what kind of audience we're in for. Secondly it lets me know what kind of material has been talked about. If the guy before me does a twenty-minute set about Eighties music, I might wanna reconsider doing my material about Eighties music.

This night, I watched for a whole different reason. Here's what happened.

As the lights went down in the venue, which by the way, was an enormous marquee set up in the middle of a snow-covered field, a voice-over began.

'Ladies and gentlemen, please welcome a very special guest – Spike!'

The lights came up to reveal a lone microphone, surrounded by a bass drum, a small road case, a briefcase, a suitcase (each one a little taller than the other), and a stool. The front of the bass drum fell open, to reveal a real, live, breathing, white rabbit.

The audience 'awwww'ed, as the rabbit nimbly hopped up onto the small road case, then onto the briefcase, then onto the suitcase, then up onto the stool. The floppy-eared opener then stood on his hind legs, reached up, placed his two front paws on the microphone, put his little bunny mouth up to the mic, and started to move his lips.

Through the speakers came the words, 'Good evening, everyone. My name's Spike, it's good to be here.'

For the next five minutes, the rabbit ripped off some absolutely killer material, all delivered while standing on his hind legs, cradling the mic in his front paws, and moving his mouth to the words.

'I'd like to point out that I am not a "rabbit comedian". I am a comedian who just happens to be a rabbit.'

The crowd were in hysterics. From where I stood, it was a vaguely surreal sight. A four-hundred-strong audience, comprising some of the biggest wigs in the entertainment industry, were watching a fluffy bunny 'tell jokes'.

Eventually the rabbit began to wrap things up.

'Listen, you've been great, but I gotta get out of here. I've got a wife and ninety-seven children to feed. Thanks a lot, my name's Spike, good night everybody.'

With that the rabbit immediately stopped 'talking' and dropped to his haunches. He stayed there as the audience applauded, then reached up to the mic again for a final, 'Thank you, thank you very much. Enjoy the show everybody.' He then hopped down off the stool, onto the suitcase, onto the briefcase, onto the road case, and back into the bass drum, which was all then wheeled off stage.

It. Was. Beautiful.

My guess is that the 'cord' leading up to the microphone pumped a liquid solution of food to the rabbit. For as long as it was pumped, the rabbit would nibble. As it nibbled, an unseen performer backstage would deliver the jokes.

As soon as the supply was cut off, the rabbit would return to his haunches, and the performer would stop the jokes. What I can't work out is this: how did the rabbit know to reach up to the mic again for the final thank you?

Again, I can only guess that the rabbit knows that thirty seconds after the initial cut-off, the food is re-pumped, just for a few seconds. Through rigorous training, he knows to reach up one last time.

I could be completely wrong, though. Maybe the rabbit only happened to jump up again, and the guy doing the voice ad-libbed an extra thank you.

Or maybe, just maybe, the rabbit is a master of stage technique and knew exactly what he was doing. Come to think of it, I never did see the guy doing the voice-over.

Hang on, maybe the rabbit actually was talking. I may have witnessed the first ever talking animal act.

On the other hand, perhaps I had a little too much oxygen backstage before the show.

Greatest Hits

Thankfully, the majority of the funniest *Spicks and Specks* moments happened on camera, and ended up on air.

That's the way a TV show should work.

Like the moment Frank Woodley re-enacted Little Nell's appearance on a British TV show.

Little Nell Campbell is most famous for playing the role of Magenta in the original *Rocky Horror Picture Show*, but also had a hit single, called 'Do the Swim'.

We had found a somewhat famous blooper from a show on ITV in the UK, in which she sang the song while laying on the floor on her stomach, pretending to swim. Unfortunately, every time she raised her arms, one of her nipples slipped out the top of her one-piece bathing suit, resulting in a good few minutes of Nell bravely singing, swimming, and desperately trying to tuck a nipple back into a swimsuit.

Clearly, we wanted to play this back to her on the show, but the cost of buying the clip from the British producers was absolutely exorbitant. Turns out, it's in quite high demand for bloopers shows worldwide, and the producers of the original were making a lovely living from it.

So we thought it might be funny to ask one of the comedians on the show, Frank Woodley, to re-enact the scene. He could jump up on one of the desks, reveal he was wearing a swimsuit, and replicate the entire scene, with his own nipple popping out at the appropriate moment.

Frank agreed, and as far as I knew, that was what was going to happen.

At the appropriate moment in the show, I brought up the topic of Nell's appearance, and she cringed. I then explained that we couldn't afford the rights to the clip, so Frank was going to re-enact it.

And he did. He stripped down to a swimsuit, hopped up on the table, mimed the song, pretended to swim, and then made sure his nipple popped out.

All funny, and as expected.

However, as Frank stood back up, it became slowly apparent that something else had fallen out of the swimsuit. Something much lower than a nipple, and bigger, with a bit of hair on it.

One of Frank's testicles had fallen out of the side of his swimsuit, and was now dangling like the last avocado on the branch.

Some audience members had noticed, but not all, and a few of the guests had spotted it too. Frank seemed oblivious, though, and kept on explaining how embarrassing it must have been for Nell to have that happen on live television.

I tried to get Frank's attention, to alert him to the on-air mishap that was even more embarrassing than the one he was describing, but he just ignored me and kept talking. I tried again, and still he ignored me, all the while speaking genuinely and eloquently, as the audience grew more and more hysterical.

He then threw me the tiniest glance, that seemed to say, 'I can hear you, but I'm ignoring you,' a glance that said, 'You don't need to tell me my testicle is out, I know my testicle is out,' a glance that I interpreted to mean, 'My testicle is out on purpose.'

Safe in the knowledge that Frank was in control, I sat back and watched the carnage unfold. He paced along the stage, then sat up on the desk and crossed his legs in a way that put his testicle in full view of the audience, all the while pretending not to know it was on display.

Myf laughed so hard I thought a lung was gonna come up, the audience were in absolute spasms of laughter, and Frank maintained his innocent, wide-eyed, boyish face throughout the whole thing.

I later found out that he had not only planned it, but rehearsed it with the director, the producer and the cameraman, to make sure it was all covered properly. However, they had kept it a secret from those on the panel, to make sure it also looked as genuine as possible.

It remains one of the funniest moments I've ever experienced on television, and it all came about because we weren't able to run with our original idea.

Look up both these clips on YouTube. They are totally worth it.

I Just Called to Say I Love You

After the first year of *Spicks and Specks*, I was invited to a meeting with the big boss of one of the commercial networks, where I was asked if I'd like to leave the ABC behind, and come play with the big boys.

When I asked what show they had in mind for me, I received the answer, 'Oh, I'm sure you've got some ideas, and I know we've got some ideas, and I'm sure if one of those ideas matched up, we could all walk hand in hand into the sunset together.'

What?

Truth is, I already knew what one of their ideas was, and it was a game-show format that had just failed in America, in which scantily clad women removed layers of clothing to reveal how much money contestants had won. I wasn't filled with confidence.

My manager and I left the meeting with a promise to consider 'joining the network'.

As we walked to his car, he said, 'As your manager, I have to tell you that the amount of money they're offering is five times what you currently earn at the ABC. But I don't think you should take it. Right now you host a hit show that you love making, and could last for a number of years. There's no guarantee that will happen at the commercial network. You could sign to them, then be forced to make something that's not as good, and you'll be out on your ear after a year.'

Flattered as I was by the commercial offer, staying at the ABC was the right thing to do. I absolutely loved every second of making *Spicks and Specks*, and can't imagine my life without it.

Like I said earlier, the majority of the funny stuff happened in front of the cameras, and I don't want to be one of those people who recap past glories, when they've all been seen anyway. But a few little bits and pieces, or spicks and specks, never made it to TV.

Like the time one of our guests took a phone call during the show.

Now, we've all had our phones go off at inopportune moments. When I worked in radio, one of the other announcers was renowned for leaving his phone on during his shift. We would occasionally call him while he was on air, so we could hear it ring in the background as he spoke.

I still owe a case of beer to the Triple M Grill team in Sydney after my own phone rang during a live radio interview. (By the way, the unspoken rule is that if your phone goes off when you're on air, you owe the crew a case of beer.)

Once I was watching coverage of the Australian Open tennis, and was laughing hard at the commentary of former players John Fitzgerald and my tennis hero, Henri Leconte. Someone had the bright idea of teaming them up to do late-night commentary of a men's doubles match and it was genuinely some of the funniest TV I had seen.

I had become friends with Fitzy, and I texted him to tell him how much I was enjoying the commentary. Fifteen seconds later, Henri said out loud, on air, 'Did you just get a text message?'

Flustered, Fitzy responded, 'Um, well, um, yes. There's a comedian here in Australia called Adam Hills, and he just messaged me to say that he thinks you're really funny.'

So it wasn't massively surprising that someone's phone went off during a filming of *Spicks and Specks*. In fact, it's a miracle it only happened once.

I won't name names, for reasons that will become clear, but let's just say he was a performer who was internationally famous. I think I was mid-way through asking a question when it rang.

'Hi.'

'Yep, I'm filming it now.'

'OK, I'll see you when it's done.'

'OK, bye.'

Apologies were offered, we all made a few jokes about it, and the show resumed.

After we'd finished recording, the star in question approached our producer.

'Are you gonna edit out the bit where my phone rang?' he asked.

'Probably,' said our producer, 'but I'll see how funny it looks in the edit.'

'Well,' began the star sheepishly, 'I'd prefer it if you did edit it out, if that's OK.'

'Sure,' replied our producer, a little confused.

'See, that was my girlfriend on the phone,' stammered the star, 'but when the show goes to air, I'll probably watch it with my wife.'

We edited out the phone call.

Rockin' All Over the World

Rick Parfitt and Francis Rossi from Seventies stadium rockers Status Quo walked onto set like two men who had opened Live Aid, sold 118 million albums and had sixty UK hits.

Mainly because they had.

They had absolutely nothing to prove, and were one-hundred-per-cent comfortable in their own skins. Within seconds they were laughing, telling stories, and charming everyone within a fifty-metre radius. Especially the women.

'We'd love to,' I heard Meshel Laurie say, as I was collecting my thoughts.

Turning towards her, I saw the smiles beaming on her and Myf's faces.

'Love to what?' I enquired.

'Rick just asked if we'd like to spend an afternoon on his boat,' said Meshel.

Rick smiled like a Cheshire Cat.

'Nice,' I said. 'Where's your boat?'

His smile somehow broadened, as he replied, 'On top of me neck.'

It took a few seconds for my vague knowledge of cockney rhyming slang to kick in.

Boat.

Boat race.

Face.

He just asked Myf and Meshel if they'd like to spend an afternoon on his face. And Meshel said they'd love to.

And yet, no one was offended. In fact, I think the girls kinda admired that he got away with it, then fessed up to it.

I, however, refused to be charmed.

Later as I visited the communal toilet for a quick pre-show wee, I was joined at the urinal by Rick.

'Ah,' he said conspiratorially, 'this must be where all the big nobs hang out.'

Damn, Parfitt, you got me too.

Dad's Autographs

My dad was known by all who worked with him as 'the nicest man in Qantas'.

Always charming, permanently friendly, he travelled the world ensuring that everyone else who travelled the world was well fed, well rested, and well looked after.

He was a member of the Qantas cabin crew at a time when the airline regularly won awards for their inflight service. Rain Man knew that Qantas never crashed, but was he aware that Qantas also never left anyone hungry or uncomfortable?

My dad often said that the Qantas inflight motto was, 'If it moves, call it sir. If it doesn't, put parsley on it.'

As kids, we became accustomed to him being away. We'd all pile into the car, Mum would drive him to the airport, then we'd sit by Botany Bay eating ice cream and wait for his plane take off. A few days, or sometimes weeks later, he'd return home with bags under his eyes and a swag full of stories.

He'd also come home with autographs.

Dad took two autograph books on the plane with him, and if there was anyone famous and friendly on board, he'd get a message for my brother and me. A quick flick through my book right now reveals the scribbles of snooker champion Eddie Charlton, Aussie cricketers Rod Marsh and Ian Chappell, two members of the Harlem Globetrotters, plus the 1981–82 West Indies cricket team (including Viv Richards, Michael Holding, Malcolm Marshall, Desmond Haynes, Andy Roberts and Joel Garner).

I've got a birthday message from cricketer Dennis Lillee, and notes from Formula One champion Alain Prost, actor Jack Klugman, and comedian Dick Emery, who my dad informed me, gave an inflight announcement in character.

Later in life, when I became the one travelling the world making people happy, I always told him when I had a celebrity encounter. For example, when I met Robin Williams in a men's toilet in Shepherd's Bush Green.

It's not what you think.

There was a club called Ginglik in Shepherd's Bush that had a regular comedy night. It held about a hundred people, and drew some big-name acts. It was also in a converted men's toilet underneath the Green.

I knew Robin Williams was in town, and had heard he was trying out material at some local clubs, but this was the last place I expected him to turn up. As it happened, it was the nearest club to the BBC, where he had just filmed a TV spot.

I still have a photo of the running order, which said:

MC: Micky Flanagan
1st Act: Lenny Henry
2nd Act: Adam Hills
3rd Act: Rob Rouse
Robin Williams to go on whenever he gets here.

I confirmed with the venue owner that this wasn't a joke, and crossed my fingers that Robin would turn up in time to see my set.

He really was my comedy idol. I had literally dreamt of doing my set with him in the audience. And I don't mean 'literally' like a teenager who thinks it means 'almost'. I mean literally, in that, I actually had dreams of doing my set while Robin Williams was in the audience.

I performed that night with one eye on the back of the room, hoping to spy that familiar face, but alas, I didn't see him walk in.

I finished my spot and walked through the crowd into the dressing room, and there he was. I introduced myself and in that very soft, quietly spoken way that I knew he could have, he said hello.

I didn't know what to say next, but thankfully Rob Rouse had met him at the BBC show, and started the conversation.

'I just want to tell you that you're the reason I do comedy,' Rob began.

'Yep,' I added. 'Me too.'

Robin stood tall and accepted the compliment.

'Thank you, gentlemen, that means a lot.'

We engaged in small talk, and before we knew it the break was over, and Micky Flanagan was telling the audience that something special was about to happen, and asking them to put their phones away and simply enjoy it like we used to do in the old days.

The next twenty minutes was like being in comedy heaven for me. I saw my comedy hero absolutely destroy the audience, in a tiny room. He ad-libbed about the venue, and London in general, then launched into a routine so tightly packed with laughs I thought the audience was going to asphyxiate.

A few nights later, I saw him do his full-length solo show in a proper theatre, and as great as it was, it couldn't match the up-close-and-personal treatment of meeting the man back-stage, then watching him perform from twenty feet away.

I was devastated when he died, and made sure to pay tribute to him on air. More than anything, I wanted to meet him again and say the phrase, 'Robin, we met in a men's toilet in London.'

*   *   *

Then there was the time Chris Rock turned up at the London Comedy Store.

This time I was the MC, and I had been warned there was a chance he might drop in.

Drop in he did, so I introduced myself.

'How do you want to be announced?' I asked in jest. 'Have you done anything big I can tell the audience about?'

I was kidding of course. One of the finest comedians of his generation, he was fresh from hosting the Academy Awards, and virtually embodied the phrase 'needs no introduction'.

I think he took me seriously. Unless I misread his tone. In what I took to be genuine humility he said, 'I dunno man. Do they get the Oscars here?'

I assured him they'd know who he was and I took to the stage.

'Ladies and gentlemen, we would normally have a break now, but a big international act has just dropped in, and really wants to do a spot. Do you wanna see him?'

They cheered.

'OK. I can't believe I'm about to say this. Your next act has hosted the Oscars.'

People laughed, assuming I was kidding.

'He's written his own TV show called *Everybody Hates Chris*.'

They realised I wasn't kidding.

'He's one of the biggest comedians on the planet.'

They dared to believe me.

'Please welcome to the stage, Chris Rock!'

The audience lost their minds. He received a standing ovation onto the stage. *Onto* the stage! People were high-fiving each other, hugging, and still applauding.

Eventually they returned to their seats, and Chris Rock performed a great set, stopping occasionally to ask one of his friends, 'Which bits should I do next?'

Problem was, there were still three more acts to go on stage, and even though there was an interval about to happen, I knew the rest of the show was in danger of becoming an anti-climax.

When I opened the second half, I told the audience of my concerns. I then suggested it was only fair to give every act a standing ovation as they came on stage, just so they felt as loved as Chris Rock.

The audience were totally on board and rose to their feet as each act came to the stage, as if they too had hosted the Oscars and was the voice of a comedic generation. This was particularly helpful for the second act in the half, who was doing a try-out spot at the Comedy Store, had only been performing comedy for a few months, and was, I think, a baker by day.

Despite this, I gave him the kind of rousing introduction I would give to a megastar.

'Ladies and gentlemen, your next act works by day as a baker! You may have seen his bread rolls in your local shop window! This is only his third ever comedy gig! Please welcome to the stage . . .'

The final act of the night, a Canadian by the name of Craig Campbell, was so good, he received a standing ovation when he left the stage as well.

* * *

As much fun as these celebrity moments were, they pale in comparison to the night I introduced my dad to one of his heroes.

I had been invited to the VIP lounge at the Australian Open tennis, where I also had tickets for the men's semi-finals. I asked Dad if he'd like to come with me, since he was the person who taught me tennis. Oh sure, I had lessons, but Dad played, and played well, and when he wasn't serving Chardonnay to John McEnroe over the Pacific (he did do that by the way, but decided not to ask for an autograph), he would often take my brother and me to the local courts for a hit.

We had dinner in the VIP lounge, during which we were joined by my mate John Fitzgerald. He also happened to be one of the people Dad had persuaded to sign my autograph book some twenty years earlier.

After the meal, I was interviewed on stage about my love of tennis, and it was as I made my way back to the table that it happened.

Rod Laver came over.

The greatest tennis player of all time, the man after whom the stadium we were about to sit in was named.

'I'm afraid I don't know who you are,' he said, as politely as possible, 'but the people at my table would like a photo with you please.'

How could I say no to that?

After posing for selfies, Rod asked what I did for a living. Halfway through my reply, I stopped my own sentence, then said, 'I'm sorry. Do you mind if I introduce you to my dad?'

I knew my dad would love it. He had grown up idolising Rod Laver.

Dad was genuinely excited. Properly chuffed. Over the moon. Smiley as all shit. Laver was the very epitome of the word 'gentleman'. We had such a lovely chat, and I got to ask a few questions I'd always wanted answered:

'I heard that you were once locked at two-sets all in a match, but had to stop play for bad light. Since the next morning was virtually a one-set match, I heard you played a full pro set before the game to warm up?'

'That's true. I was always a slow starter, so I played a proper set against my practice partner to get myself up to speed.'

Is it true you used to down a beer before each match just to steady your nerves?

'No.'

As we walked away, my dad had a grin a mile wide on his face.

'I can't believe I just met Rod Laver,' he said.

It was the first and only time I ever saw my father genuinely starstruck.

We took our seats in the Rod Laver Arena, and watched Rafael Nadal and Fernando Verdasco play the longest-ever singles match in the history of the Australian Open (at that point in time).

During the latter stages of the match, a swarthy Argentinian gentleman took his seat at the end of our row. Dad recognised him as former tennis pro Guillermo Vilas, another of his heroes.

Later I returned from the loo to find Dad beaming like the Cheshire Cat.

'I just met Vilas,' he said.

'How?'

'I just walked over, introduced myself, and told him I always admired the way he played the game.'

It was a side of my father I'd never seen – the awestruck schoolkid.

It was past one a.m. when the match finished, but we stayed until the bitter end. The next morning Dad looked tired. He told me he didn't get to sleep until four, because he was so excited to have met Laver and Vilas.

I've met a lot of cool people thanks to my job, and had so many incredible experiences because of what I do for a living.

But without a shadow of a doubt, not even for a second, the best thing this crazy career has ever allowed me to do, is say the sentence, 'Dad, this is Rod Laver.'

Para-Dise

When I was around twelve years old, my mum asked me if I'd like to attend a trial day for something called the Disabled Games.

I said no.

Mainly because I didn't think I was disabled.

Sure, I'd been born without a right foot – although technically I did have a right foot, it was just shorter than my left, and had two weird toes on it. But as I said very early on in this book, it didn't dis-able me from doing anything, therefore I wasn't disabled.

You may remember the one thing I couldn't do was wear thongs, but as far as I know there isn't a Paralympic event for that, regardless of which country's definition of thong you use.

It didn't seem fair to me that someone missing an entire leg would have to run against me, who was about ninety-five per cent still there. I had no idea there were such things as Paralympic categories, and that if I did compete, it would be against people with a similar bit missing.

It never occurred to me that somewhere in the world there might be a kid with the same length leg as me. The only disabled people I'd ever seen were the old blokes at the clinic where I had my prosthetic made. And none of them looked the faintest bit sporty. Had there been a Jonnie Peacock or an Invictus Warrior in sight, I might have foreseen a different future for myself.

Plus, I was never really into running for the sake of it. I'd happily chase after a tennis ball or a rugby league ball all day long. But athletics was never my bag.

I told my mum that if I ever competed, it would be against able-bodied people, and that was that. I mean, I was playing competitive tennis on a weekend, and winning a few matches. If I was gonna win Wimbledon, it would be against Ivan Lendl.

Truth is, I also didn't like the word disabled, I didn't consider myself to be disabled, and I didn't want to be categorised as disabled. I wanted to be like every other normal kid.

Let them have their disabled games, I'll compete against the 'normal' people.

If only I'd known.

Sixteen years later I received a call from my agent, asking if I'd be interested in presenting the opening and closing ceremonies of the 2008 Beijing Paralympic Games for the ABC in Australia.

By this stage, I'd become more aware of the Paras after the 2000 Sydney Games. It was the first time that the Olympics and Paralympics had been staged by the same organisers, and for the first time, the Paralympians were treated like equals.

I'd heard stories that in Atlanta four years prior, some athletes had to sleep on bare floors, with no bedding, and that timing equipment had been removed from some events before they even started.

The great bit about the Beijing offer was that I'd have ten days off between the opening and closing ceremonies to explore China. I had visions of a boat trip up the Yangtze, maybe take in a few Taoist temples.

Ha!

I spent every minute of every day at the Games.

It all began for me at a briefing for all ABC staff. The person speaking was the Chef de Mission for the Australian Paralympic Team, a man by the name of Jason Hellwig. Everything I learned about covering Paralympic sport came from him, and most of it from that briefing.

'The first thing you need to know,' he started, 'is that this is elite sport. Paralympians are elite athletes. They don't want sympathy, they're not brave, and they're not here to inspire anyone. They're here because they are the best in the world at their chosen sport, and that's how they want you to see them. So all I ask is that you treat them like you would treat any other elite athlete. Cos they've worked bloody hard to be here.'

It was such a brilliant thing to be told. Every Australian presenter went into those Games with exactly the right attitude, although truth be told, a lot of them had covered the Paras before.

The next ten days were to be the most influential of my life, not that I was to know it. If I had to pick a moment that summed up my Paralympic experience personally, it was walking through the athletes' village on the first day, and passing a young female Paralympian with a below-knee prosthetic on her right leg.

It was the first time I'd ever seen someone younger than me with a similar prosthetic, and I wanted to approach her and say, 'Hey, we're missing the same bits.'

I'm serious. It was that much of a novelty.

Actually, now that I think of it, I had already met someone younger than me with a similar prosthetic. She was about seven years old, and I spotted her hiding from her parents in a video store.

(Anyone under the age of twenty may want to Google the words 'video store' at this point.)

I was in my twenties, and was struck by this cheeky little girl, crouching behind the New Releases, with a prosthetic right foot.

I can't remember who spoke to whom first, but I had a great old chat to her and her mum. After I left, I kicked myself for not exchanging numbers. In the days before mobile phones, it felt a little weird to meet someone in a video store, then ask for their home number so you could keep in touch with their seven-year-old daughter.

It turned out we went to the same prosthetic clinic, though, so whenever I was there, I'd ask about my little mate. The staff would tell me tales of how she lit up the room whenever she entered, and that they always looked forward to her visits. I asked them to pass on my best wishes and they promised they would.

Then one year I arrived for my appointment, to be met by some sombre news. My little mate had originally lost her leg because of a tumour, and since I had last been in to the clinic, the cancer had spread.

She didn't make it.

The first young person I meet with a leg like mine, and she didn't even make it past the age of ten.

Maybe that's why the Paralympian surprised me so much. A healthy, active woman in her twenties, competing at a world class event – and she had the same kind of foot as me.

I didn't approach her, because as I looked around me at the different shapes and sizes walking, rolling, and being led past me, I realised that for the first time in my life – I wasn't different.

It wasn't such a big deal to meet someone with a below-knee amputation in a Paralympic Village. They were every-where! Not only had I found my people, until now I didn't even know my people existed.

A similar thing had happened the day before when I entered the Bird's Nest Stadium. In an incident that has now become part of my act, my prosthetic set off the metal detec-tor. Knowing how much consternation that usually caused in airports, I did my best to explain to the Chinese security guard that it was a prosthetic leg, but he just waved me through.

When I offered to lift my jeans to show him, he spoke in carefully considered English: 'It's OK. Thank you for your cooperation. Welcome to Beijing. You may go through.'

As I walked through unimpeded I wondered why it was so easy. Then I realised.

I'm at the Paralympics. There's a queue of amputees behind me thinking, 'You're not special, princess.'

And I wasn't! I was just another average below-knee amputee.

In fact, I learned there's even a term for people like me, who have birth abnormalities – 'Les Autres' (The Others). I decided that if I ever get famous enough that I need to check into a hotel under a pseudonym, I would call myself Les Autres.

Professionally though, it was the swimming that really opened my eyes. Fit, young athletes, stripping down to their swimmers, removing their legs, placing them alongside their sports bags, then hopping to the pool.

And not just people missing legs – there were people with one arm, no arms, no legs. Dwarves, blind people, those with cerebral palsy. People that hobbled to the pool then swam like dolphins.

As a child, whenever I swam, I was painfully aware of the looks I'd get as I made my way to the water. It didn't hurt me, or offend me, or even annoy me, but I was aware of it. I used to joke that I'd love to walk out of the surf one day hopping on my one good leg, with tomato sauce covering my right stump, just to see people's reactions.

But here. This was a place I could have quite easily ripped off the leg, and waddled over to the pool, without anyone giving a second glance.

To paraphrase a clickbait video, however, 'what happened next amazed me.'

The same people I'd been watching, marvelling at, and comparing myself to, then hopped into a swimming pool and, to use a technical term, swam like the clappers. Once again, it was the first time I'd seen people who looked like me do anything sporty. And not just a bit sporty, properly elitey sporty.

I loved it.

I think I may have spent the entire day in the Swimming Cube, watching Australia's Matt Cowdrey, America's Jessica Long, and a young Ellie Simmonds representing Great Britain.

I learned the categories – S1 to S10 were physically disabled, S11 to S13 were blind or visually impaired, and S14 was for those with an intellectual disability.

I watched a man with no arms swim the fastest fifty metres I'd ever seen swum, and a man with no arms or legs bring the crowd to their feet when he completed his race well after his competitors had finished.

Until that moment, I don't think I really 'got' the Paralympics.

It's something you can't explain to another person, you have to see it for yourself. And once you've witnessed it, you're in a secret club, with a knowledge no one else has.

The next day I visited the wheelchair basketball, and once again my mind was blown. It was a women's game first up, and I was immediately struck by both the speed and the fluidity of the game.

I was also shocked when a member of the Aussie team (known as the Gliders) was knocked out of her chair. It was a heavy collision, and the crowd gasped as her wheelchair tilted, then tipped completely.

I don't know the Chinese for 'you poor fragile thing', but I reckon it was uttered hundreds of times around the stadium. I certainly thought it.

In an instant, though, the 'poor fragile thing' was back in the chair, and with the help of a team-mate, back on her wheels. No injury, no stoppage time, not even a wince – only a glare of determination to get back into the game.

That was the moment that I stopped seeing the disabilities. Until then I was watching disabled people who were also elite athletes. After that, I was watching sport.

I spent the rest of the match with an eye on the scoreboard and an eye on the game, all the while on the edge of my seat. More wheelchairs tipped, and each time the tippee was back into the game within seconds.

The Gliders won, and I went to every game they played over the next ten days.

I also went to every sport I could. More swimming, wheelchair rugby, cycling and athletics, where I witnessed Oscar Pistorius win the one hundred metres in a race that remains one of the best sporting moments I've ever seen.

I got to know some of the Aussie Paralympians, and even performed a gig for them in the athletes' village.

Aside from the sporting events, what impressed me was the effect that the Games had on the people of China. Before the Games, China was not known for its brilliant treatment of disabled people. But if you want to host the Olympics, you also have to prove you are willing to do a good job of the Paralympics, and you can start by making your city accessible.

Which is tough in a city as ancient as Beijing. But they did it. For the first time in its history, the Great Wall of China became accessible to wheelchair users. As did all the city's major tourist attractions.

On my final day I took a trip to the Forbidden City and noticed an elderly gentleman being pushed around in a wheelchair. He may have spent his entire life unable to get a glimpse inside this iconic Chinese palace, if not for the Paralympics.

Oh sure, there were a few mistakes.

Like the disabled toilets I saw that had signs on them saying: 'Special, for the deformed'. Or the unfortunate choice of music to fire up the crowds at the cycling – the Black Eyed Peas song, 'Let's Get Retarded'. Or even the ultra-politeness of the Chinese people generally, which led them to want to push every wheelchair user they came across, unaware that people in wheelchairs hate being pushed against their will.

I came to realise that the Paralympics enlightens the world to the realities of disability, one country at a time.

As I sat in the Bird's Nest Stadium, for the closing ceremony, I reflected on the life-affirming event of which I had just been a part. Thousands of man-made 'cherry blossom leaves' fell from the roof of the stadium, in an artistic display representing the changes of the seasons.

In a lovely touch, everyone entering the stadium that night had been given a postcard and a pencil, and requested to write a message to a loved one on the card. We were then told to place those cards in special post boxes on the way out of the stadium, and they would be duly sent.

I thought of my mum, and the seemingly endless hours spent in clinics and waiting rooms, doing crosswords, or noughts and crosses, while we waited for a cast to be made of my stump, or a niggle to be repaired.

I reflected on what it must have been like for her to have her baby taken away from her immediately after it was born, as a group of physicians gathered around and debated whether to amputate his leg.

I remembered her telling me that she sometimes wondered if my birth deformity might have been caused by her lifting boxes when she was pregnant, as she and my dad moved into their new family home.

I was having one of the most uplifting experiences of my life, and all because I'd been born with one foot. It didn't matter how I ended up here, what mattered was that I'd made it.

I addressed the card to my parents and wrote, 'Thank you for whatever you did that led to me being here.'

I recently reminded my Mum of the card and the message on it, and explained what I meant by it, in case it wasn't clear. She replied that since it was addressed to both her and Dad, she thought I was referring to something way more intimate.

P.S. (Paralympic Sights)

Later that night, at the 'End of Games' party for the Australian team, I marvelled at the sights before me. With the pressure of competition off, and the introduction of alcohol for the first time in months for some, it was like a nightclub for disabled people.

A blind guy was chatting up a girl in a wheelchair; someone with CP was dancing with a guy with one arm; a dwarf was getting cosy with a leg amputee. One team official sidled up to me, surveyed the room and said, 'Mate, can you imagine the new categories that are gonna be born out of tonight?'

See, that's the other thing you need to know about Paralympians – they make the most offensive disabled jokes ever.

Over the course of the Games, I heard some of the wrongest jokes of my life. One official described their state of drunkenness as S13 and a half. When I asked what that was, they replied, 'Halfway between blind and intellectually impaired.'

I was still recovering from the joke about the categories when one of the team coaches wandered over.

'I hear you play tennis,' he began.

I confirmed that I did play competitively and used to be a coach.

'Wanna play wheelchair tennis?'

I was kinda confused, mainly because I didn't need a wheelchair.

'That's alright,' he replied, 'you don't have to. As long as your disability is considered restrictive enough, we can just put you in one.'

My eyes lit up, but I was also conflicted.

I'd feel bad about playing in a wheelchair, but at the same time I loved the idea of being a part of all that I had just seen. The next Games were four years away in London. Maybe I could actually represent Australia.

By the end of the party, word had passed around that I was considering competing in 2012. Once again the Chef de Mission, Jason Hellwig, stepped in. He'd seen that look in my eyes before.

'How about we talk about this when we're back in Australia, and the excitement of the Paralympics has worn off,' he said. 'A lot of people decide they're gonna compete on the last night of the Games.'

On the flight from Beijing to London, I grabbed my notebook. I wasn't sure why, but I wanted to document what I had seen.

I took pages of notes. I wrote of the wheelchair athlete I overheard telling a friend she couldn't understand why there's braille on the buttons in the elevators, because 'how do blind people know where the buttons are'. Her friend replied that they like to mess with blind people by gluing poppy seeds on the buttons.

I transcribed jokes I had thought of, but knew I could never make on TV, like at the opening ceremony: 'If you think you recognise the Chinese athlete without any arms, he's the drummer that screwed up in the opening of the Olympics.'

I remembered the Chinese swimmer with no arms, who was just beaten to gold by a guy with half an arm. I thought of the punchline that had been offered to me by a colleague: 'How often in life does a guy with half an arm get to think, well, that was handy?'

The night after I returned from Beijing, I was booked to perform a twenty-minute spot at a club in Chiswick.

'I've just got back from the Paralympic Games in Beijing,' I told the audience, 'and I have to tell you what I saw.'

Thus began a new bit of my stand-up act, about the life-affirming joy that is the Paralympic Games.

When I finally got back to Australia a few months later, I had lunch with Jason Hellwig to talk about my wheelchair tennis aspirations.

'Before you make a decision,' he warned, 'let me tell you what you're in for. Normally we have to teach a wheelchair user to play tennis. You know how to play, so we need to teach you how to use a wheelchair. It has to become second nature. So you're gonna have to use a chair for at least thirty hours a week. At work, at home, out and about. You need to use a wheelchair more than you walk.'

He saw the look in my eyes again, but this time it was a different look. A look of hesitation.

I couldn't spend the next four years in a wheelchair. I was writing and hosting a TV show, while also doing stand-up comedy. Plus there was the time I'd need to spend training, travelling, competing in international events.

Before I could answer, he intervened.

'Listen,' he said, with a reassuring hand on my shoulder, 'the best thing you can do for the Paralympic movement right now, is tell people about it.'

But how? London 2012 was still four years away.

Would the ABC ask me to cover it again? Would the experience match that of Beijing?

And who am I supposed to tell about this anyway?

If only I'd known.

Happy and Glorious

'What's the purpose of your visit?' asked the immigrations officer at Heathrow Airport.

'I'm performing for the Queen,' I said proudly, handing over my official letter of invitation to the Royal Variety Performance, with the gold-embossed letterhead, saying, 'Her Majesty ER II'.

'Go on then,' he sighed, with the hint of a smile.

A week later I was standing on a Blackpool stage, shaking hands with a middle-aged stage manager, bowing and saying, 'Your Majesty.'

Because you don't just meet the Queen. You have to rehearse how to meet the Queen. Which means you and everyone else on the bill line up in an enormous semi-circle on stage, in the middle of the afternoon, and you pretend to meet the Queen.

There are rules: Don't speak until spoken to. Bow deeply. Refer to Her Majesty as 'Your Majesty' the first time you address her, then as 'Ma'am' every time afterwards. Remember, it's pronounced 'Ma'am as in Ham, not Ma'am as in Smarm'.

It's weird to do all that to a male stage manager wearing a T-shirt, jeans, and a headset. Mind you, it would be stranger if they made you do it to a Queen lookalike.

Adding to the bizarreness of the scene is that you are surrounded by some of the most famous people in the entertainment industry, all in their everyday clothes, some without make-up, and not one of them is acting like a star.

Because we're all a little in awe of Her Majesty. Even the bloke pretending to be Her Majesty has somehow inherited some of her majesty.

A quick scan of the stage revealed Whoopi Goldberg, Anastacia, Twiggy, Miley Cyrus (before she started licking sledgehammers and swinging naked on wrecking balls), the dance group Diversity, Lady Gaga, me, Bette Midler, and the host of the show, Peter Kay.

We lined up in the order we were due to perform, and since I was due to go on after Lady Gaga, I was now standing next to her.

'G'day,' I said, 'I'm Adam.'

'Oh, hi,' she said. 'I'm Gaga.'

Well, of course you are.

I decided to chat to Gaga for two reasons – one, she's a person and I'm a person, so why not have a chat? And two, she was the one performer that no one else was talking to. Maybe they were all too scared – she did have an aura about her.

I didn't want her to go through the day without chatting to anyone, so I told her how much I liked her new music video, which at that stage was 'Bad Romance'. She thanked me, we chatted about the song, and even a little about her family. I think her dad may have flown in for the show.

It was brief, but she was lovely.

One day I hope to meet her again, purely so I can say, 'I stood next to you when you met the Queen.'

After rehearsing how to meet the Queen, we rehearsed our performances, which again is a strange one, because it's to a mainly empty theatre. Only the other performers watch, and even then not all of them.

That's alright for a singer, but for a comedian, it's horror. Normally they tell the comics to do their opening and closing line, but in this case they made us do our entire routines, word for word, to forty people in a three-thousand-seat theatre.

The real eye opener was Lady Gaga, who was supposed to be singing alone while playing piano.

However, once she found out there was a full orchestra there, she set about transcribing the music for them, so they could play with her. It took her a while, but she was determined that it would sound better. A few rehearsals later, and she was proven right.

I hung out in the dressing room with the other comedians on the bill – Hal Cruttenden, Paul Zerdin and Bob Golding, who had played Eric Morecambe in a one-man play at the Edinburgh Fringe, and was reprising Eric's classic Royal Variety routine tonight – and shared a lovely dinner chat with comedy legend and *Catchphrase* host Roy Walker.

Roy was booked to keep the audience entertained in between the acts, and I'll say this for him – he got a lot more laughs than I did. They absolutely loved him, and I felt bad that he wasn't to be on the televised show.

The time came for the show, and we all gathered in the green room to watch it on the TV. Except that it wasn't a traditional green room, it was a ballroom. The ballroom of the Blackpool Opera House.

Everyone who was far enough away from their performance time that they could relax, was gathered in front of one massive television, and there in her tracksuit bottoms and UGG boots was Bette Midler.

No airs or graces had Bette, she was just one of the cast, and she chatted to anyone and everyone.

The person I most wanted to meet was Whoopi Goldberg. I mean, she was the Queen of Comedy. *Sister Act*, *Jumping Jack Flash*, *Ghost*, *The Color Purple* . . . so many great movie roles, plus she hosted years of Comic Relief shows in the US with Billy Crystal and Robin Williams.

Those albums were my entrée to a lot of contemporary American stand-up, well before the days of YouTube and Netflix specials, and it's where I first heard routines by Jerry Seinfeld and Paul Reiser, before they had their own sitcoms.

So when I heard her voice behind me say, 'Excuse me, is anyone using this chair?' my heart skipped a beat. Realising she was talking to me, I offered her the chair, and she sat next to me.

No more was said until Whoopi left to do her bit, which was to say a few words, then introduce the cast of *Sister Act*, the musical about to take to the West End.

'Have a great one,' I offered, as if she was doing five minutes of new material at the King's Head in Crouch End.

'Thanks,' she smiled, and we all gathered around the TV to watch her set. It wasn't really a set as such, more a brief chat to introduce a number from the musical, but still very funny.

When Whoopi returned, I complimented her on her bit, and like almost every comedian I've ever met, she said she didn't think it was all that good. We went back and forth as I persuaded her that it was great, and that she set up the musical number perfectly, and she reluctantly took my point.

Eventually my name was called, and as I made my way to the stage, Whoopi instructed me to 'Kick ass, baby!'. I watched from the wings as Lady Gaga played a piano while suspended from the ceiling. She was dressed in an Elizabethan outfit (because she was performing for Queen Elizabeth II) and even quoted John Lennon from when the Beatles played the Royal Variety.

I looked down at my unpolished shoes, and thought I could probably have made more of an effort. Bobby Chariot would have been appalled.

Gaga finished, Roy Walker kept the audience entertained while the piano was removed, then Peter Kay introduced me by saying, 'He just landed this morning.' (Not entirely true.)

I strode on stage and opened with a joke that the producers had asked me to do. For some reason they thought it would be funny to reference that I was going home for Christmas in Australia.

I asked why, to which they replied, 'Because it'll be summer there, won't it?'

'Yes,' I admitted.

'Hilarious!' they guffawed.

'Good evening, ladies and gentlemen, my name's Adam Hills. I'm flying back to Australia tomorrow, so I can have a *real* Christmas. You know, where you get Santa and a suntan.'

It. Got. Nuthin.

Not a sausage.

Nada.

Zilch.

Thankfully my second joke got a laugh, and the routine built from there. I ended on a high, but it certainly didn't feel like one of my best gigs. I returned to the green room and was casually watching the rest of the show, when Whoopi came back in, and straight up to me.

She opened with, 'Has anyone told you, you killed yet?'

'No, not yet,' I said.

She looked me straight in the eyes and said, 'You killed.'

'I'm not so sure . . .' I began, but she did to me what I did to her only an hour earlier.

'Your set was like one of those Japanese lotus flowers that started small, then opened up beautifully so that at the end of the set, it was in full bloom. It was perfect.'

OK, she did it to me with a lot more eloquence and grace, but she managed to convince me that I had a good set.

Eventually we were all ushered back to the stage for the most important part of the show – meeting Her Majesty – but not before Whoopi turned to me and said, 'How's your memory?'

'Pretty good.'

'OK,' she replied. 'I'm gonna tell you my email address and I want you to stay in touch.'

I promised I would, then we hugged, and went off to meet the Queen of England.

A few minutes later we were on stage, in the familiar semi-circle from rehearsal, but this time it was real. Gradually Her Majesty made her way around the stage, from Whoopi to Miley to Twiggy to Diversity, and eventually Gaga.

All eyes were on the two of them, and indeed the enduring image of the night, the one that made all the papers the next day, was of Her Majesty the Queen meeting Lady Gaga. And there, just to Gaga's left, was me, desperately using my left suit-sleeve to mop up the sweat from my right palm.

The time came and I finally met the Queen. I waited for her to extend her hand, shook it, bowed, and smiled.

Then she looked away! Just blanked me.

Was I that bad? Did my Christmas joke die that hard she didn't want to talk to me?

I found out later that this is what the Queen does. She meets people, then looks ahead to see who the next person is, presumably to think of something to say to them.

While she's talking to you, she's thinking of what to say to them. Then when she meets them, she looks ahead to the next person, and so on and so forth.

Her Majesty turned back to me and offered either the weakest compliment I've ever received, or the best diss: 'The audience were very helpful, weren't they?'

I think what she meant was, 'You were shit, but we got you through it.'

I stumbled for a reply, and for some reason said, 'Yes, I think when one makes the effort to travel so far from London, the audience often appreciate the effort one has gone to.'

Why did I say 'one'?

Twice?

Something in my brain clearly thought, 'Better talk posh, mate, you're yakkin' with the Queen.'

Her Majesty looked a little bemused by my answer, probably wondering why the Australian sounded so weird, and seemed about to move on when she stopped and asked, 'Did you really fly here this morning?'

'No, Your Majesty,' I admitted. 'I have actually been here for a week. But I am flying home first thing tomorrow morning.'

'Ah yes,' she replied with a royal twinkle in her eye, 'so you can have a *real* Christmas.'

Then the Queen of England smiled at me and walked away. I mean she may as well have dropped the mic.

I stood there, taking in one of the most bizarre moments of my life. I met the Queen and she made a joke about my act. Can life get any weirder?

Then Prince Philip appeared.

The Queen's husband, the Duke of Edinburgh, and the holder of about fifteen other titles, Prince Philip had become known for his wildly inappropriate comments at moments like this.

For instance, I'd heard that the Queen and Duke had once met a military veteran, who had lost most of his eyesight while defusing a bomb. Proudly wearing the colourful tie of the regiment, he was presented to Her Majesty, who asked, 'How much eyesight do you have?'

To which the Duke piped up, 'Not much by the look of that tie.'

I had forgotten he was coming, but remembered at least to call him Your Highness. He shook my hand, looked down towards my unpolished shoes, and chuckled.

Damn, I thought, I knew I should have polished those shoes. I'm an idiot. Oh well, strap in, here it comes.

But it wasn't the state of my shoes that tickled the Prince's fancy.

'You fly home tomorrow, do you?' he enquired with a grin.

'Yes, Your Highness.'

The Duke leant in conspiratorially, then said, 'You could smuggle something out of the country in that leg of yours.'

I laughed embarrassingly loudly, after which he added, 'Put a bottle of gin down there, eh?'

A few days later, that conversation appeared in the papers, with the headline 'Comedian Offended by Disabled Joke', but I can tell you nothing could be further from the truth.

It was a well-needed tension breaker after the high-pressure stakes of meeting the Queen. In fact, I'd go so far as to add that may be why the Duke says what he does. He knows how weird it must be for people to meet Her Majesty, so he brings them back to earth with a laugh.

Who knows? What I do know is that in one day I met the Queen of England, became friends with Whoopi Goldberg, chatted to Lady Gaga, and Prince Philip made a joke about my prosthetic foot.

As The Queen and Prince Philip shook the final hand, that of the host Peter Kay, and left the stage, the audience who had sat through the entire meet and greet, applauded politely.

Lady Gaga leant in to me and said softly, 'The audience don't stand for the Queen? That is one tough motherfuckin crowd.'

Emailin' Whoopi

Whoopi Goldberg and I emailed each other every day for the first month after the Royal Variety Performance.

It was as though we started a conversation on the night that was interrupted by the Queen of England, and now we were going to continue it, despite being on opposite sides of the planet.

She sent me photos of her Christmas decorations, I sent her shots of friends' children that I'd been playing with – like two mates who'd known each other for years.

Once she emailed me in a panic, because her tour bus had broken down, and she was going to have to take a plane to her next gig – and Whoopi hates flying.

'Pray for me,' she wrote, to which I responded, 'You just opened *Sister Act* in the West End. I'm pretty sure God owes you one.'

'That really made me laugh,' came the reply. There aren't many feelings in the world that can compete with knowing you just made Whoopi Goldberg laugh.

Over time the emails dwindled, but when my first daughter was born, a beautiful package arrived of bibs, washers, and toys that we still have today.

Every now and again we'd stay in touch – Whoopi did a Skype interview on my Aussie chat show, and I sent her a link to my rant about the Westboro Baptist Church's threat to picket Robin Williams' funeral.

'Tell your wife it's OK for me to say this, but I couldn't love you more,' was her response.

Seven years went by without Whoopi and I seeing each other, until one year at the Montreal comedy festival, I noticed she was judging a comedy show called 'Roast Battle'. I dropped her an email, asking if there was a chance we might cross paths, and got an immediate response: 'I will find you.'

That night I arrived at the venue where I was doing my solo show, to find a somewhat shaken venue manager.

'Um,' he began, unsure of whether to believe what was coming next. 'I think Whoopi Goldberg is coming to your show tonight.'

'Yeah, she said she'd find me,' I said.

It's worth knowing that in Montreal, I don't perform in the same size theatres as the UK or Australia.

I was in an out-of-the-way little studio theatre that held around 130 people at the most. It was a twenty-minute walk from the centre of the city, down a back alley, and yet tonight, someone had called ahead to set aside three seats for Whoopi and her managers.

Come showtime, though, and there was no sign of Whoopi. No worries, I figured she got caught up somewhere and couldn't make it. I started the show, but before long there were latecomers.

I looked up hopefully, but still no Whoopi.

The way the venue was set up, they had virtually to walk across the stage to get to their seats. Which may be why one of the latecomers did a jaunty little step to style it out.

Which is why I decided to make every latecomer style it out.

A few more came, and a few more (turns out traffic was rough) and each time I explained that a previous latecomer had styled out their entrances, so now everyone has to. It was then that I noticed a familiar figure off to the right of the seating bank, unseen by the audience.

'And here's another latecomer. What's your name, Madam?' I asked.

'Caryn,' she replied truthfully, since that is Whoopi's given name.

'Well, Caryn, everyone who came late has styled it out on the way to their seats, so I'd like you to do the same, please.'

'OK.'

Whoopi and her managers then walked across the stage, past the first few seats, and up the aisle to the back row.

I'm not sure what the world record is for the largest synchronised double-take in history, but I reckon we came close, as one hundred and twenty-odd people looked up, applauded the stylish lady walking in late, then looked back to me, then looked confused, then looked up at the lady again, then back to me with faces that said, 'Sorry, was that just who we thought it was?'

There was now a weird unanswered question in the room, so I let everyone know that yes, Whoopi Goldberg had just arrived.

Then there was another unspoken question, so I told the audience about the time Whoopi and I met at the Royal Variety Performance.

I then did my show, trying desperately not to do the whole thing to Whoopi. People think you can't see anyone in the crowd when you're on stage, but occasionally one face stands out, and it's impossible not to check in with them during the show to make sure they're still laughing.

Show over, and it was hugs all round as Whoopi and I finally saw each other for the first time in seven years. She saved an extra huge hug for Craig Coombes, a cancer survivor who was a major part of my show that year.

'What are you doing later?' asked Whoopi.

I told her that was my last gig for the night.

'Come backstage at the Roast and hang out with me.'

So I did. Although I still wasn't sure where our friendship was at. Was I thinking we were better friends than we actually are, because she's famous? Should I go backstage? Am I over-thinking this?

I turned up to the Roast Battle, and Whoopi spotted me across the room, waved me over, and cleared a space next to her on the couch.

I could see other comedians, friends of mine, looking on in shock as I was invited to an audience with Her Majesty of Comedy.

For the next hour or so, we chatted like two old friends that had grown up together. And about the most normal things – how we've both started wearing reading glasses, how we celebrated our birthdays, what plans we had for the rest of the year.

'I gotta go do the show,' Whoopi said eventually. 'But be here when I get back.'

The show was great, and I was chatting to Whoopi's manager afterwards, when a relatively official-looking stage manager approached us.

'Is there an Adam here?'

I replied that I was called Adam.

'OK. I just tried to put Whoopi Goldberg in a car to go back to her hotel, and she said, "I'm not going anywhere without Adam." Can you come with me, please, sir?'

He led me to the stage door, where Whoopi exclaimed, 'Let's go eat!'

We exited the stage door, and for the first time I realised how ridiculously famous my friend Whoopi is. Until then I'd only ever seen her backstage in theatres – this was the first time I'd seen her in public. And the public love her!

We literally couldn't get to her car, such was the throng of people outside the venue. All wanting autographs, photographs, a hug, anything. It would have taken an hour at least to keep everyone happy, and although Whoopi did stop for a few people, the decision was made to go back inside for a while.

For the rest of the night, I was Whoopi's wingman, as she introduced me to all and sundry with the phrase, 'This is my friend Adam. We performed for the Queen of England together.'

At one point, she said to Louis CK, 'Have you met Adam Hills?' to which Louis took me in and exclaimed, 'Yeah, we played football in Kilkenny! Your fuckin' leg nearly came off.'

Eventually it was time to say goodbye, and once again we hugged and promised to keep in touch.

And we have. I now consider Whoopi to be a wonderful, lovely, fabulous friend, and every time we get together, it's like we've been buddies since birth.

The Two Men I Admire The Most

Two of the most influential people on my career in the last few years have been Kermit the Frog and His Holiness the Dalai Lama. One of them is a born entertainer with the heart of a child and a wise head on his shoulders. And so is the frog.

I met them both within the space of fourteen months.

Some of what happened made it into my stage show *Happyism*, but not all of it.

His Holiness the Dalai Lama was doing a tour of Australia, and had been booked to give a speech at the Burswood Dome in the morning.

My guess is, they had the venue for the whole day, and rather than leave it empty in the afternoon, they decided to throw a concert for His Holiness. Although I can't imagine any of the bands they booked were on his playlist.

Tim Rogers (of You Am I), the Baby Animals, Tex Perkins and the Dark Horses, Katie Noonan and Luka Bloom. There was also a band made up of lookalikes of Nobel Prize winners – Einstein, Mother Teresa, Gandhi, as well as a lookalike of the Dalai Lama.

It was a strange line-up, and I was asked to host the whole thing.

Years before, I had watched with good-natured envy as my friend Wil Anderson had hosted a youth forum with His

Holiness in Sydney. I even gave Wil a joke with which to introduce HHDL: 'Please welcome to the stage, with the sound of one hand clapping, His Holiness the Dalai Lama.'

This time we were ushered together in the green room before the show for a private audience with His Holiness, although I don't think the Nobel Band were in attendance. It might have been too much for the leader of Tibetan Buddhism to be confronted by an Einstein, Gandhi, Mother Teresa, and himself. I'm pretty sure he wasn't expecting to be reincarnated within his own lifetime.

His Holiness spoke softly, and calmly, with an almost permanent smile on his face.

'I am a simple Buddhist monk,' he explained. 'I do not listen to music.'

(Someone should have told the organisers.)

'But I will tell you this,' he continued. 'You have a microphone. Use it to say something.'

After a few minutes he took questions, and kept looking to me for some reason. I didn't know what to say. He'd been blowing his nose and snuffling throughout our session, and all I really wanted to know was if he was alright. Could I really ask the Dalai Lama how he was? I wasn't sure of the protocol.

Eventually His Holiness left the room, and I was whisked backstage. My job was to introduce the Dalai Lama onto the stage, invite him to speak, then host the rest of the afternoon's festivities.

I was told what to do, where to stand, and what to say, then stood behind the giant curtain separating the dozens of people backstage from the thousands in front of the stage, and waited.

Then it happened.

His Holiness the Dalai Lama was ushered over to me, and his aide introduced us. He looked me in the eyes, smiled, and shook my hand. A stage assistant placed a headset microphone on him, and we stood in silence. So I asked the question.

'How are you?'

'I'm fine,' he replied nonchalantly, wiping his nose with a tissue.

I explained that I would walk on stage and introduce him, but once his assistant translated it, there was some discussion.

'His Holiness would like to walk out with you, please,' he explained. 'He may need some assistance.'

How does one assist the Dalai Lama? Do you put your arm around him? Offer up an elbow on which to steady himself? Again, I wasn't sure of the protocol.

I needn't have worried.

A stage manager approached us and told us it was time to go on, at which His Holiness the Dalai Lama smiled at me again, then took my hand in both of his, and that's how we walked on stage. Holding hands.

I cannot describe to you the joy I felt walking on stage holding hands with the Dalai Lama. I led him to his seat, then wandered to the lectern, and began. With a joke. That wasn't a joke.

Earlier in the week, His Holiness had appeared on a breakfast TV show, where the host tried to tell him a joke.

It went: 'The Dalai Lama walks into a pizza shop, and says, "Can you make me one with everything?"'

It had to be translated as it was delivered, with His Holiness asking for clarification of the word 'pizza'. His response once the joke was complete?

'It is possible.'

It was an hilarious, cringeworthy moment of car-crash tele-vision, and was replayed constantly in the days following.

So I began, 'Today some of Australia's best musicians are here to play songs for His Holiness the Dalai Lama.'

I then turned to him.

'Your Holiness, I'm not a musician, I am a comedian. But I promise not to tell you a joke.'

There was a pause, as his assistant leant in and translated my words. Then the Dalai Lama laughed out loud. At me not telling a joke.

I think I may have achieved the Zen of Comedy – I made the Dalai Lama laugh by doing nothing.

I introduced His Holiness, who then delivered an address to the audience from where he was seated. Once he was done, I introduced Irish musician Luka Bloom, who played a couple of songs.

As instructed, I made my way to the far side of the stage and remained there as the musicians on the bill were presented with silk scarves by His Holiness. As he came to the end of the presentation, his assistant looked towards me and raised his eyebrows.

My orders were to stay put as His Holiness left the stage, and I obeyed. Again he raised his eyebrows, and I assumed he was asking me what to do next, so I nodded my head in the direction of the wings. Confusion became frustration as he motioned me over, and at last I obliged.

I crossed the stage, to be met by His Holiness, holding out a scarf for me. Overwhelmed, I bowed my head, while he placed the scarf around my neck, then I stood, looked him in the eyes, smiled and said thank you.

His Holiness didn't stay for the show, although I heard as he left the venue he came face to face with the Dalai Lama impersonator. From all reports, His Holiness laughed, and said, 'Is this a mirror?'

I've spoken to other people who have encountered His Holiness and they have described a kind of glow that lasts for days afterwards. A lightness. A sense of joy and compassion.

I felt it, too.

*   *   *

It's not quite the same feeling I got after meeting Kermit the Frog, but it's not far off.

Twelve months after hosting 'Songs for the Dalai Lama', I was invited once again to the Just for Laughs festival in Montreal, where I was due to perform in one of their Comedy Galas.

A quick perusal of the website (hahaha.com) told me that one of those Galas would be hosted by the Muppets.

Oh my Frog.

Do I need to tell you how much I loved the Muppets as a kid? They were my, and everybody else's, favourites. We owned *The Muppet Show Album*, watched *The Muppet Movie*, and my dad did a pretty mean impression of Animal the drummer. I didn't do a bad version of the Swedish Chef either.

In fact, I now had a five-minute stand-up routine about the Swedish Chef. If only there was some way of ensuring I was on the Muppet Gala. I couldn't simply ring the organisers and ask them, mainly because that's what everyone else would be doing.

I had to find a way.

As often happens with the Just for Laughs festival, I was asked to submit in writing the routine I wanted to perform at the Gala. As I was mulling over what material would be suitable for the Muppets, I thought, hang on, why don't I submit the bit about the Swedish Chef? Maybe the bookers will see it, and say, 'Hey, that guy should be on the Muppet Gala.'

That's exactly what happened.

But there was a hitch.

My spot was seven minutes, so I had thrown in a couple of jokes from my current stand-up show to fill the other two minutes, and one of those jokes was considered inappropriate for the Muppets.

The bookers asked if I'd be willing to drop the joke.

I said I'd have to think about it.

I realise now how ridiculous that sounds. That I wouldn't ditch one joke in order to appear on stage with the Muppets.

For some reason, I thought it was an important joke that made a salient social point about the blah, blah, blah, blah of the state of the world in which we yada, yada, yada as we all face this eternal – oh my God, sometimes comedians can be so full of themselves.

I genuinely considered pulling out of the show, rather than dropping one joke.

What a dick.

At breakfast the next morning, I told my predicament to Aussie comedian Brendon Burns, a man known for his uncompromising comedy, and dedication to saying it like it is.

He mulled it over.

'If you do the show, will you get to high five Kermit?' he asked, thoughtfully.

'Probably,' I replied.

'Then touch the frog, you idiot!' he shouted.

'I'm sorry?'

'It's just a fucken joke, you can do it any time. Touch the frog, dickhead.'

Still unconvinced, I tweeted my quandary.

'I've just been asked to remove a joke from my set in order to work with the Muppets. What should I do?'

Every comedian I know replied that I should drop the joke. The final answer came from Dara O'Briain. It said: 'Yes. Comedy is Truth, but it's also a way of meeting Kermit the Fucking Frog.'

That sold it. I'd drop the joke and touch the frog.

I'm so glad I did.

There were two shows that night, both hosted by the Muppets, but with different comedians. When I arrived at the stage door, I could hear the first show coming to an end, as the Muppets sang 'The Rainbow Connection'. I couldn't believe I nearly passed this opportunity up.

I was told that I would be going on stage directly after the Swedish Chef, and that Kermit would be introducing me.

Seriously, how on earth did I even consider pulling out of this show?

An hour or so later, I stood in the wings as the Swedish Chef prepared a dish of Montreal's finest poutine (hot chips, gravy and cheese curds). As is always the way with the Swedish Chef, he threw his wooden spoons over his shoulder, and I noticed that one of them landed about five feet in front of me.

He finished his bit, left the stage, and Kermit began his introduction while a stage hand swept up the left-over props.

The wooden spoon was missed, however, and lay directly between me and the microphone.

'This next act has come all the way from Down Under to Montreal,' the frog said. 'Or as he likes to call it, Up Over. Please welcome, Adam Hills, yayyyyyyyy.'

I walked out from the curtain, picked up the spoon, carried it to the microphone, and placed it purposefully in my jacket pocket.

The rest of my act is on YouTube, and I won't bore you with it here, but I started by saying how cool it was that Kermit had said my name. I was proud to have written a line just for the occasion: 'You know the difference between the Kardashians and the Muppets? The Muppets are real.'

I happily skipped over the joke I'd been asked to drop, and launched straight into my bit about the Swedish Chef.

I finished my set, thanked the audience, and tried to leave the stage, but couldn't. Someone was in my way. Someone in a white cooking apron and a chef's hat.

The Swedish Chef had come out on stage and was standing in front of me.

I went in for the hug, but he stopped me, leant into my jacket pocket, pulled out the spoon, then hit me with it. I hung my head in shame.

The Chef then looked at the spoon, said, 'OK,' and gave it to me, then left the stage.

It was one of the best moments of my life.

I followed the Chef off-stage, and immediately hugged him. Kermit called me back out for a bow, which I took, but before heading off-stage, I ran over to Kermit and held out my hand for a high five. He obliged.

I touched the frog.

When I returned to the wings, I was met by a collection of people in black shirts and trousers, standing and applauding me. It took me a good thirty seconds to realise they weren't a bunch of well-dressed stage hands, but were in fact the people that handled the Muppets.

One of them, a lovely guy called Dave, asked, 'Did you improvise that whole set?'

I felt bad when I admitted that I hadn't, and that the routine had been part of my stand-up for years.

He was even more amazed.

'You have a five-minute routine about the Swedish Chef?'

We all hugged, the Chef signed the spoon for me, and the show carried on.

As the show ended, and we all joined the Muppets on stage to sing 'The Rainbow Connection', I gazed in wide wonder at the pure joy they had put into the room. No cynicism, no snark, not a trace of arch, just one-hundred-per-cent unmitigated happiness.

I made a note to remember that feeling. To try to replicate it as often as possible.

The Muppets all stayed around for cast and crew photos afterwards, and were incredibly patient with the amount of people asking for selfies.

As we all left the stage, I found myself completely by chance in the wings with Steve Whitmire and Kermit. Steve complimented me on my set and I thanked Kermit for the introduction.

I then asked if there was any way Kermit would mind filming a message on my phone for my daughter, who was two at the time. Steve and Kermit obliged, and happily recorded a cheerio.

As Steve packed up his gear, I watched the video and found that with all the on-stage noise, it was hard to hear Kermit.

Steve noticed the look on my face, and said, 'Is everything OK?'

'Oh yeah,' I said. 'There's just a lot of background noise.'

'Let's do another one then,' he said, and he whisked me off somewhere quieter, where Kermit recorded another message.

It had been an incredibly long day for the Muppets and their handlers. They had rehearsed the entire show, then performed it twice, and stayed around for photos with every crew member and comedian, and yet at the end of it all, Steve still offered Kermit's services for a second video.

I was absolutely astounded at the amount of goodwill everyone associated with the Muppets exuded. The path out of the stage door was packed with fans, and as I left, I noticed Steve stopping once again to sign autographs, or pose for photos.

Back at the hotel bar I spied Bill, the Swedish Chef's handler, who offered to buy me a drink. I agreed to let him, and he invited me to join the rest of the team. Again, I agreed.

The rest of the night was spent sipping whisky and chatting with Bill and Dave (who I found out later has been Gonzo's handler since the beginning), as well as the people that take care of Miss Piggy, Fozzie and the rest.

The weird thing was, without the Muppets around, no one knew who these guys were. Anyone I knew in the bar was wondering who the strange guys were that Adam was hanging out with.

A former WWE wrestler by the name of Mick Foley, whom I had met a couple of nights earlier, wandered over to tell me he'd been at the Gala and enjoyed the show. Six foot two, with long hair, and a huge beard, he was dressed mainly in a checked flannelette shirt and tracksuit pants.

'Who are these guys?' he asked.

'They're the people who handle the Muppets.'

'Oh My God.'

Mick was as starstruck as I was, and he was surprised that no one was mobbing them.

As Mick left, Dave turned to me and asked, 'Who was that?'

When I explained who he was, Dave said, 'Oh my God. I thought he was just some homeless guy.'

We ended the night by swapping email addresses and promising to stay in touch, and in the days that followed, I began to piece together my next stand-up show.

I'd try to combine the spirit of joy that came from both a frog and a Buddhist monk. I'd use my microphone to say something, and that something was: 'Touch the frog'.

Twelve months later, I performed my show *Happyism* at the Edinburgh Fringe Festival. In the audience one night was the cast of an improvised puppet show called *Puppet Up*, who were on after me in the same venue.

I finished the show by telling the story of the Muppets, of the Gala I nearly pulled out of, and the advice given to me by Brendon Burns. I ended with a gospel choir on stage, in white robes with green Kermit ruffles, as we sang, 'Glory, glory hallelujah – you gotta touch the frog.'

After the show, the cast of *Puppet Up* came backstage, joined by their boss who had just flown in from the States – Brian Henson, son of Jim Henson, the man who invented the Muppets, and created Kermit.

A few nights later, I joined them on stage in their show and improvised a scene with a Scottish puppet called Jock on the end of my arm, as Brian operated the puppet next to me.

It was the end of a long journey that began when the Dalai Lama held my hand, and Kermit the Frog gave me a high five.

And I've saved my favourite bit of the story till last.

When I left the stage after my set in Montreal, I didn't hear what Kermit said about me. It was relayed to me later by my manager, who was in the audience.

Apparently, Kermit's words were: 'That guy was great. We should fluff him up a bit and make him a Muppet.'

* * *

P.S. (Pinewood Studios) I kept in touch with Bill and Dave, and when they came to London to film the movie *Muppets Most Wanted*, they invited me to the set. I spent an entire day with them in Pinewood Studios as they filmed with Fozzie and Walter on a train.

Bill even asked if I'd like to sit with the handlers as they filmed a scene.

I scurried over to the set, boarded the train, and crouched at the feet of the handlers, who were standing in a hole in the floorboards. I got to watch them all in action as they plotted scenes, and improvised jokes.

I also chatted with Fozzie between takes.

That's right, just me and Fozzie Bear, hanging out on set. He even asked me for advice on how to play a particular moment, and demonstrated a couple of walks for me to choose from.

The next time you watch that movie you won't see me, but just know that when Fozzie and Walter are on the train, I'm crouched at their feet, under the floorboards, having the time of my life.

When Barry Met Hillsy

I first met Barry Humphries at a Retail and Traders conference in Ireland. An unlikely sentence I know, but sometimes you come across comedy legends in the strangest of places.

I had been booked to perform at said conference for a group of mainly whitegoods sellers from Australia, who had all been flown to Dublin for the weekend. My job was to sit through the entire conference, then perform a routine about it on the final day, before introducing Dame Edna Everage as the 'piece de flamboyance' at the final night dinner.

And let me tell you, you haven't lived until you've tried to write twenty minutes of comedy about a whitegoods conference. Luckily, I had five minutes of material about being Australian, and five more about being in Ireland, so I only really needed ten minutes of new jokes.

I still charged them for twenty though.

After two days of riveting whitegoods talk, I delivered my routine, and introduced the star attraction, Dame Edna. And that's when things got weird.

Dame Edna Everage, the housewife superstar, nay, megastar, is one of the greatest comic creations of all time. An uncle of mine once told me he saw an early performance of Edna's in Sydney, and half the room walked out in disgust, while the other half thought it was the best thing they had ever seen.

Over time, Edna graced the stages of the world, hosting her own hugely popular talk show in the UK, and appeared as a regular character on the US TV series *Ally McBeal*. As a young 'un, I was more partial to Barry's foul-mouthed Sir Les Patterson, but as I grew older, I came to appreciate the quiet genius of Dame Edna.

She took the stage in Dublin to a rapturous reception, and began to make jokes about the executives at the front table that were so offensive they should have caused them to stand up and walk out. And yet they loved every second of it.

One of the beautiful facets of Dame Edna is that even when she is being horrifically offensive, you can't really get angry, because deep, deep down, you know you're getting angry at a grown man, dressed like a frumpy housewife who thinks she's a megastar.

It'd be like punching a clown – you're the one who looks stupid.

Eventually Dame Edna decided to call the family of one of the guests, back home in Australia.

This was apparently a regular Dame Edna 'bit', and involved a phone number being dialled by a technician at the back of the room, who would then put the call through the speakers on stage. Dame Edna had a microphone attached to her glasses, by which the receivers of the call could hear her.

She took aim at a couple at the second table and asked them a few personal questions, then asked if she could call one of their parents back home.

Of course, they replied yes, so Edna asked for their parents' number.

However, the ins and outs of international dialling codes, combined with the effects of copious amounts of alcohol, meant that the couple in question couldn't quite remember the actual number of either of their parents. It didn't stop them having a few guesses, though.

This resulted in a few failed 'the number you have called is not connected' announcements, one wrong number, and even a recording in a foreign language – all of which Edna made hilarious.

I can't remember what she said, and even if I did I wouldn't be able to do it justice, but the more it went wrong, the funnier it got.

Eventually Edna moved on to a second target, who turned out to be as fruitless as the first, then a third, who thankfully was able to recall her parents' phone number.

Finally a connection was made, and somewhere in Adelaide, an unsuspecting older lady answered a phone call from Dame Edna.

By this stage, the euphoria of the previous fifteen minutes of madness had combined with the relief that the end was in sight, and the audience cheered.

The call went ahead, and again, was funny as hell. Just as Edna was about to wrap up though, the mum in Adelaide said, 'Hold on, I'll put you on to my husband.'

Once again, the audience lost it. Only an elderly Aussie mum would have a long-distance phone call with Dame Edna Everage, then make sure her husband gets a word as well.

'Hello,' a gruff voice said.

'Hello, possum,' said the Dame.

'Who's this?' said Dad.

'It's Dame Edna, possum.'

'No, it's not.'

Massive laughter from the audience.

'I'm fairly sure it is, possum.'

'It can't be Dame Edna,' Dad continued.

'Why not, possum?'

'Cos you sound like a woman, and it's a bloke that does Edna.'

At this point the audience virtually exploded. After failed call after failed call, drunken misunderstandings and in-jokes, this was the icing on the cake.

Somehow Edna managed to wrap up the call, and exited the stage to a standing ovation.

Later, as we posed for photographs with the corporate honchos, Edna put her arm around me and leaned in close.

'Were you watching that?' she asked in a voice that sounded more Barry than Edna.

'I was,' I affirmed.

'Good,' replied Barry/Edna. 'The lesson there is – always drive through the skid.'

Barry then looked at me through Edna's eyes, to make sure I knew what he was saying.

I remembered my first driving lessons, and being taught that if you start to lose control of the car, don't give up and let it crash. Put your foot on the accelerator, and drive firmly through the skid.

Or in comedy terms: when things start to go wrong, don't abandon the routine. Put your head down, commit to the bit, and it will get funnier.

Always drive through the skid.

*   *   *

Three years later, Dame Edna was booked as a guest on the *Spicks and Specks* Christmas show.

I was in the ABC make-up room when Barry entered.

'Barry,' I said, 'I'm Adam, I host the show.'

'I remember you,' he replied quietly, 'from Dublin.'

'Always drive into the skid,' I added, and he chuckled softly.

Later when the show began, I was sure to direct my first question to Dame Edna, and let her take the spotlight. She ripped off three or four brilliant jokes and we were away. Or so I thought.

Ross Noble, the Geordie king of improvisation, was sitting next to Edna, and began to make a few very funny observations about our Christmas set. At one point Edna tried to say something, but Ross continued.

Undeterred, Edna looked at me and pulled a face, and once again, Ross barrelled on.

Eventually Edna got out a word, but was stopped as Ross turned to her and said 'hang on', then proceeded again on his merry surreal way. Finally, Ross finished his bit, and *then* we were off.

Later I asked Ross what was going on, and he explained.

'Well, I know what Edna's like, and she always has to put everyone in their place. That's fine, but I wasn't just going to be her whipping boy for an hour. So I wanted to let her know I was going to do my thing, and I wasn't gonna let her dictate how I do it. So I purposely went off on one at the start of the show, and I refused to let her get in my way. That way we both knew where each other stood.'

It was remarkable to watch, like two antelopes locking horns, or two clowns honking each other's noses. It was effective, though. Each of us was put in our place by Edna that show, but not Ross. To her, they were equals.

Having said that, both Edna and Barry were indefatigable. Being our Christmas Special, it took two and a half hours to record, as we had bands, guests, choirs, changing sets, and of course, Santa.

Throughout it all, Edna was on fire.

It started with her observation on our 'Christmas on the beach' set: 'It looks like one of those nasty old tsunamis has gone through.'

When Alan made a joke about the size of the two baubles above his head making him feel like he was sitting under King Kong, Edna paused for the laughter, then added, 'Yes, we all *thought* that joke, Alan.'

When one of the guests held up my released-just-in-time-for-Christmas live DVD, the Dame simply said, 'Adam Hills? It must be awfully embarrassing to know there's a *comedian* with the same name as you.'

Even during the pauses in filming, when every other guest would switch off for a few minutes, Edna kept going.

'It is hot in the studio,' Edna said to Myf, sitting alongside her. Then, gesturing to a rather large woman sitting in the front row in a kaftan, she added, 'The dwarf under that woman's muumuu must be sweating.'

Two and half hours of filming, constant jokes, and at the end of it all she donned the high heels and took centre stage to sing out the show.

Remarkable.

A few years later, Barry appeared as himself as a guest on a short-lived talk show I hosted on the ABC, called 'Adam Hills in Gordon St Tonight' (later renamed 'Adam Hills Tonight').

I took the opportunity to ask him to sign something for me – a photograph taken by one of my best mates, Rich Hardcastle. Rich is an astoundingly good photographer, and has undoubtedly taken some of your best-loved shots of your favourite comedians, even if you don't know it, including the cover photo for this book.

He had taken a beautiful portrait of Barry, standing side on to the camera, fedora askew, with both hands behind his back, holding Edna's glasses. I had it delivered to Barry's dressing room, with a black pen, and the request for a signature.

It was returned after the show with the words, 'To Adam, a joyous heart always, Barry Humphries.'

The most recent time I worked with Barry was at Australia House in London, home to the Australian High Commission (and also Gringott's Bank, for any Harry Potter fans).

The South Australian Club was putting on a showcase of food, wine and entertainment, which included Vili's Pies, FruChocs, Cooper's Ale, and separate performances by my wife Ali McGregor and myself, all hosted by Barry Humphries.

Ali and I had met on the set of *Spicks and Specks* when she was booked as a guest. At the time she was one of Australia's leading sopranos, but since then has turned her hand to, and reinvigorated, the world of cabaret. In a lovely connection to one of my adopted hometowns, Ali had become the Artistic Director of the Adelaide Cabaret Festival, hence the invitation to the South Australian Club.

Naturally, we invited everyone we wanted to impress, and the guest list included our favourite authors Kathy Lette and David Sedaris, Bill Oddie from the Goodies, and my mum.

The show went well, and later as I was chatting to the head of programming at Channel 4, a wonderful whirlwind of a woman by the name of Jay Hunt, Barry approached to say his goodbyes.

'Before you go,' I interrupted, 'I'd just like to introduce you to Jay. She's the boss of Channel Four, and is the person that gave me a job.'

'Pleasure to meet you,' said Barry. 'You're his boss, are you?'

Jay nodded.

Barry paused.

'He's very good, isn't he?'

Jay nodded.

Barry paused again, and a twinkle appeared in his eye.

'He'll be the next Rolf Harris, you know.'

Barry winked, then left.

The First Leg

After seven years and nearly two hundred and eighty episodes of *Spicks and Specks*, Alan, Myf and I decided it was time to play our final note.

At the end of each year we'd get together to decide if we were gonna go round again, and we always said that if one of us left, we'd all go. At the end of year six, we were starting to feel a little stale.

The viewers still loved the show, and we were still enjoying it ourselves, but Alan's theory was, 'I'd rather they're grumpy at us because we finished early, than angry because we stayed on too long.'

I was spending half the year in London, but when I returned to Oz at the end of 2010, it was to film our final season. An announcement was made that 2011 would be our final year, and a live 'Farewell Tour' show was organised to say goodbye to our fans in person.

We were on tour when the final episode went to air, but decided it would be weird to do a live show on the same night, so we had a free day in Sydney.

While Alan had returned to Melbourne Myf and I booked a double-room hotel suite, overlooking Sydney Harbour, invited some friends around, and watched the last episode together.

It was an hour-long extravaganza with all our favourite guests, including Geoffrey Rush, Hamish Blake, Dan Sultan, Megan Washington, and a final performance by Brian Mannix as he sang the Uncanny X-Men classic, '50 Years'.

As we hugged and cried and said goodbye on screen, Myf and I hugged and cried together on the couch.

The live tour finished where it all began, in Melbourne, as we played three shows to five and a half thousand people a night. In total, over eighty thousand people came to the farewell shows.

It had been an amazing ride, featuring some of the biggest names in music and comedy – Meatloaf, Weird Al Yankovic, Steve Coogan, Martha Wainwright, Darlene Love, Ben Folds, Suggs, Steve Lukather from Toto (who also played guitar on the *Thriller* album), the keyboard player from America, the guy who told the audience at Woodstock not to take the brown acid, and Frank Zappa's keyboard player.

We also showcased some of Australia's biggest and brightest and paid homage to the legends – Peter Garrett, Molly Meldrum, Doc Neeson, Chrissy Amphlett, Guy Pearce, Denise Scott, Sarah Blasko, Tim Minchin and Jon Farriss from INXS.

I met my wife-to-be Ali in Series One, and by our final episode we were married with a daughter.

The crew of producers and researchers that worked on the show were like a family, and each and every one of them made an invaluable contribution to our success, in particular Bruce Kane, Anthony Watt, and Paul Clarke.

Most of them came to our final live show, and I broke down as I gave a farewell speech to them all. I was recounting an email I'd received from a viewer, whose parent had recently passed away from cancer, saying that the only joy they had together in the last few weeks of their life was watching *Spicks and Specks* on the hospital TV.

What made that story harder to tell was that my dad had just been diagnosed with leukaemia and wasn't well enough to make our final show.

It was time to sit back, take a break from TV, and live the quiet life of a stand-up comic again. Oh sure, I had also started hosting my own chat show, but that was only twelve episodes a year. The rest of the time could be spent chillin'.

Or so I thought.

* * *

A few weeks later, I was sitting at my in-laws' holiday house in the beachside town of Point Lonsdale, a two-hour drive south(ish) of Melbourne, on a conference call at eleven o'clock at night, after my wife and daughter had gone to bed.

Channel 4 had won the rights to broadcast the London 2012 Paralympic Games, and were interested in me hosting a late-night highlights show, with a slight comedy angle. Was I up for it? Did I think it could be done? If so, how?

These were the questions I mulled over with a couple of Channel 4 producers.

I recited the advice I had received four years earlier at the Beijing Paralympics: 'You have to treat this as an elite sport. Because it is. Whatever we do, it has to be a show that celebrates the sport first and foremost. There is definitely fun to be had with the Paralympics, but if all you do is make jokes, it'll look like you're mocking disabled people. You have to start with the sport, respect it, then move onto the funny bits.'

I was quite sure about all of this, and I didn't want to work with people who didn't get it.

I didn't even mind if someone else was given the job, as long as the sport was respected.

A few weeks later, the offer came through: to host a one-hour Paralympic highlights show, at midnight, on Channel 4's digital offshoot, More 4.

It sounded fun, so I said yes.

Some months after that, I was asked to host Channel 4's publicity launch of their Paralympic coverage. A few hundred members of the press were invited to Channel 4's Horseferry Road headquarters, as every member of their Paralympic broadcast team was presented to the world.

I began the show by relaying all the stories I had gathered from Beijing, which had now become a pretty tight, twenty-minute routine. I talked about the opening ceremony, the joy of the athletes' village, my own prosthetic, and finished with the story of the Chinese swimmer with no arms.

I then introduced the Channel 4 presenters, many of whom were disabled themselves, and had been trained up to cover the Games. One of them was a young sports journalist called Alex Brooker, who moaned light-heartedly that I did all the jokes about my missing foot that he was gonna do about *his* missing foot.

I thought, welcome to Disability Showbiz, mate. It's a guide dog eat guide dog world out there.

Later at the pub, I took a shine to the chatty bloke at the end of the table with one foot and hand deformities, who tried to 'nick' my material. I noticed how comfortable he seemed using his teeth to open a packet of crisps, or holding his pint with his two 'fingers'.

He seemed, well, natural. A gregarious, and funny bloke. I liked him.

A few weeks later, I got a call from my manager. This time I was in Malta, filming an episode of *Who Do You Think You Are?* for Australian TV.

The show traced my ancestors back to the Maltese city of Mdina, where my eleven-times great-grandfather turned out to be one of the richest men on the island. Mainly because he owned shares in two pirate ships.

It took me an hour and a half before I realised, 'My ancestor was a pirate? That explains why I've got one leg.'

The producers told me they'd been waiting for me to make that joke on camera, but at the time it didn't come to me. They were too scared to prompt me in case I took offence, so they stayed quiet. It was only in the cab back to the hotel that I suddenly blurted it out.

They made sure to film an interview later, so that I could get the joke to air.

'Channel Four wanna take the show to prime time,' my manager explained.

I asked what that meant.

'The main channel, ten-thirty, right after the events finish each day.'

'Brilliant, will I get more money?' I asked, mainly joking.

'No,' was the answer, 'we've already agreed the deal. But you never know what might come of it. We just need to find a name for it, and some co-hosts.'

A few weeks down the track and I was back in London, having lunch with a sports producer called Pete Thomas. Pete was going to be the brains behind the show, so we sat down with a mate of mine who was also a great comedian, Adam Vincent, to flesh out some ideas.

Pete agreed that the show had to revere the sport first, and be a comedy show second. He said he'd like to achieve the same cult status that a couple of Australian comedians called Roy and HG had done back in 2000, when they hosted a late-night show for the Sydney Olympics.

I loved that he knew of Roy and HG, and casually dropped into conversation that the guy who played Roy had been my substitute teacher back at high school.

We vaguely fleshed out a plan for the show, including an introduction to the items on the show.

'A bit like the old *Wide World of Sports* used to do,' said Adam, 'back in Australia.'

'Or the Twelfth Man,' I added, alluding to the Australian comedy parody of the same sports show.

'I love the Twelfth Man,' Pete joined in, and then began to quote the lines.

Now I really loved him.

'So what kind of set do you think we should have?' I asked.

'I dunno,' said Pete, 'but I can see it in my head.'

Brilliant. I really admire people that can 'see things in their head'. He was completely the right man for the job.

Now down to the hosts.

'I've been thinking of that guy who was at the press launch,' Pete said, 'Alex Brooker.'

This is ridiculous. Now he likes the same bloke that I liked at the press launch.

I had a good feeling about this.

We talked about various celebrities we'd like to have as guests, and discussed having a segment where people could feel free to ask any questions they wanted about disability. We knew that the viewers would have questions about the categories, the disabilities, and the athletes, and that answering those questions would make the Paralympics a whole lot more fun to watch.

Pete suggested we think of it as a 'Paralympic surgery', much like an MP's surgery, in which they answer the public's questions.

Channel 4 liked our ideas, but insisted on filming a fifteen-minute 'pilot episode' to see how it would work.

Before that, though, was a trip to LA for my brother's wedding. While I was flitting around the world talking on a microphone, Brad had relocated to Los Angeles to follow his acting dream. He'd been Best Man at my wedding, and now it was time to return the favour. Of course I also managed to squeeze in a few gigs, including at one of my all-time favourite places: the Comedy & Magic Club in Hermosa Beach.

The Comedy & Magic Club has played host to every major US comedian, and was where Ray Romano and Jay Leno would regularly test their material. I had become friends with Richard, the manager, who on this particular night introduced me to a young up-and-comer, and told me he was gonna be huge. He was right – Trevor Noah now hosts *The Daily Show*.

'I got some spots next week if you wanna come back,' Richard offered after the show.

'I can't,' I moaned. 'I have to go back to London to film a pilot for a TV show.'

Richard sized me up, and immediately called me out.

'Oh, you poor thing,' he said, dripping with sarcasm. 'You're gonna be famous in *another* country.'

I stopped my whining.

I returned to London and Pete, Adam and I set to work on the pilot. It was basically a wee example of how the show was gonna run. By this stage the channel had suggested a young comedian by the name of Josh Widdicombe as a regular guest.

I had met Josh earlier in the year at The Cat Laughs Comedy Festival in Kilkenny, Ireland, and I'd enjoyed both his routine and the chat we had afterwards.

I had only one question: 'Does he like sport?'

Apparently he did.

Problem was, Josh had a gig on the day of the pilot, and we couldn't afford to book a guest. So it was decided that I would interview Alex Brooker, as if he was one of the guests.

Before the show, Alex and I began chatting about our prosthetics. I later found out it was the first time he had ever talked to someone of a slightly similar age about his leg, and for me, it was a very rare opportunity to do the same.

We compared amputations, prosthetic feet, fake toes, and bruises. We laughed over shared experiences that no one else would understand – like the exquisite pain of getting an infected hair follicle on your stump, and I offered some ways to avoid it.

All the while, Pete stood watching, jaw agape.

'This is the show!' he said. 'You and Alex talking about stumps and prosthetics. This is amazing.'

What felt to Alex and I like a completely normal, yet joyous, conversation was to the casual observer a revelation about disability.

We recorded the pilot with Alex playing the guest role, and although we didn't repeat our backstage chat, we did recreate a joke he told me about how he always wins rock, paper, scissors, because nobody can tell which symbol his fingers are forming.

It was clear that there was a real chemistry between us. He was like my disabled brother from another mother.

Channel 4 were happy with the pilot, but they were reluctant to let Alex out of his trackside reporting duties. They wanted him by day, we wanted him by night.

The pilot shot, I then flew straight back to Montreal for another week at the Just for Laughs Comedy Festival. By now, my body was in jet-lag shutdown.

In four months I had flown from Melbourne to London, to Prague, Germany and Malta (the last three for *Who Do You Think You Are?*), back to London, then back to Melbourne, on to LA, back to London, then to Montreal.

I walked around Montreal in a daze, sleeping by day, awake all night, and managed to completely miss all coverage of the 2012 Olympics. From what I've heard, the opening ceremony was quite good. I've never seen it.

I left Montreal with an offer from the owners of the Comedy Cellar in New York. It's the venue that featured in Louis CK's sitcom, and most nights showcased some of the biggest names in comedy. The last time I'd been there, Chris Rock had just dropped in.

The owners had come to my solo show, enjoyed it, and asked if I'd like to do a residency there. I jumped at the chance, and it was decided I'd head to NYC in October to perform six nights a week at the world-famous Comedy Cellar.

Meanwhile Pete and I had been going backwards and forwards over email about the name of the show. Channel 4 had sent through a whole bunch of selections, and when I say they were spitballing, I mean it.

Clearly no suggestion was considered a bad suggestion. Some of the options included:

Amputee and Scones
They Deserve a Medal
Dwarves Aren't Magic
and
Mobility Scooters Are for Fat People.

I suggested the name 'Ramped Up', but Channel 4 preferred 'The Last Leg'.

I wasn't sure about that one, for a few reasons. Firstly, I didn't want the name of the show to be a joke about my leg. It should be about the athletes, not me. Plus, when someone is on their last legs, that's never usually a good thing.

For me, there needed to be a good reason for the name. One that would exist even if it wasn't a show about disabled sports, or hosted by a guy with one foot.

'There is,' said Pete, who once again had seen the whole thing in his head. 'You just start the show by saying, "Welcome to the last leg of Channel Four's coverage of the Paralympic Games."'

Oh yeah. I had missed that one.

Now I was on board.

I returned to London, then took the train to Edinburgh to do a shortened run at the Fringe. I can still remember the day the Olympic rings were removed from in front of my venue at Assembly Hall, on a hill that overlooked the city, and were replaced by the Paralympic symbol, known as the Agitos.

That's when I knew showtime was near.

Then billboards went up in the middle of London advertising the Paralympics. They said: 'Thanks for the warm-up.'

That's when I knew it was gonna be cheeky.

In amongst it all, Channel 4 had released TV ads, proclaiming 'Meet the Superhumans'. It was the first time I'd ever seen disabled people look edgy, as images of athletes flashed on the screen, accompanied by Public Enemy's 'Harder Than You Think'.

In the middle of the ad, everything stopped as a car flipped, a soldier was blown up, and an ultrasound appeared on the screen. Then just as suddenly, the music kicked back in, and the Paralympians returned to the screen.

It was astounding.

What a beautiful, powerful way to remind the viewers that every athlete had a story, was there for a reason, and had moved on from it in the best possible way.

The ad finished, and I sat back with tears in my eyes, and a swelling in my chest.

That's when I knew something special was going to happen.

The Middle Leg

'A Paralympics show called "The Last Leg"? Typical Channel 4.'

'I can't believe there's a show about disabled sports called "The Last Leg". Such bad taste.'

'Poor form by Channel 4 to call their Para sports show "The Last Leg". I'm disgusted.'

These were the basic sentiments expressed on Twitter when the ads for *The Last Leg* started running on air. A month earlier, I had filmed a couple of little bits to camera about the joy of the Paralympics, and Channel 4 had packaged them up into some fifteen-second commercials.

They did not go down well.

I was pretty sure from my years of talking about Paralympic sport on stage that once the audience heard what we were actually saying, we'd be OK. I also knew from experience that once they became aware of my prosthetic foot, they'd proba-bly cut me a bit of slack.

Still, though, it wasn't a great start.

On the day of our first show, I still didn't have any co-hosts.

Alex Brooker was booked as one of the guests, alongside ex-cricketer Andrew Flintoff and blind judo champion Simon Jackson. Josh Widdicombe would have his own segment late in the show.

For the most part, I'd be up front on my own, in a show called *The Last Leg with Adam Hills*.

We were due to go to air after the day's events, at ten thirty.

At ten twenty-five, we were still rehearsing.

'You can rehearse the final segment, or go to the toilet,' I was informed by our director, 'but there's not enough time to do both.'

I went to the toilet.

I stood there at the urinal, trying to comprehend what I was about to do. In three minutes I'd be live on Channel 4, hosting a TV show across the UK. I was strangely calm.

Possibly because my two hundred and seventy-something episodes of *Spicks and Specks* had prepared me for TV, but also because we didn't really have an audience in the studio. The only people in there were a few staff members of the produc-tion crew, who'd been roped in to stay behind after work.

I made sure to mention my prosthetic within the first few

minutes of the show starting. I wanted the audience to know that I was also missing a bit, and therefore not an able-bodied person mocking those supposedly less fortunate than me.

The show itself went well, I think, as Alex and I recreated some of the jokes we had performed during our pilot episode, and Alex played rock, paper, scissors with Andrew Flintoff – who had absolutely no idea how to react.

Could he laugh? Was it distasteful? Was it OK?

The final segment of the show (the unrehearsed one) was slightly chaotic, but in a good way, and it was clear that the show was at its best when Josh, Alex and I were all on set at the same time.

After the episode I took to Twitter, and thankfully the reaction was overwhelmingly positive. It seemed the gamble had paid off.

In amongst the praise, and a couple of complaints, were some questions.

'Is it okay to ask what some of the Paralympians' disabilities are, because some of them don't look disabled at all?'

'Is it alright to think that some of the athletes are quite fit?'

This was exactly what we were hoping would happen, when Pete came up with his 'Paralympic surgery' idea. In all the excitement of the opening episode, however, we had forgotten to ask for people's questions, or even set up the segment.

Now the questions were coming in anyway.

The following day, it was decided that I would read out the tweets on air, answer them, then ask for more.

'If there's anything you want to know about the Paralympics, or disability in general, tweet your question to us @TheLastLeg,'

I said out loud in the meeting room, as an example of how it would sound on air.

It was our director Jules who then offered up the phrase, 'Hashtag isitok.'

And a segment was born. A segment that became the highlight of the show.

The next night we answered the questions as best we could, while also trying to be funny: 'It is definitely okay to ask what some of the disabilities are. Sometimes a person with cerebral palsy may swim okay, but when they get out of the pool their disability becomes clearer – and yes, some people do find amputees attractive, thank you very much.'

The questions also gave Alex and I the chance to have the type of discussion Pete had witnessed backstage before we shot the pilot, and was convinced should be in the show. One of those discussions involved Alex and I answering the question, 'Do you take your leg off to have sex?'

I already had stand-up material about that very topic, and trotted it out on camera, but genuinely laughed in shock when Alex replied, 'Depends whether or not it's a quickie.'

We were later told by a Channel 4 presenter that at that very moment, the Prime Minister David Cameron was watching the show in bed with his wife Samantha, and particularly enjoyed the 'quickie' joke.

When we asked how he knew, he replied, 'Because David Cameron told me.'

At the time, though, we didn't really know if anyone was watching the show. The ratings told us that around nine hundred thousand people saw the first episode, but we had absolutely no clue if that was a good or a bad figure.

The highest-rating episode of *Spicks and Specks* was 1.6

million people, but that was in a country with a quarter of the population of Great Britain.

To make matters worse, the day after episode one, we received a visit from 'someone from the channel'. We sat like chastened schoolchildren as we were told what was wrong with the show, and how to fix it. One of the suggestions was to have Josh and Alex on the couch for the whole show, which was what we had wanted all along.

What we didn't realise was that the powers-that-be at Channel 4 had loved the first episode, and saw the potential for the show to continue long after the Paralympic Games had ended. That's why they sent down one of their entertainment commissioners to polish off the rough edges. But at the time, we all thought we were in trouble.

Gradually we found our feet (pun absolutely intended), and the audiences slowly increased, partly because the Paralympics GB Team were doing well, but also because the three of us together made for a better show. There was something about our three personalities – the older, responsible, overly earnest Aussie; the young, keen, almost naive puppy that was Alex; and the token able-bodied, yet world-weary voice of Josh.

We were like a three-part harmony of comedy accents – Aussie, Cockney, and West Country.

One tweet in particular told us we were doing the right thing. It said, '#isitok to ask how a man with no arms gets out of the pool?' What made that tweet stand out was the sender: the captain of the US wheelchair rugby team.

Ever since Pete and I had bonded over the Aussie comedians Roy and HG, we had hoped that Paralympians would get into the show. At the 2000 Sydney Olympics, Roy and HG's show *The Dream* became a cult hit amongst the athletes, some of whom got into trouble for taking the show's mascot onto the podium with them.

Although we would never copy their format, we certainly hoped to achieve the same notoriety amongst the athletes.

What we didn't account for, was that every athlete had a strict curfew until their particular event had finished. That meant they were in their accommodation at the end of each day's action, with nothing else to do but watch TV.

So they all watched *The Last Leg*.

They laughed, they cheered on their friends, and just as importantly, they asked us questions, too. As I've said on stage since, 'We've never seen that many disabled people in a room either. We're as freaked out as you are.'

The biggest ratings boost came from a complete accident, though some thought it was a canny piece of publicity. I can assure you it wasn't.

One of the difficulties of doing a live show is that you have to edit as you go. Sometimes a segment goes longer than planned, so you have to wind it up early. Sometimes you have to drop the next segment altogether. Occasionally, you have to change the order of the show completely.

This was all communicated to me through an earpiece, by Pete. That earpiece also carried comments from the director, as well as a countdown to the ad breaks whenever they approached.

Add to that the voices of Josh, Alex and the guests, and the words on the autocue in front of me, plus the cards on the desk, and it's little wonder I struggled to wind down after each show.

Sometimes I'd get home, go to bed, drift off to sleep, then wake up with a shudder as I dreamt the words, 'and go to the break in ten, nine, eight, seven . . .'

So it was on this fateful episode that Pete was calmly guiding me through the isitok segment. We always prepared more tweets than we needed, in case we were running under time, but on this occasion we didn't need them all.

On around the third one, Pete said to me, 'This is the last one.'

Unfortunately, either Josh or Alex was talking at the same time, and their voices mingled together. What I thought I heard was, 'Skip to the last one.'

So I did. We discussed the final tweet, then moved onto the next segment.

The graphics supervisor, however, had followed Pete's lead, and rather than putting the last tweet on the screen, had put the *next* tweet on the screen, which read:

'#isitok to punch a disabled person if they're being a nob?'

Oblivious to all this, we carried on with the show, but the next day the press were up in arms (this pun is actually unintended but let's keep it) – Were we encouraging violence against disabled people? (No.) Were we trying to be sensationalist? (No.) Was it done on purpose? (Definitely not.)

It was a pure accident, brought about by a melange of voices, and my dodgy hearing.

The following night, 1.6 million people tuned in, partly because Jimmy Carr was a guest, but also because every newspaper had carried the story of the massively offensive guys on Channel 4.

In the end it was all a bit of an anti-climax. We apologised for the mix-up and answered the question by saying that although violence is never the answer to any problem, disabled people are as capable of being nobs as anyone else, and you should treat them exactly the same as you would an able-bodied person being a nob.

Despite the audience figures, we still didn't feel like a hit. Mainly because we were spending twelve hours a day in the International Broadcasting Centre.

The IBC was at the opposite end of the Olympic Park from most of the action, and had its own entrance. Rather than alighting at Stratford station, then walking through the Westfield shopping centre and on through the public entrance to the Olympic Park, I'd take a train to Hackney Wick, then walk the graffiti-soaked back streets to the IBC.

It meant we didn't get to mingle with the crowds or the athletes, who we now know were our biggest fans.

Even the IBC itself was an airless monstrosity of a building. It was like five aircraft hangars laid end to end, with one or two jutting off each side. No windows, nondescript concrete, it was easy to get lost in it.

It was also virtually empty. I imagine it was a thriving, buzzing hub of activity during the Olympics, but when the Paras were on, it was basically us and the Aussie broadcasters, for whom I was still doing some coverage.

I'd arrive at midday each day, then spend the next few hours watching various TV feeds of various sports, while we mapped that night's show. Around five, we'd all sit down for a planning meeting, and that's where the magic happened.

Those meetings have become legendary among some of the staff who were in attendance, because that's where most of the show was written. And when I say 'written', I mean, improvised around the table.

As well as Pete and Adam Vincent, there was Josh, his writer Tom Craine, Alex (who didn't have a writer, because he didn't know any), the director Jules, the Channel 4 commissioner Syeda, as well as an assortment of other producers and people from the channel. All in all, around a dozen people.

As we planned the show, we'd scroll through the isitoks, and say whatever came to mind. Everyone chipped in, and when something made the table laugh, it was followed by the direction 'Say that!', and I would duly note it down.

After the meeting, we'd all go our separate ways and prepare our own bits, and if I was lucky, I'd see some sunlight on the way to the Media Centre cafeteria.

Then back to the studio to rehearse the show, before going live to air around ten-thirty, depending on which events were still going, and whether Paralympics GB was competing in them. We'd be off air around eleven-fifteen, and I'd head to Twitter to gather some isitoks for the next show.

A car would pick me up around twelve-thirty, and I'd be home by one a.m. It would then take at least an hour to calm down enough to sleep, and after a few false starts and ad-break dreams, I'd be asleep by two. Then I'd get up the next morning at ten, leave home at eleven, and repeat the process.

I mean, it was an absolute hoot, and we loved every minute, but it was impossible to gauge the reaction of the outside world.

Until the day Josh and Alex decided to check out some of the sporting action. I don't even know what it was they went to see, but I remember their reaction when they returned.

They had been driven through the park on the back of a golf cart, and the raised position of the seats combined with the beeps of the cart brought them a lot of attention.

When people realised that the guys they'd been watching at night were right there in front of them, they went a bit over the top. That was the first time the boys discovered what the show actually meant to people, and in particular, to Paralympic fans.

'Bloody hell,' said Alex, when they returned, 'we were mobbed. It was like being in the Disabled Beatles.'

And that's how it went for ten whole days. We spent our time in a windowless aircraft hangar, doing the show to a studio 'audience' of a dozen or so people per night, while in the outside world we were being watched by athletes, their families, Paralympic fans, and the Prime Minister.

There's no doubt we were buoyed by the popularity of the Games, and the way Channel 4 covered them.

One night we went on air directly after Oscar Pistorius's race, which had attracted over three million viewers. Even if half of them turned off when our show started, we'd still have one and a half million watching.

Fortuitously, Oscar chose that moment to have a rant about the legality of the length of his opponents' blades. Which meant a lot of people watched us to see our reaction.

What would we say about the pin-up boy of Paralympic sport losing his rag on live TV?

I said the only words I could think of: 'Holy shitballs.'

I was chuffed beyond belief when the Aussie writer Clive James later praised me for using the perfect words.

So many things contributed to our success: (1) Paralympics GB had a hugely successful Games, (2) Channel 4 covered it all brilliantly, (3) The general public were on such a high after the Olympics, that they were actively looking forward to whatever came next, and (4) Jody Cundy had a temper tantrum.

It's a small thing, but when cyclist Jody Cundy stormed out of the velodrome after being disqualified from a race, people suddenly took the sport seriously. These weren't a bunch of disabled people who were just happy to be there. These were serious athletes who had trained their asses off for the past four years to compete at the highest level possible. And they got angry when something went wrong.

The British public had gone through the same process that I did in Beijing. They came to see past the disabilities and appreciate sport at its purest.

During the opening ceremony, the Paralympics GB team had entered the Olympic Stadium like no disabled people I had ever seen. Fireworks exploded, confetti cannons sprayed into the air, and the David Bowie track 'Heroes' blasted at full volume.

I watched with tears in my eyes.

I thought of every person on that team, and how at some stage in their life they must have cursed their disability. We all have. I thought of their parents, who like mine, might have been told their children wouldn't have much of a life.

Now those parents were watching their children feted like very few people on the planet. Those children were now a part of something they could never have envisaged.

Athletes like Jonnie Peacock, Ellie Simmonds, Hannah Cockroft and Richard Whitehead became household names. Children were cutting legs off their Action Man figures and Barbie dolls to make them look like Paralympians. Others were making their own prosthetics out of cardboard, or running like Richard Whitehead, because he looked cool.

During the closing ceremony, I was asked my thoughts.

'Sydney was the first time the Paralympians were treated as equals. London was the first time they were treated like heroes.'

As the Games came to an end, I was approached by a Channel 4 producer who asked what I was doing next.

'Going back to Australia,' I replied.

'No, I mean in television,' she said.

'Oh, um, well, nothing I guess.'

She looked at me sternly and stated, 'That will change after this.'

Then added, 'Make sure you talk to us before anyone else.'

The Last Leg

As I mentioned earlier, the head of programming at Channel 4 was a force of nature by the name of Jay Hunt. Originally from Australia, she is fast-talking, blunt, effusive, energetic, and great fun to chat to.

Although Joe took care of my live work in the UK, the man in charge of my TV career was Addison Creswell. Respected by many in the comedy industry, he was a fast-talking, blunt, energetic ball of charisma, who could charm the pants off a Rottweiler, then become one at a second's notice.

I sat between the two of them at Channel 4 headquarters, in a very well-lit meeting room, and watched them discuss my future. Jay wanted me at the channel. That was her job. Addison wanted me to be well paid. That was his job.

'I mean, I've never seen an audience react to someone the way they've reacted to you,' said Jay.

She spent a good minute or two singing my praises, and that of *The Last Leg*, before looking at Addison and saying, 'I probably shouldn't be saying all this with you in the room.'

'Keep talking,' Addison smirked. 'I'm just watching his fee go up.'

Jay looked at me and said, 'Excuse me for this, Adam,' then turned to Addison with a grin and replied, 'Fuck off, you pig.'

They both burst into laughter, as did I, unsure of whether Addison had just sealed the deal or scuppered it.

We left the meeting with an agreement to have another meeting, and a possible stand-up special on Channel 4.

At the next meeting I was asked what kind of show I'd like to host.

'*The Last Leg*,' I replied, 'preferably with Josh and Alex.'

They offered up the idea of a weekly show, in which Josh, Alex and I would treat the news of the week the way we treated the Paralympics. We'd watch it, make sense of it, and deal with any tricky subjects that came up along the way.

I wasn't sure. What made us stand out was that we were talking about disability sport. There were plenty of shows that talked about the news.

We left that meeting with an agreement to have more meetings.

Later that day, Josh, Alex and I were due to film a piece for the broadcast of *Stand Up to Cancer*. We treated it like an isitok, and discussed whether it was okay to not donate. Somehow, we made it funny. More than that, we still seemed to have that on-air chemistry that we found during the Paralympics.

Later over lunch, I told them of the Channel 4 meeting.

We all had the same reservations. Do we really want to be doing a show about the news? Would people still watch it outside of the Paralympic Games?

One thing we all agreed on was that we clearly have a 'thing' between the three of us. There was definitely magic happening when the cameras were on us. I offered that I'd only ever experienced this kind of on-air connection once before – with my *Spicks and Specks* co-hosts Alan and Myf. And that show ran for seven years.

In fact, Alex even reminded me of Myf. He had never really been on TV before, and hadn't developed an on-screen persona. What you saw was what you got, and that natural charm simply oozes out of a TV screen. Josh, on the other hand, was every bit as funny as Alan.

I'd seen this before. It could work again.

We left lunch in high spirits, and later I spoke to Addison's business partner, my other manager, Joe.

'We just don't know if the show will work,' I said.

'No one knows if a show's gonna work,' said Joe. 'All you can do is roll the dice. Listen, if it doesn't work, it'll be off-air after two weeks and no one will ever remember it. If it does work, though, it could run for years.'

Well, when you put it that way.

I've been incredibly lucky to have been surrounded by some really clever people. And I'd like to think I've been smart enough to listen to them.

I listened when Joe told me to go back to Australia and learn how to host a TV show. And I listened to him when he said we should try turning *The Last Leg* into a weekly news show.

There was no doubt that my missing foot helped me get the job hosting *The Last Leg* during the Paralympics. It looked great for Channel 4 to have a disabled person who could also host a comedy show. It looked even better for them to have disabled people on-air after the Paralympics had ended.

What put me in better stead was the years I'd spent doing comedy and hosting TV without mentioning my foot. I had, as was suggested to me early on, plied my trade without the novelty of being 'the one-legged comedian'.

Now I could combine the novelty of being disabled, with the years of experience in front of audiences and a camera.

In other words, I put my *other* best foot forward.

Finding Our Feet

I never did make it to New York. I put the month-long residency at The Comedy Cellar on hold, and spent the rest of 2012 preparing for *The Last Leg*. We filmed an end-of-year special, with chef Jamie Oliver, Olympian Nicola Adams, and Paralympian Jonnie Peacock, and Channel 4 confirmed that we'd be getting a full series in the New Year.

I flew back to Australia for Christmas, to find that my Dad's leukaemia treatment was not going well. His body was struggling with a bone marrow transplant, and the combination of the copious amounts of medication he was on was making him drowsy, delirious and weak.

Still jet-lagged, I sat with him in hospital, and told him all about my overseas adventures, as he had done to me when I was younger. He smiled at the tales of the Paralympics and at the prospect of *The Last Leg*, and a few days later we opened Christmas presents around his hospital bed. As I left the room that day, he said firmly 'Good luck in London'. It was the last proper sentence he said to me.

Two days after Christmas we were told that Dad only had a few days left. He was now in intensive care, and as I explained the situation to him, I gave him a hug, told him that I loved him, and softly hit the Mel Brooks-inspired high note with which we ended every get together. Despite being unable to speak, he still managed to squeak out a high note in return. That was the last proper interaction we had.

The first series of *The Last Leg* was delayed by a week so that I could attend Dad's funeral, and make sure Mum was OK. Thankfully Brad had made it from LA to see Dad before he died, and we all spent a week together as a family, supporting each other and laughing whenever it felt appropriate.

Two weeks later I was back in London, live on air hosting *The Last Leg*. We still didn't entirely know what the show was meant to be, but Channel 4 were adamant we had to talk about more than just sportspeople with disabilities. Oscar Pistorius changed that.

We awoke on Valentine's Day 2013 to the horrific news that Oscar Pistorius had shot and killed his girlfriend Reeva Steenkamp. Alex was the only one of us who had met Oscar, but we all felt an attachment to him. He was the Paralympic Golden Boy, the Blade Runner, the face of the sport. We had to talk about him. But how?

There was absolutely no way we could make jokes about the situation, so we didn't. One of the strengths of our Paralympic coverage was that at times, we could be genuine about the sport without taking the mickey out of it. So that's what we did.

We expressed our horror at the still unfolding series of events, and told the viewers that we didn't want to make jokes about it. It was the first time we were serious on air.

As the weeks passed, we found some dim light in the situation by discussing whether prosthetics would be allowed in jail, or whether Alex and I would put our legs on in the night if we thought we heard an intruder. It was a tricky subject to cover, but I think we managed it by saying exactly how we felt.

Over time that ability to be serious meant we were able to cover the tragic events of Charlie Hebdo, the Westminster

Attack, the murder of Jo Cox, the Manchester Arena bombing, and the Grenfell Tower fire.

Of course, attempting to do that live on air can be quite precarious, and on the day of the Pistorius episode, we spent a lot of time talking to lawyers. Even though the case would be heard in South Africa, we still had to be mindful of what was said.

On the way into the studio, our Commissioning Editor Syeda took me aside.

'You know we have to cover our bases legally,' she said.

'I know' I sulked.

'Listen to me though' she commanded. 'Once you're on air, you're live. And I can't stop you saying whatever the hell you want.'

That night I went off script while discussing a magazine editor's decision to post bikini shots of a pregnant Kate Middleton without her permission. It resulted in me shouting 'Fuck Off!' quite determinedly.

It felt good.

I followed it up with a scripted rant that ended with the honest desire for us all to "just stop being dicks".

That episode was a combination of serious news, genuine opinion, a little indignation and our usual sense of silliness. Finally, we knew what the show was meant to be.

Political Pot

For some reason, I seem to get along quite well with politicians.

Once, on a flight from Adelaide to Melbourne, Julia Gillard crossed the aisle to sit in the empty seat next to me.

With a glint in her eye she opened with, 'Hello, I'm the Deputy Prime Minister of Australia. And since the Prime Minister is out of the country at the moment, I'm in charge, which means you have to do as I say. So, I'm ordering you to talk to my assistant over there, because she quite likes you.'

I did exactly as I was told, and chatted to both the Deputy PM (later to become Australia's first female leader) and her assistant. When we alighted the plane in Melbourne, we were met by a scrum of security men, who eyed me with justifiable suspicion.

Ms Gillard quickly informed them I was with her, at which point they all did that thing that security men do in movies – put their fingers to their ears and spoke into their cuffs.

Years later, when she was prime minister, Julia came to one of the *Spicks and Specks* farewell shows. It's a rare thrill to be on stage and see your own prime minister sitting in the audience.

After the show she was escorted backstage, and after chatting to us all, she admitted that her true musical loves were Bruce Springsteen and the Australian rock band Cold Chisel, but made us promise not to tell anyone.

I never understood that. Surely admitting that you genuinely like popular music would help a politician. Unlike those embarrassing election moments when they appear on radio and try to sound cool by saying, 'I'm a huge fan of the Antarctic Monkeys.'

After the group chat, I managed to get some facetime with the PM, and surprised myself by chatting to her like an old mate.

'So how has it been since you became PM?' I asked, as if we'd been hanging out together all our lives.

She confided in me that she was happy that her government had been able to implement the difficult but important things that wouldn't necessarily be popular: equal pay for women, the disability insurance scheme, a carbon tax.

'We did the things we thought needed to be done, now it's time to make sure people like us again.'

I really admired that. This was a politician who did what she thought was best for the country, regardless of how it would initially be perceived. Whatever your politics, that's really what you want from a leader.

I then got to ask her the question I've always wanted to ask a world leader: 'How do you deal with jet-lag?'

It might sound like a dumb question, but I've always wondered how a prime minister or president, or queen, or dictator can fly halfway around the world, step off a plane at the time of day they'd normally be in a deep sleep, and go straight into negotiations with another president, or prime minister, or king.

How they can then hash out a peace deal for a war-torn area, or negotiate a trade agreement, was beyond me. I can barely operate a microwave when I'm jet-lagged. Not only that, two days later, these world leaders hop on another plane, and do it all again.

'We have an amazing doctor,' the PM admitted, 'hilariously, called Dr De'ath.'

Apparently, these doctors have the best sleeping pills, and administer them as soon as the plane lifts off, in order to get the PM/President/Princess into the right time zone immediately.

Dull, I know, but my point is – I feel completely at home chatting to politicians. Maybe it's because politics has been described (by many politicians) as showbusiness for ugly people. And in some ways, stand-up comedy is politics for irresponsible people.

Oh sure, we all say we want to make the world a better place, it's just that comedians don't have to do anything once they've said it.

Anyway, over the years I've become good friends with the former leader of the Australian Democrats party, Natasha Stott Despoja, and have spent an afternoon in Parliament House watching Steve Coogan videos with the deputy opposition leader, Tanya Plibersek.

Full disclosure: Tanya was at Jannali Girls High School at the same time I was at Jannali Boys High School across the road, and we were at a few barbecues together back in the day.

I saw her again twenty years later in Canberra, when she had become the MP for Sydney. It was an ABC TV function, in which the 'stars' of the network shook hands with the MPs that funded us, and tried subtly to remind them why the Government gave money to the ABC in the first place.

We were warned ahead of time that every politician would only half look at you when they spoke, as they casually scanned the room for the real stars of the day – the Bananas in Pyjamas.

I'm not kidding – the seven-foot high children's characters bounded into the room halfway through a previous function, and every politician of every persuasion immediately stopped whatever conversation they were having and made an instant beeline for the giant yellow rock stars. They all claimed it was for their children, but I know for a fact, some of them didn't have kids.

It really does remind you where you stand in the pecking order, when two enormous bananas, who not only didn't dress up for the occasion, but refused to even change out of their bedclothes, take your spotlight.

Thankfully, I bumped into Tanya before the Bananas had made an entrance, and reintroduced myself. It's a weird sensation to say to a politician in Parliament House, 'Remember me, we were at a barbecue at Dicko's place back in 1987?'

We exchanged a few pleasantries, and upon finding out I spent a lot of time in the UK, Tanya asked how Aussie humour translated to the British, and vice versa.

'Funny you should ask,' I replied. 'Because I've just been contacted by Steve Coogan's producers to take a look at his scripts for his upcoming Australian tour show. He'll be on stage as Alan Partridge and a few selected characters, and they've asked me to look at the script and weed out the Englishisms.'

'Oh my God,' she suddenly lit up. 'I love Steve Coogan. Do you know the character Tony Ferrino?'

I explained that although Tony Ferrino was in the script I had been sent, I wasn't actually aware of the character.

'Stay here!' Tanya countered. 'I'll be back in five minutes.'

She then spent approximately five minutes doing the obligatory lap of the room, shaking the hands she had to shake, then came back and said, 'Let's go to my office.'

We strode the halls of Parliament House together, stopping only for Tanya to deflect a complimentary but entirely inappropriate comment about her legs from a well-known male MP.

'Does that happen often?' I asked.

'Every day,' she replied wearily, 'every single day.'

Onwards we trudged, until eventually we came to her office. Inwardly giggling, but outwardly composed, I tried to pretend I always sneak off to MPs' offices in Parliament House to watch comedy videos.

Oh sure, remember that time Bob Hawke invited me into his chambers to watch an old episode of *Are You Being Served*? Nothing so base for Paul Keating, though – no, he was more of your Monsieur Hulot kinda guy.

And so it was that Tanya Plibersek, the now Deputy Leader of the Opposition in Australia, sat with me in her parliamentary office, and watched an entire Tony Ferrino video. I'm not sure which one of us shirked their duties more, but I have a feeling it was me.

I returned to the function after an hour, feeling guilty that I hadn't worked the room appropriately, and that I had jeopardised the future funding of the ABC.

Fortunately, I was greeted by the sight of around fifty politicians and their staff madly gathered around two giant bananas, trying desperately to get photos. I doubt if anyone even noticed I was gone.

I had a point here, I'm sure . . . oh yeah, I like politicians. I get along well with them.

So I didn't find it all that strange when I asked the Deputy Prime Minister of Great Britain if he wanted to come to a Prince concert with me.

Nick Clegg was the leader of the Liberal Democrats party, who had formed a coalition government with David Cameron's Conservatives in 2010. When he appeared as a guest on *The Last Leg* in 2015, he was the serving deputy prime minister.

He was also, as my research told me, a huge Prince fan, having seen the Purple One playing live several times back in

1990, when he was on a fellowship at the University of Minnesota.

A week or so before his appearance, I was offered tickets to a private Prince gig in London, and for some reason I couldn't find a date. Not one.

Everyone I knew who was of an age to love Prince, all had kids, or partners, or commitments. Anyone I knew who was young enough to have a free night that didn't require permission, a babysitter, or a cancelled gig – simply wasn't that into Prince.

So, partly at my wits' end, and also because I thought it would make for a fun story – I asked the Deputy Prime Minister if he'd like to come to a Prince concert with me.

I remember we were in the make-up room of the London Studios, where we film *The Last Leg*. We had already filmed a sketch together earlier in the day, and got along really well, both on camera and off.

'You like Prince, don't you?' I asked, fully aware of the answer.

'When was the last time you saw him live?' I asked, pretending again that his answer was a surprise.

'I've just been offered two tickets to a private Prince gig on Monday. (*Pause for effect.*) I don't suppose you want to come with me, do you?'

If I'm honest, I thought he'd say no immediately. But he didn't.

'I'll have to check the diary,' he started. Then a glint entered his eyes. 'But I'd love to. Can I let you know over the weekend?'

I gave him my number and expected that was the end of that. I mean, if my married mates can't clear the diary with a week's notice, what chance does the Deputy PM have?

Not only that, one of the segments on that night's show involved Alex Brooker grilling Mr Clegg while occasionally pushing a 'bullshit' button whenever the answers got too politiciany.

While harsh, and a bit of a trap, it did cause Clegg to reveal that he felt a 'nine-and-a-half out of ten' bad about reversing his promise not to introduce student tuition fees. In fact, I'd go so far as to say that interview showed a more human side than most people had seen of any politician for a long time.

Still, I wasn't sure Nick Clegg was entirely happy with the way he had been treated.

Two days later I noticed a missed call on my phone and checked the message.

'Adam, it's Nick Clegg. I'd love to come to the Prince gig with you. Someone from my office will be in touch to get the details.'

Two hours after that, I got a call from Nick's assistant to ask the location of the venue. And where we would be standing in the venue. And how many people does the venue hold? And where are the exits? And how many exits are there? And is there a back entrance? And how many security guards will be there? And all the questions you would ask if you were the Deputy Prime Minister of Great Britain going to a Prince gig with a comedian you met two days ago.

It may not surprise you to know, I didn't have the answers to any of these questions. So I did what any self-respecting artist would do. I rang my manager. On a Sunday. To tell him to expect a call from the Deputy Prime Minister's security detail.

On the day of the gig, I got another call from Nick's lovely assistant, asking if I'd like to arrive with the DPM.

Sure.

In that case, he'll swing by and pick you up. If he's caught up in Parliament, though, he might have to pick you up around the corner from the venue and you'll drive the last few blocks together.

Of course.

So it was that I found myself taking a taxi to a restaurant in Camden, only to alight the taxi, and stand outside the restaurant, to wait for a government car to come get me.

As I stood in the freezing night air, a well-built, well-dressed, well-spoken man approached me from across the street. He was in a suit and tie.

'Mr Hills?'

'Yes.'

'Good.'

He then did that thing I have only ever seen once before, when the deputy PM of Australia had walked off a plane with me.

Do it. Do it now, so you know what I mean.

Put your right hand over your right ear.

Go on. No one's watching.

Now pull your left hand to your left cheek, and talk quietly into your cuff.

Trust me, you look massively cool.

'I am with Mr Hills, I'm with Mr Hills,' he murmured.

Pause.

'OK – Mr Hills, the DPM will be with you in five minutes.'

I then spent the next few minutes standing in the street with a man in a suit, having a perfectly lovely conversation about how busy we both were, how cold it was, and whether or not he'd be allowed into the Prince gig.

Turns out, there were more than a few volunteers to keep the DPM safe that night, and they somehow all needed to be inside the venue, with a good view of the stage. And who could begrudge them?

Mid-sentence, he stopped, did the cool talk into the cuff thing again, and informed me the DPM was behind the next bus. And he was.

A big red London bus trundled past, and a sleek black government car pulled alongside me. Out jumped Nick's assistant, who had to walk to the venue, and in jumped muggins.

We took a left, a right, another left, and we were at the venue. Once again, my complete lack of appreciation for the circumstances kicked in, as I saw the size of the queue.

'Oh man, we're gonna have to stand in the cold for a while,' I moaned.

'It's OK,' said Nick with a wry grin. 'I reckon I can get us in.'

At this point my ignorance of who I had asked to accompany me on a man-date was painfully clear.

I was about to explain to Nick that I thought we should probably do the right thing and wait in line like everybody else; that everyone on the guest list was a VIP, so there was no point pulling the 'Do you know who I am?' card; and that I'm too self-conscious to do that anyway.

Then the man in the suit from before suddenly appeared at the front of the queue, motioned to us to follow him, and escorted us through the foyer, up the stairs and onto a roped-off VIP balcony.

Of course, the Deputy Prime Minister gets a security escort through the venue! I think that was the moment I realised how wildly inappropriate my original invitation had been. I had asked the second most powerful person in the country to come to a Prince gig with me.

Thankfully, however, he wasn't the most important person in the room, and within minutes we were both mere mortals worshipping at the feet (well, above the head) of the Maroon Deity.

From the second Prince took to the stage and hit the first bars of 'Purple Rain', we were both star-struck fans.

'Oh my God,' I turned to Nick and exclaimed, 'you know this is gonna be a good night when he OPENS with "Purple Rain".'

What followed was an album of Prince's greatest hits, played live, by Prince. 'Little Red Corvette', 'Raspberry Beret', 'When Doves Cry' all followed in quick succession. Down below in the crowd I spotted Alan Carr and Noel Gallagher, while alongside us on the balcony were Jonathan Ross, Michael McIntyre and Naomi Campbell.

All the while Nick and I chatted (turns out he quite likes a female drummer), laughed, and at one point caught ourselves singing along to 'Kiss', in falsetto.

Two things stood out for me about that night, and in particular, the life of a politician. One came as Nick and I were casually chatting before the show started.

From below I could hear someone calling Nick's name.

'Nick! Nick! Nick!'

We were in mid-conversation, and it seemed rude to stop talking, so we ploughed on, both aware that someone was trying to get the DPM's attention.

Like a scene from an episode of Alan Partridge, it persisted.

'Nick, Nick, Nick, Nick . . . Nick!'

Honestly, the guy must have yelled Nick's name at least twenty times.

Ever the gentlemen, Nick finished his sentence to me, before politely looking below him to where the person was yelling his name.

That person then shouted 'Wankaaaaaa' and made the universal sign for 'wanker' to ram the point home.

What struck me was how quickly Nick shook that off and returned to the conversation.

If that was you or me, we'd probably have responded with a single finger, or a 'fuck you', or depending on your attitude, a glass thrown back in reply. At the very least, I'd look back to the person to whom I was originally talking, and acknowledge it somehow. Maybe raise an eyebrow, laugh it off, say something like, 'One of the perks of the job, I'm afraid.'

Because for you or me, that would be a strange thing to have happen to us. It would warrant some sort of reaction. Nick was so used to that kind of treatment, he simply resumed his conversation, as if the person had said, 'Sorry, thought you were someone else.'

How many times has that happened to him, I wondered, that he can shake it off as an everyday occurrence?

The second glimpse into the life of a high-profile politician came towards the end of the gig.

Prince had started the show by saying, 'I'm gonna play all the hits for an hour and a half, then we'll just see what happens after that.'

With the hits done, and the newer stuff being shown off, the venue was still packed. Nick and a few of his staff were having a ball, safe on the balcony, champagne in hand. Everyone was beaming.

Subtly I noticed the man who met me on the street, the same man who talked into his cuff, approach Nick and murmur something in his ear.

Nick's face dropped.

He turned to me, put his half-drunk glass of champagne on a ledge, and said, 'I think I better go. The press have got hold of me being here, and have surrounded my car by the back door. If I stay here any longer, they'll write a story about how late I stayed out, how many drinks I had, and generally suggest I was skiving when I should have been working.'

At this point it was around ten-thirty on a Monday night. In what other career does a glass and a half of champagne on a Monday night count as 'skiving'?

'Is it really that bad?' I asked innocently.

'Oh God, it's constant,' he replied.

'Does it get you down?'

'You know,' he said, 'you get into politics for certain reasons. Because you really want to make a difference, and you think you can. But when you get as close to the top as I have, you see how things really work, and who really has the power. And it's a lot different to how you thought it would be.'

'Does it make you lose your faith in politics?' I wondered.

'Actually, no,' he said steadfastly. 'It reaffirms my faith in what my party stands for. It makes me realise more than ever that we need to keep doing what we do, because no one else is.'

Still, I suggested, it's a tough way to live.

'You know what?' he began. 'You get one knock after another. The press turn on you, the lies come out, and then one day your press secretary says, "Do you wanna go on *The Last Leg*?" And you think, fuck it. Why not? It couldn't get any worse.'

With that, we laughed, exchanged numbers, and the Deputy Prime Minister snuck out the back exit of a Prince gig while it was still going, in case anyone might think he was slacking off on the job.

The following day, photos of us arriving at the gig appeared in one of the tabloids. I was described as wearing a 'colourful scarf and a dark blue shirt'.

Dark blue? It was purple! For Prince!

Bloody journos.

Last Foot Standing

Occasionally I'm asked if I ever wish I'd been born with two feet. The answer is always no.

Because if I had, I wouldn't be where I am right now. And right now, I'm in a pretty good place.

Literally.

I'm sitting on a train to Warrington at 8.40 a.m. on a Sunday, where I'll be playing in the UK's first ever game of Physical Disability Rugby League.

Less than a year ago someone tweeted me, asking if I knew there was a South Sydney Rabbitohs physical disability team. I should explain that I've been supporting the Rabbitohs since birth.

When I was three days old, my dad brought a red-and-green toy rabbit into the hospital to ensure I'd be a South Sydney fan for life. His dad supported the Rabbitohs, he supported the Rabbitohs, and that toy rabbit now sits in my daughters' play-room, reminding them to carry on the family tradition.

The story goes that the team got their name because many of the original members were rabbit sellers by day, affection-ately known as 'Rabbitohs'. They'd walk through the streets of inner-city Redfern in green smocks, with rabbits over their shoulders, shouting 'Rabbitoh!' Once the bunnies were sold, they'd turn up to rugby league training with blood stains on their smocks, which is why the club colours became red and green.

Anyway, as is the way between men and boys, I always felt that the South Sydney Rabbitohs became the glue that bonded my dad and I together.

When they played in the 2014 Grand Final, I flew from London to Sydney for the weekend to watch them win, and when they did, I shed a tear that my dad wasn't there to share it with me. He died with his Rabbitohs cap next to him on the bed.

In 2015 I sent an invite to the South Sydney club to see if anyone wanted to come to my show at the Sydney Opera House. As well as the CEO, and chairman, two of the players came – Adam Reynolds and Luke Keary.

I was like a giddy kid. I could actually see them from the stage, and spent the entire show checking to see if they were laughing, while reminding myself there were two and a half thousand other people there as well.

They came backstage afterwards for a chat, and again I was like a teenager. Until my manager entered the room to tell me I was due on stage again in five minutes to do the show to a second crowd.

I'm telling you all this to give you an idea of how much I love the South Sydney Rabbitohs. They represent a link to my dad, a huge part of my childhood, and also the history of a proud part of my hometown.

I was intrigued when I heard of the disability team and found a contact online. I had two questions: what can I do to help support the team, and can I play?

To be honest, I wanted to ask question two before question one, but thought I should offer my support first.

Ever since the Beijing Paralympics, I've been itching to get into disability sport (although once you've been hit hard in a tackle by an above-knee amputee, you come to realise that no one playing the sport is really disabled).

My dalliance with wheelchair tennis didn't last long, and although last year I started training for a celebrity para triathlon, it turned out I only had to run a kilometre, while two disabled kids completed the other legs.

I still ran the fastest kilometre I could, and I got the taste for sport again. Plus I think deep down, I still regret my refusal to try out for the Disabled Games when I was a teenager. Could I finally make amends for that decision?

I was told by George Tonna, the man behind the Physical Disability Rugby League, or PDRL as it is known, that the main thing preventing me from playing with the Rabbitohs was that they are based in Sydney, whereas I am based in London. He said it in a way that suggested my disability might not be purely physical.

However, he'd just been contacted by the Warrington Wolves Charitable Foundation, who wanted to set up a PDRL team in the UK. Maybe I should contact them. So I did. And asked the two big questions again.

The man I spoke to was called Neil Kelly, and he is a walking reminder that there are some truly good people in the world. He runs the Wolves Foundation, which provides dance classes for the community, support groups for men's mental health, and a soccer team for kids with disabilities.

For some reason, they'd never thought to start up a rugby league team, despite Warrington being your typical Northern working-class, rugby league-loving town.

He suggested I come to Warrington to raise some publicity for the PDRL team, and lined up a game between a few of the disabled members of the club, against the actual Wolves first grade team.

I took a cameraman and a director with me, in the hope that this might be something worth documenting. If all goes well, the journey will be turned into a proper documentary, so I won't bore you with all the details – suffice to say it has been one of the most rewarding things I've done in my life.

Since that first publicity day, we've held an open trial, formed a team, and had three training sessions.

I've met Keith, a guy with Down's Syndrome, who is the unofficial mascot of the Wolves. He works for the foundation with Neil and is known to come to work dressed as either Elvis or George Michael, depending on who he saw on TV the night before.

When the Wolves made it to the final at Wembley a few years back, the team chipped in and bought Keith and his carer tickets to London. Keith repaid them by giving the pregame speech in the dressing room.

He said simply, 'You lose, I quit,' then left.

I've met Dan, a twenty-six-year-old, above-knee amputee, who lost his leg in a cycling accident four years ago. When he arrived for the open trial, he hadn't played rugby since his accident. His first words to me were, 'I'm gonna sit you on your arse.'

He thought he'd never play rugby league again.

I've met Jamie, a fourteen-year-old with a degenerative condition that means he can play like a champion now, but may have only a few good years in him.

345

He doesn't know how much longer he can play league.

Meanwhile the Leeds Rhinos have formed their own team, including Chris, a former professional rugby league player, who left the field in protest after being hit illegally in back-play, collapsed, was rushed to hospital, died twice on the operating table, and suffered a permanent brain injury.

Like Dan, this is the first time he's played league since the accident.

And then there's Simon Brown, a forty-year-old war veteran, who has limited eyesight after being shot in the head in action in Iraq. His reason for playing league again after all this time? 'If I'm going out, I'm going out on my terms.'

And in amongst it all, there's me. Forty-seven-year-old Adam, who was born without a right foot. He loved the Rabbitohs and played rugby league throughout high school.

I never thought I'd play league again.

I'm absolutely loving it, and since each PDRL team has two able-bodied members, I'm playing alongside a former England Fullback called Shaun Briscoe, who's teaching me the finer points of the game.

I was never the best kid on the team, even when playing for the Jannali Boys High B-Side, and was always worried that my prosthetic might cause more damage than it would take.

This is, after all, a sport that entails tackling people below the waist – as my dad always told me, 'they can't run without legs' – and the last thing you want to throw into that mix is a solid lump of virtually indestructible carbon. That fear of causing injury was one of the reasons I stopped playing. That, and I wasn't particularly good.

I'm still worried about the damage my prosthetic might cause, but at least now there's a similar chance someone else's leg will do the same to me. Plus, on a team of disabled people, I'm no longest the slowest on the field.

In fact, I've been playing on the wing. Turns out you *can* run without legs.

On the other hand, Dan, the above-knee amputee, has been running into tackles harder than any kid I ever played against. He's an absolute machine, and I'm still sore from trying to stop him in training.

I know the look in his eyes, though. It's the same look I saw in Beijing among the wheelchair basketballers and rugby players. Finally, they can smash someone or get smashed, without the people around them rushing in with kid gloves saying, 'You poor fragile thing.'

Personally, I'm happier than I've been in years, and can't stop talking about this new venture. I'm fitter, I've lost weight, and I'm enjoying the camaraderie that comes from being part of a team.

Oh sure, as I sit here typing on the Virgin Trains Pendolino to Glasgow, my right wrist hurts, my left shoulder is sore, and my left hamstring is very, very tender, but I feel alive.

And that's why I wouldn't want to have been born with two feet. Because I wouldn't be where I am right now.

My mum used to tell me that God had taken away my foot, but he made me smarter than the other kids. I don't know if that's true, but I reckon my lack of a foot made me look at the world a little differently.

It also made me determined not to let anything stop me achieving my goals.

Those two traits led me to stand-up comedy and made me doggedly pursue it. To be as good at it as I could possibly be, without relying on my foot as a prop.

Then, when I worked out how to do this crazy thing called comedy, I put my second-best foot forward, and realised it was my best foot after all. I found a way to help people accept disability, and in the process, came to accept mine. While confirming what I'd thought all along – that I'm not really disabled.

More than that, I'm proud of being different. I like being part of this weird secret society of amputees, wheelchair users, blind people and cerebral palsy peeps.

My funny little right foot has made me determined, positive, and literally forces me to look at the world from a different angle. And what makes you different, makes you unique.

It's watched me go from the Sydney Comedy Store to the Sydney Opera House, where I walked in the same stage door as Billy Connolly all those years ago, and from the dressing room window could see the house my grandfather grew up in, under the shade of the Sydney Harbour Bridge.

It came with me to Adelaide, where I recently received a star on the Adelaide Festival Centre Walk of Fame, then to the Edinburgh Fringe, where a local magazine once declared me such a festival regular that I was one of their Top Ten Scots.

It followed me back to Australia to host a TV show, then took to the stage itself, although in a supporting role, as I hosted Paralympic broadcasts from Beijing to London and Rio.

Now it's taking me to Warrington, to play a competitive rugby league game again, for the first time in over thirty years, against my *Last Leg* co-host Alex Brooker.

By the way, before writing this entry, I texted Neil at the Wolves to say my train is on time, and that I am sore and tired. He just responded that Josh, who has cerebral palsy and joined the team last week, has given him some of his CP medication, and said that once I take it, I won't feel a thing.

Later in the year, we hope to take the Wolves team to Sydney, to play an exhibition match against the South Sydney Rabbitohs PDRL team, at the former Olympic Stadium, before an actual Rabbitohs First Grade game. Ideally, I'd finally pull on the red-and-green jersey and fulfil that childhood dream of representing South Sydney, but I've a sneaky feeling I'd find it too difficult to go up against Dan, Jamie, Jason, Jensen, Knocker, Chris, and my newly acquired Wolves team-mates.

Besides, I don't want to miss out on Keith's team talk.

But now my left foot's getting jealous. Isn't it the one that's kept me stable all these years? Sure, my right foot kept me on an angle, but my left also kept me level.

I have a stunning and talented wife, two gorgeous and wonderful daughters, and I'm lucky enough to have a life split between Australia and the UK.

Somehow between my funny right foot, and my reliable left one, I've managed to tread a decent path, and from here the view is pretty good.

Perhaps I don't have a best foot after all.

Maybe they're both great, and together they make a brilliant team.

Epilogue

Big Yin and I (Part Three)

Recently two things happened that led me to contact Billy Connolly.

The first was an invitation to do an interview for an ITV show, in which famous and not-so-famous people talk about how much the Big Yin meant to them.

The producers of the show had heard of my meetings with Billy over my career, of the time he told me to follow my dream of comedy, as well as his appearance at the London Comedy Store the night I happened to be on, and they wanted me to tell those stories on camera.

The strange part was, they had heard the stories from Billy.

Apparently they had interviewed him for the show as well, and he had mentioned the time he met me.

I turned up for the interview and checked if he had actually brought the story up himself, and they confirmed it.

Later that week I was having dinner with the author and all-round good egg Kathy Lette. As we swapped stories of growing up in the Sutherland Shire of Sydney, and of how far we'd come since then, I told the story of Billy telling the story of me.

'Oh, I know Billy, I email him every day,' she squealed.

I asked her to pass on an email from me to him, and this is what I wrote:

Dear Billy,

I've been wanting to send you a message for a while now, but didn't know how to get to you. Thankfully our mutual friend Kathy has stepped in to save the day.

I was recently asked to say a few words for an ITV show about you, and was chuffed to find you had mentioned our meeting at the Comedy Store a few years ago, and our meeting in Adelaide many years before that.

Your words to me back in Adelaide were instrumental in my decision to quit my job as a radio DJ and head to the UK to follow my stand-up dreams, and led me to where I am today.

In fact, I am currently writing a book about my comedy 'career' and it occurred to me you have popped up at just the right time, to say the right things to send me on my way.

Anyway, I wanted to let you know how much those little nuggets of encouragement mean.

I do hope you are well, and would love the chance to buy you a cup of tea whenever we happen to be in the same country.

Until then, though, I just want to thank you eternally for being such an inspiration, both on stage and off.

Huge love to you and yours,
Adam Hills xxx

The following day, I received this reply:

Dear Adam,

How nice to hear from you. Your success in Britain makes me very happy. It couldn't happen to a nicer guy. I love your Ozzie optimism.

Good luck to you,
    Billy Connolly xxx

Acknowledgements

I would like to thank every single person I've come across in the world of comedy, as well as every one of my family and friends. In particular, but in no particular order, enormous thanks go to – my first manager Ingrid, and my subsequent managers Kevin, Dioni, Flee, Richard, Christina, Eavan, Joe, Danny, Addison, and Jodi. Everyone at Off The Kerb, Lisa Richards Agency and Token Artists.

To the team at Hodder and Stoughton, and Hachette Australia, for asking me to write a book, bearing with me while I did, saying nice things about it and moulding it into shape.

To my close friends who have put up with an intermittent relationship, punctuated by long periods of time on the other side of the world, I love you dearly.

And to my family, who are an unrelenting source of support. From grandparents past – Ron, Mary and Beatrice – and present – Dool – to my mum and dad, my brother, my gorgeous wife and my incredible daughters. I couldn't have done all this without you, nor would I have wanted to.

I love youse all.

Picture Acknowledgements

The author and publisher would like to thank the following copyright-holders for permission to reproduce images in this book:

SECTION 2
Page 2: Copyright © Rolling Stone LLC 2008. All Rights Reserved. Used by Permission.
Page 4, top: ©Jim Lee/AUSTRALSCOPE
Page 4, middle: ©Leon Neal/AFP/Getty Images
Page 4, bottom: ©Rusty Stewart/AUSTRALSCOPE
Page 6, bottom: ©Flynet – Splash News

All images are courtesy of the author.

The author and publishers have made all reasonable efforts to contact any copyright-holders for permission and apologise for any omissions or errors in the form of credit given. Corrections may be made to future printings.

Text Acknowledgements

Copacabana by Barry Manilow

I Get Around by The Beach Boys,
written by Brian Wilson and Mike Love

Ob-La-Di, Ob-La-Da by The Beatles,
written by John Lennon and Paul McCartney

Sellotape by Flight of the Conchords,
written by Jemaine Clement & Bret McKenzie